A FORGOTTEN FREUDIAN

The History of Psychoanalysis Series
Professor Brett Kahr and Professor Peter L. Rudnytsky (Series Editors)

Other titles in the Series

Her Hour Come Round at Last: A Garland for Nina Coltart
edited by Peter L. Rudnytsky and Gillian Preston

Rescuing Psychoanalysis from Freud and Other Essays in Re-Vision
by Peter L. Rudnytsky

Ferenczi and His World: Rekindling the Spirit of the Budapest School
edited by Judit Szekacs-Weisz and Tom Keve

Freud in Zion: Psychoanalysis and the Making of Modern Jewish Identity
by Eran J. Rolnik

Ferenczi for Our Time: Theory and Practice
edited by Judit Szekacs-Weisz and Tom Keve

The Clinic and the Context: Historical Essays
by Elisabeth Young-Bruehl

Sandor Ferenczi–Ernest Jones: Letters 1911–1933
edited by Ferenc Eros, Judit Szekacs-Weisz, and Ken Robinson

The Milan Seminar: Clinical Applications of Attachment Theory
by John Bowlby, edited by Marco Bacciagaluppi

Ferenczi and Beyond: Exile of the Budapest School and Solidarity in the Psychoanalytic Movement during the Nazi Years
by Judit Mészáros

Looking Through Freud's Photos
by Michael Molnar

Psychoanalytic Filiations: Mapping the Psychoanalytic Movement
by Ernst Falzeder

The Abandonment Neurosis
by Germaine Guex (translated by Peter Douglas)

The Life and Times of Franz Alexander: From Budapest to California
by Ilonka Venier Alexander

Freud and the Dora Case: A Promise Betrayed
by Cesare Romano

The Freudian Orient: Early Psychoanalysis, Anti-Semitic Challenge, and the Vicissitudes of Orientalist Discourse
by Frank F. Scherer

Karl Abraham: Life and Work, a Biography
by Anna Bentinck van Schoonheten

A FORGOTTEN FREUDIAN
The Passion of Karl Stern

Daniel Burston

Routledge
Taylor & Francis Group

LONDON AND NEW YORK

First published 2016 by
Karnac Books Ltd.

Published 2018 by Routledge
2 Park Square, Milton Park, Abingdon, Oxon OX14 4RN
711 Third Avenue, New York, NY 10017, USA

Routledge is an imprint of the Taylor & Francis Group, an informa business

Copyright © 2016 by Daniel Burston

The right of Daniel Burston to be identified as the author of this work has been asserted in accordance with §§ 77 and 78 of the Copyright Design and Patents Act 1988.

All rights reserved. No part of this book may be reprinted or reproduced or utilised in any form or by any electronic, mechanical, or other means, now known or hereafter invented, including photocopying and recording, or in any information storage or retrieval system, without permission in writing from the publishers.

Notice:
Product or corporate names may be trademarks or registered trademarks, and are used only for identification and explanation without intent to infringe.

British Library Cataloguing in Publication Data

A C.I.P. for this book is available from the British Library

ISBN-13: 9781782203469 (pbk)

Typeset by V Publishing Solutions Pvt Ltd., Chennai, India

Dedicated to Gregory Baum, for a lifetime of service to all humanity

CONTENTS

ACKNOWLEDGMENTS   ix

ABOUT THE AUTHOR   xi

SERIES EDITOR'S FOREWORD   xiii

PREFACE   xix

A NOTE ON ABBREVIATIONS   xxiii

CHAPTER ONE
Early years: 1906–1932   1

CHAPTER TWO
Psychiatry, psychoanalysis, and politics: 1932–1935   31

CHAPTER THREE
London to Montreal: 1935–1949   49

CHAPTER FOUR
The Pillar of Fire: 1950–1955   81

CHAPTER FIVE
Through dooms of love: 1955–1967   105

CHAPTER SIX
A legacy lost: 1968–1975   143

CHAPTER SEVEN
Freud, faith, and phenomenology   161

CHAPTER EIGHT
A Hebrew Catholic   181

CHAPTER NINE
Judaism and Catholicism in Stern and Lacan   221

AFTERWORD   231

REFERENCES   235

INDEX   247

ACKNOWLEDGMENTS

This book would never have been written without the kindness, co-operation and steadfast support of Katherine (Stern) Skorzewska, Professor Gregory Baum, and the late Dr. Noel Walsh. The insights, information, and encouragement they gave me have been invaluable. I am also deeply indebted to Karl Stern's daughter-in-law Lilian (Stern) Kapp, her daughter Eva Marie Stern, and Lilian's sons Philip and Stephen Stern. The many hours I spent in conversation and correspondence with them inform every chapter of this book.

Also, my heartfelt thanks to Katherine's husband Olaf Skorzewski, and to their daughter Dr. Anna Skorzewska and her partner, Dr. Andreas Motsch, and to a long list of generous and insightful Montrealers, including Professor Sherry Simon, Professor Robert Schwartzwald, Professor Andrée Levesque, Dr. Maurice Dongier, Dr. Israel Libman, Dr. Brendan and Mary Campbell, and last but not least, Deborah Ostrovsky. Warm thanks to Professor Emeritus Donald Carveth, of York University's sociology department, and to my fellow Yinzers (Pittsburghers) Dr. Carlos Placci and Professor Paula Kane, Marrous Professor of Catholic Studies at the University of Pittsburgh, and to my colleagues Marie Baird, Aimee Light, and Laura Edwards, who read and commented on various chapters. Their scholarship and support have been invaluable.

Next, I'd like to thank Dr. James Swindal, Dean of Liberal Arts, at Duquesne University, and Dr. Jeffrey McCurry, Director of the Simon Silverman Phenomenology Center, and Angelle Pryor, the Phenomenology Librarian, for their steadfast encouragement and support. I am also grateful for the generous help I received from Susan Wadsworth Booth, of Duquesne University Press, and two outstanding archivists, Dr. Thomas White, who curates the Karl Stern Archive at the Gumberg Library of Duquesne University, and Phillip Runkel, who curates the Dorothy Day-Catholic Worker Collection in the Department of Special Collections and University Archives at Marquette University in Milwaukee, Wisconsin.

Finally, I must thank my wife Sharna, and my children Adam and Gavriela, for their patience and encouragement, and their willingness to put up with me while my mind wandered to remote times and places for long periods over the last seven years. This book is a labor of love, and would never have been possible without theirs.

ABOUT THE AUTHOR

Daniel Burston is an Associate Professor and former chair of the Psychology Department at Duquesne University in Pittsburgh, PA. He was raised and educated in Toronto, Canada, and is married with two children. He is the author of numerous books and journal articles on the history of psychology, psychiatry and psychoanalysis, including *The Legacy of Erich Fromm*, *The Wing of Madness: The Life and Work of R. D. Laing*, and *Erik Erikson and the American Psyche: Ego, Ethics and Evolution*.

SERIES EDITOR'S FOREWORD

After many years of sustained labor by a small number of devoted scholars, the history of psychoanalysis has finally become a proper field of study. Once the preserve of a tiny group of archivally minded psychoanalysts, this discipline has, in recent decades, become an increasing area of interest to mental health clinicians, professional historians, biographers, memoirists, journalists, and academics of all persuasions.

The history of psychoanalysis now boasts not one, but two, superb periodicals—the English-language *Psychoanalysis and History*, and the German-language *Luzifer-Amor: Zeitschrift zur Geschichte der Psychoanalyse*—which suffer from absolutely no shortage of truly first-class contributions. And likewise, through the generosity and foresight of Oliver Rathbone, the publisher of Karnac Books, we also have a "History of Psychoanalysis Series," which, since its launch in 2011, has produced nearly twenty titles, authored by scholars from Australia, Canada, Hungary, Israel, Italy, the Netherlands, the United Kingdom, and the United States of America.

And yet, in spite of the growth of this field of endeavor, as emblematized by a stack of books on my desk so tall that I wonder when I shall ever have the time to read them all, we still have many *lacunae*, not least a series of proper studies of those members (or near members) of the psychoanalytical community who, for one reason or another, have fallen off the radar.

Whilst sitting in our consulting rooms, psychoanalytical practitioners devote ourselves to helping patients remember the long-forgotten past; but outside of office hours, many of us often engage in the diametrical opposite, by helping to *repress* the memory of those who displease us in some way. When, for instance, Peter Gay's (1988) stalwart biography, *Freud: A Life for Our Time*, appeared in print in 1988, it received a great deal of much-deserved praise for its meaty coverage, its use of archival materials, and its graceful prose. But few critics at the time had dared to mention publicly Gay's grossly partisan denigration of the work of Paul Roazen and, also, Gay's complete suppression of any mention of Wilhelm Reich. In many respects, Professor Gay's attack on Roazen's scholarship, and his failure to remember Reich's role in the Viennese psychoanalytical community remind one of Ernest Jones's (1957) earlier assassination in print of some of his sibling rivals, most especially Sándor Ferenczi. Thus, in spite of our clinical wish to embrace the past, members of our community will, from time to time, engage in acts of *damnatio memoriae*.

When Professor Daniel Burston, a distinguished American psychologist and historian, approached Karnac Books about the possibility of writing a biography of Karl Stern, even the most historically savvy members of staff blurted out, "Karl *who*?" No one seems to have heard of this man. And yet, Stern, a Bavarian Jew, had begun studying the ideas of Sigmund Freud, Carl Gustav Jung, and Alfred Adler, in the mid-1920s, while still a teenager; and then, while working as a psychiatric intern for the eminent physician Dr. Kurt Goldstein at the Moabiter Krankenhaus in Berlin, Stern and his young colleagues enjoyed psychoanalyzing one another out of hours! Eventually, Stern underwent a formal psychoanalysis and became increasingly immersed in its study and practice. Although never a formal member of the Deutsche Psychoanalytische Gesellschaft, Stern did, nevertheless, utilize Freudian concepts in his medical work over a long professional lifetime.

As a Jew, Stern had to flee Continental Europe while still a young man. Perhaps if he had trained ten years earlier, he might have become a member of one of the psychoanalytical societies and would, perhaps, have secured his reputation within the field more squarely; but as a refugee—and a young one at that—he developed his work in his own creative way. And though Stern never became a formal psychoanalyst, he did pioneer the field of psychodynamic psychiatry in Canada, in which capacity he exerted a huge influence on many future psychoanalytically orientated physicians.

Stern's marginalization from the psychoanalytical core may have resulted from his turn towards Catholicism in later years. Indeed, those atheistic psychoanalysts who did know of Stern and his work may have harboured suspicions towards a former Jew who had come to embrace Christianity. In many respects, Stern reminds one of Dr. William Brown, the noted British medical psychologist—one of the earliest and most dedicated disciples of psychoanalysis during the 1910s (e.g., Brown, 1913a, 1913b, 1913c, 1914a, 1914b, 1914c, 1914d)—who fell foul of Ernest Jones (1920, 1921, 1922, 1923, n.d.), at least in part, because of his religious devotion (e.g., Brown, 1925, 1929, 1946). The repression of such figures certainly raises questions about our capacity to tolerate difference.

Over many decades, Daniel Burston has become one of the most highly respected historians of psychoanalysis, having written deeply engaging and trustworthy studies of such marginalized figures as Erik Erikson (Burston, 2007), Erich Fromm (Burston, 1991), and Ronald Laing (Burston, 1996), helping to restore their substantial intellectual and clinical contributions to the mainstream once again. Now, Burston has turned his special scholarly skills to the work of Stern, and in doing so, he has undertaken an even more challenging task, because Stern had never become part of the psychoanalytical mainstream; in fact, in spite of his deep sympathy to Freudianism, Karl Stern had always maintained his own maverick presence, writing in his own voice in the most authentic and individual of manners.

In this wonderful book, *A Forgotten Freudian: The Passion of Karl Stern*, Burston has brought this much-neglected figure to life in the most readable and enjoyable manner. Drawing upon a range of neglected source materials, Burston has reconstructed Stern's unique journey from the small Bavarian town of Cham to his full flourish as a leader of Canadian psychiatry and spirituality. Burston has not only recreated the Stern story for those of us who have lived in ignorance of this remarkably insightful man but, also, he has deftly traced the links between Stern's work of the mid-century and the contributions of such unexpected figures as the French psychoanalyst Jacques Lacan, helping us to appreciate the contemporaneity and challenge posed by this much-overlooked Bavarian-Canadian forefather.

I thank Daniel Burston for sharing with us this compelling story in such a generous manner, and I hope that Burston's biography and critical study of Karl Stern will serve as an exemplar to other scholars who wish to resurrect other forgotten Freudians, who, in spite of their death and repression, still have much to teach.

Professor Brett Kahr
Series Co-Editor
London, England

References

Brown, William (1913a). Freud's Theory of Dreams. *The Lancet*. 19th April, pp. 1114–1118.

Brown, William (1913b). Freud's Theory of Dreams. *The Lancet*. 26th April, pp. 1182–1184.

Brown, William (1913c). A Case of Extensive Amnesia of Remote Date Cured by Psycho-Analysis and Hypnosis. *British Medical Journal*. 8th November, pp. 1217–1219.

Brown, William (1914a). What is Psycho-Analysis? *Nature*. 5th February, pp. 643–645.

Brown, William (1914b). Psycho-Analysis. *British Medical Journal*. 7th February, p. 341.

Brown, William (1914c). Discussion. *Proceedings of the Royal Society of Medicine*, Section of Psychiatry, 7: 78–79.

Brown, William (1914d). Freud's Theory of the Unconscious. *British Journal of Psychology*, 6: 265–280.

Brown, William (1925). Religion and Psychology. In Arthur James Balfour, Bronislaw Malinowski, Charles Singer, Antonio Aliotta, Arthur S. Eddington, Joseph Needham, John W. Oman, William Brown, Clement C. J. Webb, and William Ralph Inge. *Science Religion and Reality*. Joseph Needham (Ed.), pp. 301–327. London: Sheldon Press, and New York: Macmillan Company.

Brown, William (1929). Religion and Science: A General Survey. *Journal of Philosophical Studies*, 4: 39–49.

Brown, William (1946). *Personality and Religion*. London: University of London Press.

Burston, Daniel (1991). *The Legacy of Erich Fromm*. Cambridge, Massachusetts: Harvard University Press.

Burston, Daniel (1996). *The Wings of Madness: The Life and Work of R. D. Laing*. Cambridge, Massachusetts: Harvard University Press.

Burston, Daniel (2007). *Erik Erikson and the American Psyche: Ego, Ethics, and Evolution*. Lanham, Maryland: Jason Aronson/Rowman and Littlefield Publishing Group.

Gay, Peter, (1988). *Freud: A Life for Our Time*. New York: W. W. Norton and Company.

Jones, Ernest (1920). *Treatment of the Neuroses*. Covent Garden, London: Baillière, Tindall and Cox.

Jones, Ernest (1921). Book Review of William Brown. *Psychology and Psychotherapy*. International Journal of Psycho-Analysis, 2: 133–135.

Jones, Ernest (1922). Letter to Sigmund Freud. 26th January. In Sigmund Freud and Ernest Jones (1993). *The Complete Correspondence of Sigmund Freud and Ernest Jones: 1908–1939*. R. Andrew Paskauskas (Ed.), pp. 454–457. Cambridge, Massachusetts: Belknap Press of Harvard University Press.

Jones, Ernest (1923). The Nature of Auto-Suggestion. *International Journal of Psycho-Analysis*, 4: 293–312.

Jones, Ernest (1957). *The Life and Work of Sigmund Freud: Volume 3. The Last Phase. 1919–1939*. New York: Basic Books.

Jones, Ernest (n.d.). Letter to Sigmund Freud. n.d. Quoted in Vincent Brome (1982). *Ernest Jones: Freud's Alter Ego*, p. 167. London: Caliban Books.

PREFACE

Karl Stern was born in the little town of Cham, Bavaria in 1906, the eldest son of assimilated Jewish parents. He trained in medicine and neurology in Germany, and moved to Montreal, Canada on the eve of World War II. His memoir, *The Pillar of Fire*, published in 1951, was an international bestseller, and was greeted by many Catholics as a worthy successor to Thomas Merton's *The Seven Storey Mountain* (Merton, 1948). One reason for the book's spectacular success was that it was written by a convert from Judaism who was also a respected man of science. After all, when *The Pillar of Fire* appeared, Stern was an Associate Professor of Psychiatry at McGill University, and had already published fifty-two articles on neuroanatomy, neuropathology, and several psychiatric disorders in prestigious medical journals (Shaw, 1951). In *Seminars in Neurology*, published a half century later, David Goldblatt paid tribute to his former teacher, noting "How unusual it is for one man to have such a thorough understanding of both the corpus callosum and Corpus Christi" (Goldbaltt, 1992, p. 282).

In addition to being a seasoned clinician, brain researcher, and lecturer, Stern was an accomplished musician. His passion for music is reflected in a remark of the Dean of Graduate Studies at McGill University in 1951, who quipped that: "Dr. Stern is a musician whose hobby is medicine." There is truth to that remark. Carlos Placci, a retired psychiatrist now living in Pittsburgh, recalls journeying from his native Argentina to study with Stern as a young man in 1962. Days after his arrival in Canada, Placci spent Christmas Eve with Stern and family. He recalls many portraits and autographed pictures of musicians and composers on the wall of Stern's home, including an autographed copy of "Till Eulenspiegel," by Richard Strauss. Placci was impressed by the fact that, while touring Canada, Rudolph Serkin visited Stern's home, and played for him for over an hour. As the evening unfolded, Placci and Stern played Brahms' *Variations on a Theme by Haydn* for two pianos—Stern on the grand piano, Placci on the upright nearby. And when the party was over, Stern gave Placci Glenn Gould's recording of Bach's Goldberg variations as a Christmas gift.

The Pillar of Fire was translated into German, French, Spanish, Dutch, and Italian, and reprinted many times. As a result, by the end of the sixties, Stern was a well-known figure, a public intellectual, both in Canada and the United States. He was a member of PEN, and the Canadian representative to the UNESCO Institute for Education. In 1965, he testified as an expert on racism and prejudice in the House of Commons, and in 1968, was interviewed at length on CBC television, and awarded an honorary Doctorate by the University of Laval.

Though Catholic intellectuals like Gabriel Marcel, Graham Greene, and Dorothy Day were frequent visitors to his home, Stern was completely shunned by Montreal's Jewish community (Simon, 1999). Nevertheless, like Cardinal Jean-Marie (Aaron) Lustiger, Msgr John Öesterreicher, and other well-known "Hebrew Catholics" of that era, Stern claimed that his embrace of Catholicism did not negate his underlying Jewishness. And to prove his dogged loyalty to his ancestral faith, Stern devoted considerable time and energy to combating anti-Semitism, both in the Church and the culture at large.

But Stern's main passion—besides music—was trying to "baptize" Freud, or more precisely, to incorporate many of Freud's contributions to psychology into contemporary Catholic philosophy. Stern's second book, *The Third Revolution: A Study of Psychiatry and Religion* (1954), explored the relationship between psychoanalysis and Catholicism, arguing that the two are quite compatible, and that scientism, the current idolatry, obscures this fact from public view—even from the intelligentsia, who should know better. Stern's third book, *The Flight From Woman* (1965a), combined Freudian and Jungian perspectives on philosophy, religion and literature. It blended psychoanalysis with existential-phenomenology to explain the rise of positivism, rationalism, and scientism as major intellectual and cultural trends, and addressed the pervasive devaluation of "women's ways of knowing"—(empathy and intuition)—and the deformations of the human spirit that follow as a consequence.

So, Karl Stern was a man of many parts. He was fluently trilingual, an accomplished researcher, clinician, teacher, and musician, and an occasional novelist and comedian, as we shall see presently. How does a man as protean, popular, and prolific as Stern was fall into such deep obscurity, especially in Canada, where he lived most of his life? Even in the Catholic world, where he is still remembered fondly, there is no serious reflection on his oeuvre, and few attempts to make it relevant to contemporary debates in the mental health field, or the interfaith dialogue between Jews and Catholics that has grown since Vatican II. In the chapters that follow, I hope to fill that lacuna.

Writing about Stern's life and work has been a wonderful opportunity because it motivated me to delve into history of psychoanalysis and psychiatry in Canada, and to befriend many of Stern's surviving family and friends. It also helped me to understand the precipitous decline of the psychodynamic psychiatry practiced by Stern, and its replacement with an increasingly vapid, materialistic pill-pushing psychiatry that is ethically compromised, spiritually impoverished and thoroughly beholden to multinational corporations (Healy, 2003; Olfman, 2007; Angell, M., 2011a; Angell, M., 2011b; Burston, 2012). Strange as it sounds to most psychiatrists nowadays, Stern was convinced that interpreted correctly, in historical context, the ideas of Sigmund Freud, could become a potent ally in the effort to develop an ethically responsive and spiritually open approach to psychiatry and psychotherapy. I do not share Stern's theological frame of reference, and have no wish to "baptize" Freud, but in many ways, Stern was quite right about this. Whatever else we make of the triumphs and tragedies of his life, we should keep this fact in mind, going forward.

A NOTE ON ABBREVIATIONS

When referencing hitherto unpublished correspondence or rough notes, the author uses the letters KSA to stand for the Karl Stern Archive, which is housed in the Simon Silverman Phenomenology Center in the Gumberg Library at Duquesne University in Pittsburgh, Pennsylvania. The Karl Stern Archive was created by a generous donation from Stern's daughter, Katherine Skorzeska, and was open to the public on October 10th, 2014. All photographic images here appear courtesy of the Karl Stern Archive.

CHAPTER ONE

Early years: 1906–1932

Infancy and childhood

Karl Stern was born on April 8th, 1906 in the town of Cham, Bavaria, a predominantly Catholic, rural enclave near the Czech border. The Stern family had lived in the region for centuries, and in generations past, had included many prominent rabbis. Bavaria's Jewish population dwindled significantly during the mid to late nineteenth century as Jews departed for urban centers around Germany, and so most of young Karl's friends were from Christian homes. Until the birth of his brother Ludwig nine years later, Karl's family consisted of his grandfather, his father, his mother and himself. They lived in an apartment above the family business; a store that supplied local farmers and tradesmen with textiles, leather, tools, machine parts and other supplies.

Adolf Stern, Karl's father, was the eldest of three sons, a man of modest means who worked alongside his own father in the family store. Stern described his father as a man of "natural humility and simplicity," "the most guileless person I have ever seen," and occasionally, as extremely naïve. Uncle Felix, the second oldest, trained in engineering and law and moved to Chicago, where he became quite wealthy. Though seldom seen in Karl's formative years, Felix was a regular

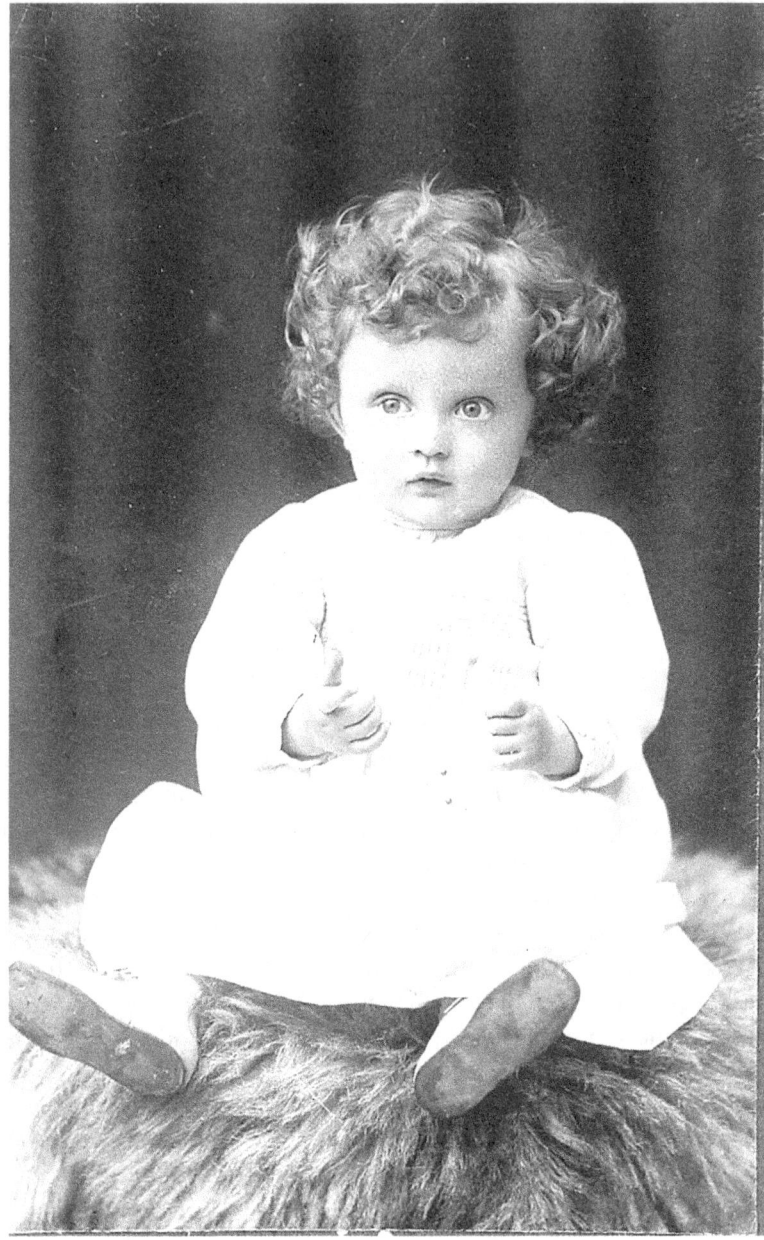

Figure 1. Karl Stern, one year old.

correspondent, sending greetings and news of his own growing family several times a year (Stern, 1951).

By contrast with Felix, the lawyer and engineer, uncle Julius was a bachelor in the printing business. Julius was often home for Passover and short, impromptu visits, and was remembered by Stern as his grandfather's favorite son, despite his socialist leanings. Julius was younger

Figure 2. Moritz Stern, Karl's grandfather.

than Felix, read widely, and travelled the world on business, sending his fond nephew postcards from exotic locales, and regaling him with stories about his travels in India, France and North America. As Stern recalled: "It seemed somehow extraordinary that he, my father's brother, supplied Chinese merchants in Ceylon with perfume labels, and that in his suitcases were literary reviews from Paris" (Stern, 1951, p. 20). By his own admission, Karl's accomplished uncles struck him as almost "mythological" figures, rendering his father's modest station in a life a source of some embarrassment. So it is probably no accident that Stern's most vivid childhood memories concern his grandfather, his mother and cosmopolitan uncle Julius.

Stern described his grandfather Moritz as a local personality who joked freely with children, customers, and friends, but was also as a strict disciplinarian when circumstances required. Though not a rabbi, Stern's grandfather led Sabbath services and holiday prayers in the local synagogue—a modest room rented above a local brewery. By contrast with his grandfather, Karl's parents were somewhat permissive, and quite distant from Jewish tradition. Neither his father or mother knew Hebrew, so on the rare occasions they prayed, they recited their prayers by rote; a fact that Stern's grandfather accepted without complaint.

Figure 3. Ida and Adolf Stern.

Christmas and Chanukah are festivals that frequently coincide or overlap, so every December, Ida Stern, Karl's mother decorated a Christmas tree in the store to celebrate the season with the family's friends, customers, and employees. And each December 5th, following Bavarian custom, his grandfather dressed up as St. Nicholas to distribute gifts to children in the neighborhood. Evidently, the idea of a Jewish community leader dressing up as Santa Claus did not strike anyone—including their Christian neighbors—as incongruous or inappropriate, and the intriguing oddity of this situation did not even dawn on Karl until he was eight years old.

Meanwhile, during these seasonal festivities, Karl often went to friends' homes or local Churches, where Christian iconography was prominently displayed. Moreover, at his mother's instigation, Stern attended a local kindergarten run by nuns. So, as he himself observed:

> [...] my first religious education was Catholic. We had no catechism but we were entertained with stories from the Bible, particularly from the New Testament, which were illustrated with colored pictures on the wall. There was also a little prayer now and then. I must have been impressed by the pious atmosphere. I have only vague recollections of the stories, pictures and [...] our Christmas play, in which I had a role. (Stern, 1951, p. 24)

When Stern started public school, the next phase of his religious education was entrusted to a local Cantor whose name he did not remember, but whom Stern described as "hateful." As World War I approached, the nameless Cantor was drafted into the Army, to be replaced by a several equally forgettable tutors, until the arrival of Cantor Mohrmann, who had an intemperate fondness for cards and late nights, but imparted a real love of music to his young charges.

While his memories of kindergarten were vague, Stern's recollections of public school in Cham were colorful and distinct. The overwhelming majority of students were children of poor farmers or tradesmen. His first elementary school teacher was a gentle giant named Kaspar Russ—an extremely shy, extremely musical, and devoutly religious man. A fervent fan of Wagner, he was nevertheless fond of Jewish children, several of whom, including Karl, received their first musical instruction from him. Karl's early education was also imbued with the love of nature and literature, imparted by the head teacher Herr Gradl, who led

Figure 4. Karl Stern as a pre-schooler.

Figure 5. Karl Stern and a childhood friend.

the school children on lengthy excursions "through the vast meadows of the Regen valley" to collect botanical specimens, and read Schiller's poetry—and occasionally, his own—when they were well behaved.

On December 5th, 1915—the Eve of St. Nicholas—old Santa Claus failed to show up on cue. Instead, Karl was ushered into his parents' bedroom to greet his younger brother Ludwig, named (for some obscure reason) after the mad King of Bavaria. By all accounts, Ludwig bore a startling resemblance to his older brother, and though Karl did not realize it at the time, his younger brother's arrival severely taxed his mother's delicate health. To lessen the domestic burden on Ida Stern, Karl was sent to a boarding school in Ebenburg, not far from Cham, the following year. From this point onwards, young Karl would live most of the year away from his parental home, only returning on holidays (Stern, 1951, pp. 31–33). Whether he realized that Ludwig's arrival and his banishment to boarding schools were connected—and if so, what sense he made of this state of affairs—is unknown.

In any case, Karl's experience in Ebenburg can be summed up in three words—lonely and boring. He and two older boys, Leo and Alex, lived on the second floor of a dismal, mouse-infested building. A dreary synagogue was downstairs, and on schooldays, they attended a school across the road. Stern described Ebenburg as "a drab industrial town," and the religious instruction he received there as perfunctory and formulaic. "There was hardly anything left of the world of Isaiah—just a little establishment for circumcisions, funerals and for singing prayers on certain days" (Stern, 1951, p. 33). Looking back, the best thing Karl could say about Ebenburg was that it enabled him to appreciate the medieval charm of his home town—which he had hitherto taken for granted. Now vacations, spent at home, seemed like "furloughs in heaven."

At eleven, Karl went to school in Munich, where he fared better. He lived with the Kohens, an orthodox Jewish family. The head of the household, "good, tiny Frau Kohen," was a widow of modest means whose children were slightly older than he was. The Kohen home was suffused with a warm, pious atmosphere that enchanted Karl, and for the first time in his life, he experienced the Passover *seder* as a moving and meaningful ritual. At synagogue services, Stern prayed alongside orthodox Jews, and was quite moved by their fervor, which contrasted starkly with the eclectic, episodic and often lackluster observances back home. In his own words:

> There is a famous story told by Perez of a Rabbi and his disciple who, while slowly starving to death, discuss Talmudic problems,

Figure 6. Karl Stern as a school boy.

with red eyes and glowing cheeks; these types really exist, I have seen them. (Stern, 1951, p. 42)

Living in Munich also afforded the eleven and twelve year old Karl undreamt of opportunities to visit theaters, museums, operas, parks, and churches. Thanks to Kaspar Russ, Stern had already heard his share of church music, and had found some of it quite beautiful. But now he thrilled to Mozart's *Magic Flute* and Beethoven's *Missa Solemnis*. He would later comment that

> [...] there is nothing like it in the history of art. It is as if you beheld European man, a late estranged European man, already half cut-off from his moorings, just once more stirred in his heart by an experience of infinite importance. (Stern, 1951, p. 39)

As music opened up new spiritual horizons, Karl started to shed his naïve egocentrism. Suddenly, he recalled:

> I was at the age during which children develop the spiritual organs of empathic perception; i.e. at the age when for the first time the strange neighbor in the streetcar becomes a feeling human being, a person who has the same eyes, the same sense of smell, the same brain, the same sensations as myself. It is the age during which the range of sympathy suddenly extends far beyond those nearest to us, in fact it runs for some time the danger of cosmic dilution. (Stern, 1951, p. 44)

"Cosmic dilution" is an odd turn of phrase, and obviously intended to convey how disquieting the suffering of others suddenly became for him. Stern's abrupt awakening also sensitized him to the horrors of World War I; a process catalyzed in part by Uncle Julius. While on furlough from the front lines, Julius praised a book called *Le Feu*, by the Marxist author Henri Barbusse. After reading Barbusse, Karl felt that "scales had dropped from my eyes." He suddenly grasped the senseless depravity of war:

> [...] the dirt of the trenches, the rain, the snow, floods, rats and corpses, the death of so many [...] human beings whom I might have known personally, and it was a fact that innocent human

beings killed one another. The fact that all these people could just as well have been friends was the most stunning insight. (Stern, 1951, p. 44)

Whom did Stern blame for this state of affairs? A "murderous clique of capitalists and industrialists" who conspired to keep peasants, workers, and artisans at one another's throats, so they would not unite and overthrow the greedy profiteers, who whipped them all into a nationalistic frenzy. And so twelve year old Stern started reading about Marxist martyrs like Karl Liebknecht and Rosa Luxemburg, and Martin Buber's beloved friend, Gustav Landauer, the pacifist anarchist murdered by Nazi thugs in 1919, mere days after Stern's Bar Mitzvah.

Looking back on this period of his development, Stern was struck by the confluence of religious piety and revolutionary fervor that suddenly animated him as his Bar Mitzvah approached. Religious piety and revolutionary fervor are often opposed, on the face of it, and a striking feature of Stern's subsequent development was the way he attempted to synthesize and reconcile these two tendencies in himself. In all likelihood, the intense emotions Stern experienced in his early teens marked the onset of an adolescent "identity crisis": a search to find his own voice, and to define his evolving sense of self through his religious and political commitments. According to Erik Erikson, the successful resolution of an adolescent identity crisis requires that adults provide the budding teenager with adequate time and space to explore and experiment with different roles and identities—a "psychosocial moratorium" that enables the young person to discover and refine the ideas and ideals he or she will embrace in the next phase of the life-cycle (Erikson, 1958; Erikson, 1964; Burston, 2007). Sadly, Stern's environment was not really suited for this purpose, and the inner turmoil provoked by his spiritual search was not really resolved till his conversion in 1943, when Stern was thirty-seven years old.

Meanwhile, young Karl's Bar Mitzvah was profoundly disappointing. As Erikson noted, rituals designed to mark significant milestones in human development should have an extraordinary, even numinous quality (Erikson, 1964). But on the day of Karl's Bar Mitzvah, the boy who preceded him on the *bima*—the podium were Torah is chanted—could not read a word of Hebrew. In fact, he was barely able to recite the preliminary prayers and benedictions. Stern was somewhat better prepared, and when his turn came, chanted a competent

Figure 7. Karl Stern approaching Bar Mitzvah.

haftorah portion from Ezekiel on the resurrection of the righteous, or more precisely, of their dry bones, on the Day of Judgment (Ezekiel 37: 1–14). The basic theme of this passage is collective renewal in the face of overwhelming tragedy; the idea that even in the face of death and devastation, the righteous can trust God to renew and restore His people.

To those conversant with the Prophets, this passage is very potent stuff, and has enormous resonance for Jews and Christians—and even to secular Zionists, who interpret it allegorically—to this day. But no one in the congregation that day was particularly moved or interested in his rendering of Ezekiel. When Karl arrived home, he received some jocular teasing from his relatives, and conventional gifts like the collected works of Schiller and Kleist, and books on polar expeditions and life in far off Tibet. Though he did not say so in quite so many words, the sense of familial indifference to (and estrangement from) his ancestral faith could not have been more pronounced. And to underscore the pervasive cultural anomie, after dinner, Stern's cousins insisted on playing a theme from Wagner's *Valkyrie* on the piano (Stern, 1951, Chapter Four).

Adolescence

Shortly after his Bar Mitzvah, Stern developed a lively interest in various German youth movements. Though differing widely on questions of race, religion and politics, as Stern recalled, these groups shared two basic characteristics: their members spent considerable time roaming fields and forests, and shared a more or less articulate antipathy toward the older generation, especially their fathers, whom they tended to blame for all the evils of modernity.

After mulling over his options, young Karl Stern joined a rather amorphous outfit called "Jung Judischer Wanderbund" (Young Jewish Wanderers) that catered to a diverse cross section of middle-class Jewish youth. With the passage of time, several members of his youth group became committed Communists or Zionists, but as Stern later recalled, most of his fellow wanderers remained decidedly noncommittal. He was the only one who turned to religion while still active in this group. Indeed, in the middle of his fourteenth year, Karl began to rise early to recite the traditional morning prayers, and put on the traditional prayer shawl (*talit*) and phylacteries (*tefilin*) he'd been given as a token of his new status as an adult Jewish male. The problem was that this sudden outpouring of piety alarmed and offended Stern's parents, and oddly enough, elicited sarcasm from his grandfather Moritz, who was easily the most observant member of the family (Stern, 1951, Chapter Five).

Perhaps Karl's family interpreted his newfound piety as a rebellion against his elders, or as a tacit reproach for their own lack of commitment to their ancestral faith. And perhaps they were right to do so. Either way, Karl's elders did not supply whatever it was he needed to navigate his way through his budding spiritual perplexities. Instead, they teased him about the pettiness of his dietary observances and his poor command of Hebrew. Ida, Stern's mother, was particularly distressed. She was convinced that her son had turned his back on "progress," or was teetering on the edge of madness. Besides, she wondered aloud, hadn't she extracted a promise from Frau Kohen the she would *not* draw her son in the direction of orthodoxy? Now, evidently, Ida felt betrayed, and complained that Frau Kohen had reneged on her part of the bargain.

As Stern points out, Frau Kohen was blameless in this respect. But even she could not help the gravitational pull that her culturally and spiritually coherent family had exerted on the impressionable boy as he approached his Bar Mitzvah. For Karl Stern, prayer that is not infused with warmth and passion was pointless and insincere. He was not content with the half-hearted recitation of verbal formulas. He was in search of "the real thing."

Fortunately for Frau Stern, Karl's orthodox phase was short lived. A family council was convened, and uncle Julius called in to sort out his errant nephew. Julius informed Karl that his belief that Jews have a unique and God-given mission to fulfill, and a special role to play in redeeming humanity as a whole, was simply delusional. No religion is as unique as it imagines itself to be, or actually better than any other, for that matter. According to Julius, a true son of the Enlightenment, fierce traditionalism in religious observance is mere superstition—an encumbrance, an atavism or an embarrassment, or indeed, all three. As they argued these points back and forth, Stern recalled:

> The thing that annoyed me was that he did not acknowledge me as an even partner in the discussion, and kept insisting on his age and greater experience. I was fifteen, and he was forty-one, and therefore he believed that I had to listen to him without argument. (Stern, 1951, p. 58)

The most remarkable thing about this episode is that his father played little or no role in this family drama. Perhaps Karl would have benefited

Figure 8. Uncle Julius.

considerably from hearing his father's views on "progress" and "tradition," and—who knows?—a meaningful compromise between the two. But that was not to be. Judging from Karl's recollection of events, his mother and uncle Julius spoke for "the family," but Adolf offered his son no insight or instruction on how to live as a Jewish man in the modern world. One wonders whether Stern's memory was selective, and he simply forgot his father's remarks—and if so, why? And if not, one wonders how the absence of the father's voice was experienced and interpreted by him at the time.

Fortunately for his elders, Karl's experiment with prayer did not withstand familial pressure, and at some point he stopped in the interests of avoiding further unpleasantness. What next? With religion out of the picture for the time being, the logical place to turn was toward Zionist youth groups. Zionism is a movement for Jewish emancipation that arose in response to the rising tide of anti-Semitism that engulfed Europe in the mid-nineteenth century, and a flurry of armed campaigns called "pogroms" that were widely tolerated, and often secretly sponsored, by European states against their Jewish citizens. Calls for the establishment of an autonomous Jewish homeland started in 1840, but it was not until five decades later, at the first Zionist Congress in Basel, Switzerland in 1897, that the Eastern and Western European branches of the movement coalesced under the leadership of Theodor Herzl (1860–1904).

Despite Herzl's leadership, Zionism is not, and never was, a homogeneous ideology. It began as a movement to resettle portions of the Ottoman (and later British) ruled territory known as Palestine, and eventually, to establish Jewish sovereignty over these territories, which were collectively referred to as the *Yishuv*. A second goal, ratified at the Basel Congress, was to revive Hebrew, then a moribund language, giving Jews from vastly different cultures a common tongue to unify them socially and politically. A third goal shared by Zionists was the desire to "normalize" relations between Jews and non-Jews. They believed that Jews' lack of national/territorial sovereignty made them exquisitely vulnerable to marginalization, scapegoating, ridicule and worse. A fourth goal was to reverse the process of deforestation and desertification that had engulfed the region, and to restore the once flourishing eco-system that had been devastated by the Ottoman Turks in the preceding centuries (Burston, 2014a).

To that end, many Jews flocked from around the world to create agricultural communes known as "kibbutzim." A kibbutz is an autonomous, self-governing community based on direct, participatory democracy, economic equality and gender equality (the first kibbutz, Deganyah, was founded in 1909, and many others soon followed).

EARLY YEARS

Unlike youth groups in the *Wandervogel* movement, the Zionist youth groups that young Karl encountered taught Hebrew, agricultural and manual trades; the basic skills needed to build new Jewish communities in Palestine. And they provided good company as well. In Chapter Sixteen of *The Pillar of Fire*, Stern described the young Zionists as

> [...] a healthy, optimistic and wholesome crowd of youngsters; they were, with the exception of purely religious groups, the only happy and well-adjusted people I encountered at that time in Germany. (Stern, 1951, p. 146)

Though alienated from conventional, middle class life, Stern conceded that these young people possessed a strong moral compass. After all:

> They felt that the peculiar nineteenth-century brand of liberalism and unrestricted individualism which was characteristic of the social strata they belonged to was a hollow structure. On the other hand, they recognized the immorality behind that new irrationalism of Klages and Spengler. (Stern, 1951, p. 145)

Nevertheless, said Stern:

> Most of them had no roots in Jewry. Its positive values, its great traditions, its spirit were entirely unknown to these people. A senseless and cruel stigma was what Jewry had become to them. (Stern, 1951, p. 145)

So while their utopian and socialist ideals were not a problem for Stern, at least initially, by the time he reached his twenties, the secular outlook of most Zionist groups left him profoundly unsatisfied. Nevertheless, while still a teenager, he disagreed vigorously with his mother's objections to Zionism. Karl's mother argued that Zionism is a form of nationalism, and therefore a betrayal of the universalistic ideals of the German Enlightenment, of the celebrated novelist Romain Rolland, and playwright George Bernard Shaw, whom Frau Stern was exceptionally fond of. The fact that Einstein was an ardent Zionist, and that the majority of German youth in the *Wandervogel* regarded her Jewish son as a misfit or a menace to society because of *her* Jewish blood made no impression on her. No doubt, it was for these very reasons that Karl initially rejected his mother's position, though her critique provoked some mixed feelings. In his own words:

> I was torn by conflicting motives. On the one hand I admired the noble (cosmopolitan) […] spirit of such people as Romain Rolland and Friedrich Wilhelm Foerster. On the other hand I thought it ignoble and cowardly not to identify oneself openly and emphatically with a despised minority. There seemed to be nothing very noble about the fact that so many Jews had a blind spot for their Jewishness. (Stern, 1951, p. 60)

To put Stern's retorts to his mother in historical context, remember that they occurred in the early 1920s, when a series of vicious pogroms against Jews in Ukraine suddenly reached a sickening crescendo. Estimates vary, but roughly 200,000 Jews were killed, and many more were injured and displaced. At the time, Ukraine was governed by General Symon Petliura, who vigorously opposed to the Bolshevik Revolution. Whether Petliura supported these vicious anti-Semitic rampages, or was merely powerless to oppose them, as seems likely, remains controversial. But in response to these events, said Stern, he and many other members of the Jewish Youth Movement canvassed the Jewish neighborhoods of Munich to raise money for the victims. The results of this campaign were quite meager, relative to the community's actual wealth. Indeed, Stern was stunned by the indifference of Munich's Jewish community, many of whom regarded their Eastern European counterparts as illiterates and peasants; someone else's responsibility. Little did they know what lay in store for them when Hitler came to power, less than ten years later.

So looking back at his adolescence, it appears that Karl's father contributed very little to his eldest son's evolving sense of self, either in a positive or negative fashion. A modest shop-keeper with no strong political or religious convictions, Adolf Stern provided his son with no firm foundation or conceptual co-ordinates by means of which to map or define his own evolving sense of identity—even a negative example, against which Karl could rebel. Meanwhile, as her health slowly deteriorated, and as the world around them became more menacing and chaotic, Karl's mother Ida seemed increasingly determined to shape her son's development by speaking out *against* two ideologies that young

Karl had tentatively embraced: that of the orthodox Jew, and that of the committed Zionist.

Fortunately, in his eighteenth year, Karl had an inspired teacher named Franz Burger. Burger taught Latin and German, and read poems by Ovid, Goethe, Werfel, and Rilke in class. Burger also introduced Stern to the ideas of Freud, Jung, and Adler (Stern, 1951, p. 61), and "instilled in us a religious sense of justice present in those socialists of the early industrial period," arguing against the rising tide of anti-Semitism that was sweeping Germany in 1924 (Stern, 1951, p. 62). Reflecting on the intergenerational estrangement so common in that era, Stern recalled that he was often taken aback by the rude and disruptive behavior his fellow classmates directed toward their high school teachers. In Burger's case, he recalled, he was particularly dismayed, because most of his classmates and contemporaries—who claimed to like and admire Burger, and behaved well in his class—treated him respectfully, but completely ignored his counsel outside the classroom, turning toward fascist and anti-Semitic ideas (Stern, 1951, Chapter Five). Despite the failure of Hitler's beer hall putsch in 1924, the transnational and universalist ideals of Romain Rolland and George Bernard Shaw, which had enjoyed such currency after World War I, and to which his own mother clung tenaciously, were being drowned in a tidal wave of nationalist resentment at the Treaty of Versailles—an ominous portent of things to come.

In the absence of a fatherly presence to guide Stern through this turbulent period of history, Herr Burger's passion for literature and social justice left a deep impression on the adolescent Karl Stern. But sometime in the early 1930s, this principled, outspoken middle-aged man suddenly succumbed to a fatal illness. As death approached, in 1933, Burger warned Karl about the approaching catastrophe, and foretold Germany's future with chilling accuracy.

Meanwhile, in March of 1925, Stern's mother Ida passed away. Her death was not unexpected. She had contracted rheumatic fever as a younger woman, and after the birth of Ludwig, had shown signs of heart disease. Even then, however, she worked long hours, and refused to take sensible precautions for her health. She succumbed to a stroke in 1923 which left her paralyzed on her left side, and her concern for young Ludwig—who was seven at the time—prompted her to elicit a promise from Karl's father that he would remarry when she passed

Figure 9. At home, 1925.
Ludwig is on the right, Karl second from right. Moritz is third from left, Adolf second from left.

away. The fact that his mother and father discussed these things openly in his presence was profoundly disconcerting to young Karl. So was her funeral, which like his Bar Mitzvah, was an awkward and unsatisfying ritual, devoid of meaning, charm or consolation (Stern, 1951, Chapter Six). Nevertheless, he described the impact of her passing on the family as follows:

> During the following year Grandfather, Father and Ludwig lived in that house like three sailors marooned on an island. When I was at home, things were even stranger. Since I was then nineteen and Ludwig only nine, there was the impression of four generations of men. It was a house of four males who appeared to walk around with an air of aimlessness. When I later read in the medical literature of the behavior of men in high altitudes, the "first stage" always reminded me somehow of us four in that house. In a sense, the atmosphere had really lost a certain amount of oxygen; all this in spite of the fact that we still had Therese, our faithful old maid-servant, and Mother, after all, had been quite out of action in the last year of her life. (1951, p. 72)

A year or so later, in keeping with his promise, Adolph remarried. Karl's stepmother, Helene, was a "roundish, jovial person with a great treasure of affection." Grandfather Moritz never warmed to her fully, but Ludwig bonded instantly, and Karl, now twenty years old, was impressed by his younger sibling's affection for her, and eventually began to address her as "Mother." With the passage of time, he even felt, in some vague way, that his mother had been instrumental in "sending" his stepmother to the four shipwrecked sailors (or stranded mountain climbers), and credited her with transforming all their lives with her "patience and kindness and warmth."

Medical school

Looking back on his years in primary and secondary school, Stern paid tribute to teachers who, despite various personal handicaps, taught by example, and made their deep love of nature, literature, music, and ideas palpable to their students. In recalling their impact on him, he noted that today's educational experts focus almost entirely on questions of curricular content and teaching methods, because they undervalue (or simply fail to understand) the less tangible or quantifiable dimension; the impact which a deeply committed teacher's presence has on the class as a whole.

Similarly, when reflecting on his medical training in Frankfurt, Munich, and Berlin, Stern stressed the importance of the personal element. Stern allowed that the preclinical part of medicine could be handled in a standardized, impersonal fashion, but insisted that medicine is an art, as well as a science. It requires knowledge and technical skill, but also intuition and wisdom. Following Karl Jaspers, he acknowledged the importance of transmitting factual knowledge, but stressed the impact of working with "the Master" and the importance of "Socratic method"—the lively give-and-take between student and teacher. As a result, more than half a century ago, Stern warned that North America was in the midst of a profound cultural transformation that spelled "the twilight of humanist medicine" (Stern, 1951, Chapter Seven).

Stern's misgivings about medicine at mid-century, which still ring true today, render his descriptions of the men who taught him anatomy, physiology, and chemistry during his twenties all the more poignant and illuminating. Their teaching approach was idiosyncratic, by contemporary standards, but effective, because it moved and motivated as well as informed students. Thus, Stern could write: "When I look back at every one of those lectures, I feel like some old opera addict when he ruminates over his evenings at the Metropolitan" (Stern, 1951, p. 75). Clearly, Stern was deeply engrossed in his studies, and enchanted by his teachers' masterful command of their subject matter. That being so, it is instructive to note that Stern inspired this very same sense of gratitude in some of his own more accomplished students, whose tributes

Figure 10. The medical student.

to him have helped keep his memory in Canada alive (e.g., Goldblatt, 1992; Goldbloom, 1999; Stahnich, 2010).

Of all his teachers in Frankfurt, the one who made the deepest impression on Stern was an internist named Franz Volhard (1872–1950). As Stern recalled, Professor Volhard possessed enormous sensory acuity, combined with the personality of an "exuberant and expansive artist." He was an excellent violinist, who did everything "in some strangely large and strong style," and refused to follow textbooks. Instead, Volhard's method of instruction was to confront students with a new patient and a new set of diagnostic mysteries to solve in each class, planting shrewd questions and patiently eliciting answers until a consensus gradually emerged.

Between 1930 and 1931, Stern also had the privilege of working with Dr. Kurt Goldstein as a resident in psychiatry at the Frankfurt Neurological Institute. Goldstein (1878–1965) was a pioneer in the rehabilitation of brain injured war veterans, practicing a kind of holistic neurology that was sensitively attuned to the nuances of the patient's experience and ongoing psychological issues. Given the importance that Stern's association with Goldstein had for Stern's career in years to come, he said surprisingly little about him in *The Pillar of Fire* (Stahnich, 2010).

Nevertheless, Stern eventually followed Goldstein to the department of neurology of the *Moabiter Krankenhaus* (Moabit Hospital) in Berlin, performing numerous brain autopsies on deceased mental patients. Much as he had relished the individuality and expressiveness of his teachers thus far, Stern now realized that medicine has another, less uplifting side to it. The Moabit Hospital was a vast and sprawling entity, a world unto itself, with a very specific and very rigid hierarchy, consisting of rules, roles and expectations. To counteract the pressure and anonymity of such a regimented environment, Stern and his peers spent many hours discussing science and politics and—above all—one another, "analysing" one anothers loves and hatreds, aspirations and blind spots This was a common enough pastime for psychiatric interns by the end of the 1940s, perhaps, but was completely new to Stern. Up until this point, Stern had shied away from this kind of freewheeling, unsupervised mutual psychoanalysis. But now, he found, "we were all inebriated by some miasma emanating from a mixture of Freud, the Russian novelists, Mann, Gide, Joyce and others" (Stern, 1951, p. 80). With all these novelists in the mix, he was suddenly in his element.

Despite his introverted personality, and distaste for the bureaucracy and anonymity, Stern thrived.

One teacher at Moabit Hospital who made a deep impression on Stern was Professor Ernst Haase. As Stern recalled, Haase was a shrewd yet compassionate doctor who conducted a clinic for alcoholics and drug addicts from the slums surrounding the hospital. Whether he was dealing with a homeless, unemployed middle-aged man or a young woman recently thrust into prostitution, said Stern

> [...] he penetrated right into the core of the psychological and social situation. When it came to find a rational solution, he seemed to have unlimited resources of imagination and "know-how." He drew an appallingly small salary for all this, but I often noticed, when he believed himself to be unobserved, that he slipped money into the hands of some alcoholic's wife. (Stern, 1951, p. 83)

Haase's charity impressed Stern deeply, but so did his political acumen—if not at first, then subsequently. Haase warned Stern that despite appearances, the Soviet experiment was a dismal failure, and that the Bolshevik revolution had turned deeply destructive. And this matters because at this point in his life, if asked, Karl Stern would have described himself as a Marxist. True, he harbored doubts about some aspects of dialectical materialism, especially with respect to what Jaspers called "liminal situations." But for the moment, his orthodox Jewish and Zionist phases seemed far behind him.

Like Paris, in those days, Munich had a flourishing café culture, and when he wasn't engaged with his medical studies, Stern was a regular at the Café Gassner, along with a diverse group of students in medicine, physics, and mathematics. One such person was Erich von Baeyer, a medical student like himself. In terms of temperament and physique, Karl and Erich could not have been more different. Erich was heavy set and muscular; a blunt extravert with no aptitude for self-reflection. Karl, by contrast, was slender, and not particularly robust. And by his own admission, despite all the adolescent "mutual analysis," he was also somewhat introverted. But Erich was a good painter, an excellent draftsman and a superb cellist; traits Stern valued highly. He also despised National Socialism, and like Stern, feared that the recent upsurge of nationalism—in Germany and elsewhere—would destroy pan-European values. In this, they were in complete agreement. But unlike Stern, who came from humble beginnings, von Baeyer came from an illustrious family. His father was a distant relative of Felix Mendelsohnn and an internationally renowned Professor of Orthopedic Surgery. Erich's grandfather had won one of the first Nobel Prizes in chemistry, and there was even a statue in his honor in one of Munich's public plazas. Finally, Erich's *great* grandfather was a famous general and geographer, who introduced the use of lines of latitude and longitude to Europeans.

Despite their different backgrounds and temperaments, Karl and Erich became fast friends, and Stern was soon paying regular visits to the von Baeyer family's home in Heidelberg "just above the Neckar River close to the old bridge." On these occasions, as a rule, Karl and Erich played chamber music together. To a shy and awkward young man unaccustomed to such opulent surroundings, there was a striking lack of formality about the place. In the von Baeyer home, as Stern later recalled, "There seemed to be an air of careless improvisation about everything." Erich's brothers came and went, sometimes joining in the musical pastimes, sometimes pausing briefly en route to other activities and destinations. At dinner, Thomas Mann or Adolph Busch might drop in unannounced for a meal and conversation.

Looking back, Stern remarked that in 1930, Heidelberg society was characterized by a mood of "esthetic aloofness." Local historians, sociologists, and philosophers were frequent guests, and often joked about Hitler, or talked "in a precious and ambiguous way about Hegel, and the idea of the state." Erich's father, a large, quiet man, was sometimes vexed by the smug or frivolous remarks of his dinner guests, and after a caustic remark, would retire to his study. And everyone took his behavior in stride.

One day, Stern recalled, he passed through a room where a young woman was doing some ornate lettering on a large piece of parchment. She did not look up from her work. Stern was uncertain of her identity until Erich entered the room and announced, "This is my sister." It is not clear whether they exchanged any words on this occasion, but Stern recalled that she was "strikingly handsome" and that her craftsmanship was superb. The next morning, apparently, she entered the room while Karl was playing piano, and they became better acquainted. They even played a duet—the second movement of the fourth Brandenburg concerto.

Erich's sister, Karl's future wife, had chosen an unusual path in life. Born into a family of scientists, and surrounded by intellectuals on all sides, Liselotte von Baeyer broke with family tradition. Instead of studying languages, philosophy, music or art, as women of her class were expected to do, at fifteen years old she left school and began a seven years long apprenticeship in a bookbinder's shop. Historically, bookbinding was a male occupation, one that involves a great deal of manual labor and dexterity. Not surprisingly, most of her fellow apprentices were from artisan families, and many were Communists. However, she flourished in this environment, which as a friend observed, "brought her closer in spirit to the scriptorium of the medieval monk than to the bindery of a modern print-shop" (Shaw, 1951, p. 429). After gaining her Master's diploma in bookbinding, Liselotte left Germany for London, where she studied the art of lettering with Anna Simon, a student of Eric Gill. Later still, in Canada, her exceptional skill in the art of restoration prompted Robertson Davies to entrust his entire collection of rare and antique manuscripts to her. Thanks to Davies, most of the ancient books in the University of Toronto's Massey College Library were re-bound and restored by her hands. The same is true of many volumes in the Ossler Library at McGill, and a leather-bound edition of Shakespeare that was given to Queen Elizabeth II on one of her state visits to Canada. This was no small achievement, which attests to her national (and international) reputation.

But these developments lay far in the future. On first acquaintance, Karl was struck by Lisellote's devotion to her former nanny—a pious, semi-literate, middle-aged spinster named Kati Huber, who ran the household with skill, assurance and a lot of color commentary. As Stern recalled:

> Her religious upbringing gave her the conviction, never formulated, that everybody has his appropriate place in life. The so-called "inferiority complex" and true humility are two opposites. She treated fellow domestics and visiting Nobel laureates to her crude jokes with naïve equality. Her warnings and criticisms were usually given in the form of proverbial "sayings"; many of these aphorisms contained dark and incomprehensible metaphors, and it was never certain how much of this was ancient folklore and how much freely improvised [...]. (Stern, 1951, p. 93)

Figure 11. Liselotte von Baeyer.

Looking back, Stern speculated that Liselotte's adolescent rebellion and subsequent career choice was due partly to her deep affection for (and perhaps identification with) Kati Huber.

In any case, in 1931, Karl returned to Frankfurt to become Professor Volhard's "Lecture Assistant"—a rare honor. At eight every morning, Karl appeared in Volhard's office to describe the patients who were available for the day's clinical demonstrations.

> Like a chef who proposes the menu of the day, I would say: "We have today a mitral stenosis, a cirrhosis of the liver with ascites, a cancer of the colon, a chronic pericardial adhesion and a spastic hemiplegia," and he would reply: "Always the same stuff. Can't you get something different once in a while, not ever?" (Stern, 1951, p. 96)

Once Volhard selected the clinical "material" for the day's instruction, the patient was wheeled into an amphitheater. No medical history was given or taken, initially. Instead, Volhard would observe the patient silently, then glance toward the residents, and ask, simply, "What do you see?" After several minutes of silence, said Stern, someone in the amphitheater would suggest a diagnosis based on a particular symptom, e.g., the patient's rate of breathing. Then, in due course, another would comment on a pallor around the mouth, or the peculiar shape of the patient's fingers, or the prominent veins in the patient's neck, and so on. The length of these preliminaries varied considerably, because it was only after the students had observed everything that could be seen from a distance that Volhard permitted them to examine the patient directly—to take pulses, palpate their bodies, examine their fingernails, peer directly into their eyes, etc.

As a point of principle, this first examination was always performed in a Hippocratic manner, without medical instruments or devices, as Volhard trained the novices' attention on the visual signs of illness, then to tactile and olfactory cues, such as different rhythms and irregularities in a patient's pulses, the different smells emanating from their skin and mouths, etc. Then—and *only* then—were the residents permitted to study x-rays, graphs, and other test data that had been acquired, enabling them to clinch the diagnosis, and then discuss their findings in more abstract, theoretical terms.

Even by contemporary German standards, Stern recalled, Volhard's teaching method was unusual. His teaching was punctuated by "volleys of cajoling, sarcasm, flattery, ridicule and praise. At some stupid

Figure 12. Stern and colleagues in the lab.

reply he would 'wince as if in physical pain'" (p. 98). But the end result, said Stern, was that he:

> [...] fixed clinical pictures in our minds with extraordinary lucidity. Pneumonia, typhoid fever, various types of cardiac lesions [...] represented not just textbook categories but acquired the vividness of drama. (Stern, 1951, p. 99)

Even patients who were subjected to this unusual kind of scrutiny were usually enlivened and intrigued by Volhard's "histrionics," which were a welcome break from the deadly monotony of hospital routine.

Fortunately for Stern, Volhard also took a strong interest in psychosomatics; a lively, growing field at that time. A decade earlier, Viktor von Weizsacker had introduced ideas from existential philosophy and Gestalt psychology into the field of medicine, and the impact of Freud and his followers was also widely felt. Though Volhard had little use for Freud personally, he required Stern to read and discuss papers on psychosomatic topics to his seminars. Moreover, Thomas Mann's book *The Magic Mountain* made a prodigious impression on doctors of that era. Even some surgeons, the most mechanistic members of the medical profession, paid tribute to the novelist, saying that Mann's psychological insights changed their outlook on health and healing.

Thanks to Volhard's enthusiasm, Stern also became an admirer of Mann. Like many of his contemporaries in 1932, Stern was distressed by the lack of coherent opposition to Hitler among German liberals. Mann's politics, as well as his literary craft, struck Stern as having great integrity. He even wrote to Mann, praising his lucid rationalism—which, he later hastened to add, was not the rationalism of eighteen century France, but a more mature rationalism, tested in the fires of German irrationalism—notably Wagner, Schopenhauer, Spengler, Klages, "and all those elements that had contributed to the rise of Nationalism." At the same time, in his letter to Mann, Stern complained that *The Magic Mountain* had lumped Marxism with Catholicism in the (rather unsympathetic) character of Naphta. How unfair to Marx and his followers! Mann replied promptly, thanking Stern for his letter, and expressing the hope that they would meet one day. In response to Stern's objections about Naphta, he noted (with characteristic elusiveness) that people often got erroneous impressions about his political position, because it often changed over time. And as it happens, Stern's did too—quite dramatically, in fact.

CHAPTER TWO

Psychiatry, psychoanalysis, and politics: 1932–1935

Psychiatry, racism, and forced sterilization: Munich

In the summer of 1932, Stern returned to Munich for post-doctoral work at the German Institute for Psychiatric Research. His work there was funded by a grant from the Rockefeller Foundation, and an American Jewish philanthropist named James Loeb. The Institute was founded in 1917 by the eminent psychiatrist Emil Kraepelin (1856–1926), and attracted students from around the world (Shorter, 1997), affording Stern the chance to work alongside people from the United States, Canada, Brazil, Scotland, Poland, Russia, Czechoslovakia, Switzerland, Turkey, Estonia, Spain, and Sweden. Judging from his lively description, this was the first time in his life he encountered such a diverse group of people.

While there was a sprinkling of faculty from abroad, Germans dominated the unit for genetic research, where various kinds of race theory flourished. Needless to say, this environment was ripe for politicization, and when Stern arrived, there were already some Nazis on staff, most of whom refused to sit with Stern (or any other Jews) in the cafeteria. Fortunately, the chief of Neurology, Professor Walther Spielmeyer (1879–1935) and his associate, Professor Felix Plaut

(1877–1940), a psychiatrist who headed up the Institute's department of serology, did their best to curtail or contain the Nazis' baleful influence. Stern started out as Spielmeyer's assistant, whose main duty was to instruct and oversee the work of other research fellows. His office was located beside that of Dr. Adam Opalski, a specialist in microscopy and neuro-anatomy. As Stern later recalled, Opalski could identify tissues or cell clusters from virtually any region of the brain except the cortex, because of the structural similarity of the cells from different regions of the cortex. Stern credited Opalski with teaching him everything he knew about neuro-anatomy, and the two would stage friendly competitions to upstage one another in front of more junior fellows (Stern, 1951, Chapter Ten). As Frank Stahnisch points out, Stern was now at the top of his field, receiving the highest level of neurological training available (Stahnisch, 2010, p. 22). But despite the earlier encouragement he received from Volhard, there was no place for psychotherapy or psychosomatics here. After all, Kraepelin had deemed them to be unscientific (Kraepelin, 1901). Not that Kraepelin had much to offer to seriously disturbed patients in their place. On the contrary, while they described the outward signs and symptoms of mental disorder with painstaking accuracy, Kraepelin and his followers were generally ineffectual in treating severe mental disorders—barring general paresis, which was caused by syphilis, and was therefore treatable with penicillin (Valenstein, 1986). The result, as Stern pointed out, was usually a dreary descent into chronicity, abetted by the tendency to warehouse chronic patients in the most appalling conditions. In his own words:

> In mental hospitals you pass rows and rows of chronically demented men and women, drooling, staring into empty space, crouched motionless or rocking incessantly. In many cases their condition goes on for decades before they die a spontaneous death. (Stern, 1951, p. 118)

Because of Kraepelin's belief that hereditary brain disorders were the root cause of most psychiatric disturbances, there was strong support within the Institute for the surgical sterilization for all schizophrenic, manic-depressive, and "feeble-minded" patients. Stern was quite disturbed by these policies. Indeed, he reflected later, German psychiatry's initial support for the Nazis' eugenics policy appeared to confer a degree of legitimacy on their later, genocidal campaigns against

Jews and Roma—a fact corroborated by recent psychiatric historians (e.g., Breggin, 1993). Stern was also quick to point out, however, that eugenics and sterilization campaigns—which did not become law until 1933, when Hitler took over—were prevalent before Hitler took power, and that comparable campaigns were afoot in other, non-fascist countries (especially the USA) at the same time.

While forced sterilization of the mentally "unfit" was quite commonplace, two cases stood out in Stern's memory. One concerned a devout Catholic spinster in her forties who suffered from severe depression. Given her age and religious convictions, the likelihood that she would ever conceive a child was practically nil. The patient's gynecologist insisted that this state of affairs was the real source of her anguish, and that a sterilization procedure was not merely unnecessary, but would deepen her depression, causing her and her family pointless suffering. Her doctor was over-ruled, and the surgery was performed, with precisely the results he had anticipated. Stern was shocked at the lack of sensitivity, the bureaucratic indifference toward the patient and her physician, who obviously knew her well.

Another disturbing case concerned a World War I veteran who initially sought medical attention for a stomach ailment. While recovering in hospital, he had shared his pacifist beliefs with other patients in his ward, and as a result, was detained for a psychiatric evaluation and later, involuntary detention. After his medical history was read aloud, the patient was brought into the conference room in pajamas and slippers. As Stern recalled, the patient gave a perfectly cogent account of his personal and medical history. In a calm, friendly way, he explained that during combat, it dawned on him that killing others is forbidden by the Gospels, regardless of circumstances, and so he resolved to devote the remainder of his life to prayer, good works, and spreading the pacifist message. Indeed, he felt it was his moral duty to do so, even if most people, including most psychiatrists, regarded him as crazy.

They did. Despite the absence of delusions and hallucinations, of incoherent thought or speech, and though his affect was quite normal during his interview, the psychiatrist in charge of this man's case diagnosed him as "schizophrenic." Moreover, this judgment was accepted as a matter of course; there was no discussion afterwards—and no opportunity for Institute fellows or interns to reflect, to question or offer alternative explanations for the patient's beliefs and utterances, despite the fact that the horrors of trench warfare had transformed many prominent intellectuals, e.g., Freud, Max Scheler, Hermann Hesse, into pacifists as well. No other treatment being available, this patient was sterilized, too. The cruel treatment of the Christian pacifist reminded Stern of a play by Leo Tolstoy, *The Living Corpse,* in which a conscientious objector is deemed delusional by a panel of psychiatrists simply to punish him for calling their own nationalist and militarist beliefs and priorities into question.

To Stern's considerable astonishment, one of his teachers, Dr. Bruno Schulz agreed with his appraisal of this patient's plight. Schulz was another brilliant eccentric—a cultural conservative with an impeccably Teutonic pedigree who, despite prevailing prejudices, frequently fudged his clinical reports to insure that patients were spared the anguish of forced sterilization. During the war, Schulz helped numerous Jewish doctors to escape the Nazis' clutches. Though not a believer, said Stern, Schulz was one of "the noblest and most beautiful souls I have ever encountered." More than anyone, Stern recalled, Schultz disabused him of his simplistic belief that the great dividing line in Europe (and in life generally) is between people on the Left and people on the Right. Clearly, the stark simplicity of this way of categorizing people is potentially misleading. In the years that followed, as war hysteria grew, and Europe was engulfed in flames, Stern found that people he thought of as "staunch liberals" frequently turned out to be rank opportunists, while former "reactionaries" or cultural conservatives (like Schultz) often ended up in death camps for their principled opposition to the Nazi regime. If nothing else, the Nazis taught Stern not to judge a person's character or motives solely on the basis of political ideology. In the end, he said, "the only thing that counts in this world is the strength of moral convictions" (Stern, 1951, p. 123).

The Nazi triumph

On April 1st, 1933, the Nazis seized control of Germany, and incarcerated Kurt Goldstein for a week, until he signed a pledge that he would leave the country. Then, on April 7th, 1933, the Nazis promulgated the *Law for the Reestablishment of a Professional Civil Service* that mandated the expulsion of *all* Jewish scientists and doctors, except war veterans, from the universities and state-funded medical institutions. Predictably, perhaps, the exemption for war veterans was extremely short lived, prompting a concerted flight of German Jewish doctors, neurologists, and psychiatrists from Germany and Austria, chiefly to the United Kingdom and North America. Indeed, by most estimates, by December of 1933 Central Europe lost *one third* of its top-notch neurological, psychiatric and psychological researchers; an exodus of medical talent which benefited the English-speaking world enormously (Stahnisch, 2010, p. 6).

However, Stern lingered on, being lucky—incredibly so. Spielmeyer detested outside interference with the Institute, and despite the adverse attention it generated, he managed to keep Stern employed—something he could still do legally, because the funding for Stern's position came from abroad. The result was that, from April 1933 until Spielmeyer's death two and half years later, Stern and Felix Plaut were among a tiny handful of Jewish men in Germany still working in a university setting—a dubious distinction, as Stern himself recognized. Much as he valued the financial stability that came with this privilege, his position also made him highly visible and exposed; a prime target for future persecution. He felt trapped, and started to think about finding a situation abroad.

Meanwhile, the relentless Nazification of Germany was frightening to behold, though the Nazi movement was less homogeneous than many of its critics imagined, at least in its initial stages. For example, Dr. Leo Mager, a senior faculty member, a geneticist, epidemiologist and an early member of the Nazi party was widely rumored by be a candidate for the Bavarian Minister of Health. But he mistook the term "socialism" in the phrase "Nation Socialism" to be more than a mere slogan. When Hitler seized power in March of 1933, the Nazi brass dispelled his illusions on this score, so he promptly handed in his membership card—an act of great courage, in the circumstances. Along similar lines, Stern encountered a group of Left-leaning Nazis who had long, loud arguments in the Institute's cafeteria. As Stern recalled, several of them held forth on Trotsky's theory of "permanent revolution" as if he was one of their own. Stern pointed out to them that Trotsky was a Bolshevik, and even worse, Jewish. How could they possibly base their political *modus operandi* on his ideas, and treat him as their "evangelist?"

> They turned to one another, laughed, and looked at me as one would look at a political yokel (which I was.) [...] they belonged to a then quite powerful wing of the Nazi party which was in favor of

an alliance between Communist Russia and Nazi Germany against what they called Western Capitalism. They claimed that very few of the Nazi leaders was really an anti-Semite, and that anti-Semitism was quite consciously used merely as a political tool to obtain the support of the petite bourgeoisie. It is quite possible, they said, that Hitler took his anti-Semitism seriously, but most Nazi leaders were not even interested in the Jewish question and employed it only as indicated. As to Bolshevism, it was the same. The anti-Bolshevik campaign was initiated only in order to obtain support from big industry, particularly in France and England. From this they proceeded to develop their own dialectics, which were, in an eerie and weird fashion, similar to yet slightly different from those of Marxism. (Stern, 1951, p. 114)

While Stern was receiving mixed signals on questions of race from Left-leaning Nazis, the messages broadcast by the Nazi controlled media were completely unambiguous. On a visit home in 1933, he noticed many large, brightly lit signs around town that read: "The Jews are our misfortune" and "In this town Jews are undesired." In the town square, a weekly newspaper carried headlines that "reported" that Jews ran call-girl operations out of synagogue basements; that Jews ran Wall Street; that Jews had orchestrated the Bolshevik Revolution, and so on. Storm troopers went to Jewish stores putting signs on windows, warning customers not to shop there. Most non-Jewish shop-keepers and former customers no longer spoke to Stern's father and grandfather. Indeed, most of Adolf's employees actually quit, rather than live with the indignity of working for a Jew.

Stern's first analysis: Rudolph Laudenheimer

Even at its best, before the Nazis took over, the German Institute for Psychiatric Research had very tangible limits for someone like Stern. Racism, forced sterilization, bureaucratic indifference, and outright hostility to patients' religious convictions—these things gnawed at Stern inwardly. But beyond that, something else was sorely missing. As he put it later:

In the department of genetics, in thousands of files, stored on shelves, in cupboards and in crates was the disease of generations.

It could be reduced to simple formulas, to graphs of predictability, and it seemed to lose all passion and the fortuitous chance of suffering which had been experienced in every single "case." In the department of Clinical Research we observed human experience and behavior. We created precious categories. In the department of Neuropathology there were hundreds of museum jars with brains, and thousands of microscopic sections, in colorful stains, mounted on glass. Most of us got out of this with some sense of assurance and power. Sickness, insanity, begetting, dying—all seemed to be objectivated and made to conform with the cleanliness and brightness of our laboratories. (Stern, 1951, p. 138)

Put differently, the hallmarks of the "classical" psychiatry Stern studied were objectivity, quantification, predictability, order, cleanliness, and for many, at least, a vague (though pervasive) sense of omniscience—one oddly at variance with the therapeutic impotence of Kraepelin's approach. The work was interesting, for the most part, but the human dimension was absent, somehow—lost in a welter of formulas and graphs. Gripped by a growing sense of bewilderment and futility, in 1932 Stern decided to undergo a personal analysis with Dr. Rudolph Laudenheimer (1869–1947).

Who was Rudolph Laudenheimer? Stern describes him as a humane psychiatrist whose Jewish parents had converted to Christianity and raised him as a Protestant. He bore a slight resemblance to Sigmund Freud, was deeply versed in the history of art and literature, and together with his wife, hosted lively gatherings of local artists, musicians, writers and scientists at his home. Stern admired and emulated his analysts' humanism and pluralism, and his refusal to be claimed or defined by any particular "ism" in the psychotherapy world—not an easy thing to do, especially in Germany in the 1930s.

Though revealing in some ways, Stern's portrait of his first analyst leaves a lot to the imagination. Stern noted (somewhat cryptically) that in his youth, Laudenheimer was "[…] associated with a group of writers and poets who later rose to fame" (Stern, 1951, p. 139)—perhaps Stefan Georg and his circle? But then, like Stern himself, Laudenheimer had trained in "classical" psychiatry, working under Paul Flechsig (1847–1929), the famous brain anatomist, in Leipzig in the 1890s. With the passage of time, Laudenheimer became disenchanted with this approach, and opened a private sanatorium that soon achieved national renown. During this period, Laudenheimer contacted Kraepelin's *bête noir*, Sigmund Freud, whom he described as a decisive influence on his work. Somewhat later, Laudenheimer also gravitated toward Jung and his circle, though without becoming a fully credentialed Jungian analyst.

In any case, when Stern first encountered him, Laudenheimer had retired from the sanatorium, but continued to see patients in his private practice. Evidently some patients, like Stern, were financially disadvantaged, so in lieu of cash payment, the normal form of compensation, Laudenheimer invited Stern to play selections from Beethoven and Schubert on his grand piano before or immediately after the analytic hour. Stern's analysis with Laudenheimer lasted two and a half years, during which time Stern was expected to keep a careful dream diary and to spend the analytic hour on the couch. Stern described his first analysis as a journey in which he "[…] was slowly and painfully taken through quagmires and seraphic regions" (Stern, 1951, p. 141). While there is usually quagmire aplenty, analytic patients seldom describe being transported into angelic realms. This metaphor is striking. Since by his own admission, Stern began his analysis as a steadfast Marxist, but emerged convinced of "the primacy of Spirit." And at the same time, it underscores the fact that Stern's description of his first analysis was actually quite short on specifics. We may know the result, in Stern's estimation, but we will never know which childhood experiences, family relationships, sexual feelings or liaisons or conflicts concerning religious and professional issues were (or were not) addressed in Stern's dreams, associations and the analysis of the transference.

Still, based on the meager information Stern did give us, we can speculate a little "around the edges," so to speak. For example, Stern remarked that Laudenheimer and his wife were childless, and that a strange sadness pervaded their lives. And he noted that when the issue of payment came up, Laudenheimer made light of Stern's poverty by saying. "I don't want your money! I am like King Saul. I want your music!" (Stern, 1951, p. 142). This was a tactful (and generous) way of circumventing an embarrassing dilemma for Stern, but this Biblical allusion may have had an additional significance. After all, King Saul demanded music from David when he was plunged in the depths of depression. So reasoning by analogy, one wonders whether Stern's analyst was depressed. Since there was obviously no Jonathan on the scene, this curious remark might also imply that Laudenheimer secretly hoped that the youthful musician—the future King David, in the Bible story—would eventually become his successor.

In any event, reading between the lines, one gets the distinct impression that whatever transpired in their sessions together, Laudenheimer served as a professional role model for Stern—the most important one after Burger, Volhard, and Schultz, evidently. After all, as his analysis unfolded, Stern became acutely conscious of something he only sensed dimly before—that a deep understanding of human experience involves things that elude precise quantification, and that our most determined efforts to isolate variables in controlled laboratory settings seldom yield the kind of knowledge we need to really ameliorate human suffering. And this was a theme he returned to frequently in the decades ahead.

Given the political climate in which his analysis was conducted, it seems likely that Stern's emphasis on Laudenheimer's humanism and pluralism were not merely intended to describe him, but to dispel any negative misconceptions people familiar with that period of history may have formed about his analyst. Why? Stern neglected to mention this, but in 1933, just one year after his analysis commenced, C. G. Jung became President of the newly created International General Medical Society. In that capacity, Jung worked closely with Matthias Göring, an Adlerian psychiatrist who was the President of the German General Medical Society for Psychotherapy, and an older cousin of Hermann Göring, a prominent member of Hitler's cabinet. Both of these Nazi-sponsored organizations were committed to purging the psychotherapy field of Jewish (i.e., Freudian) influences ideas and practitioners (Cocks, 1991; Kirsch, 2000).

Of course, Jung broke with the Nazis in 1939, and after World War II, angrily rejected the charge that he was anti-Semitic (Burston, 1999). But many former followers and admirers of Jung's remained in the Nazi fold, and these, in turn, were often attracted to the work and ideas of an eminent Swiss psychologist, Ludwig Klages, whose motto was: "The intellect (*Geist*) is the enemy of the soul (*Seele*)." A flaming irrationalist, Klages was also a neo-pagan, and a fervent apostle of Friedrich Nietzsche. Why does this matter? Well, three decades after these events, in a landmark study called *The Discovery of the Unconscious*, Montreal psychiatrist Henri Ellenberger demonstrated that Klages' ideas played a significant part in the cultural and intellectual milieu that accompanied the rise of psychodynamic psychiatry in Europe in the 1920s

Figure 13. Karl Stern circa 1935.

(Ellenberger, 1970). And more recently, in *The Jung Cult*, Richard Noll demonstrated that though they had no personal contact—or none that is documented, anyway—the "inner circle" of close friends and followers surrounding Klages and Jung in the 1930s overlapped to a considerable degree (Noll, 1994).

That being so, it seems likely that Stern's fond portrait of his first analyst was not merely an act of homage. It was also a slightly defensive gesture, intended to pre-empt the common human tendency to impute guilt by association. After all, looking back at his time at the Institute, Stern recalled:

> There prevailed at that time among the young Germans a peculiar brand of irrationalism. This was a reaction against the rationalist pragmatism which had been handed down to them. *Bios*, Life, was extolled as something that had primacy over *logos*, the Spirit. Even those who were avowedly anti-Nazi used to sit over their after-dinner coffee in the Psychiatric Institute and talk about D. H. Lawrence and Ludwig Klages, the German philosopher of the *bios*.
>
> I think that with D. H. Lawrence it had been a vigorous rebellion against an emasculated bourgeoisie. With Klages it had become a form of shadiness, one of those specifically Teutonic forms of the European illness. [...] Something similar could be found in some of the followers of Jung. It was a strange form of mysticism, which opposed itself to Reason.
>
> Although Laudenheimer belonged to the circle around Jung, he escaped this danger, perhaps because of his profound affinity to the classical, perhaps because of his strong though ill-defined Christian belief, perhaps because of his Jewishness. It seems almost as if a Jew cannot become an irrationalist [...]. (Stern, 1951, p. 142)

From Judaism to Jesus: Zionism, Buber, and advent, 1933

In addition to being a turning point in politics, 1933 was marked by great spiritual turmoil for Karl Stern. By this juncture, Stern was thoroughly disenchanted with dialectical materialism, and was restlessly seeking clarity, closure and a sense of belonging in three disparate communities—orthodox Judaism, Zionism and in a less open and public way, Christianity. On returning to Munich in 1932, Stern briefly rejoined the Orthodox synagogue he attended with Frau Kohen as a youngster, and was received with open arms. Consequently, Sabbath evenings were often spent round the table of Dr. Eugen Frankel, a man of deep faith whom Stern admired exceedingly. Saturday afternoons were often spent in synagogue, studying the Prophets and Rashi's commentaries on the Torah. The metaphysics of Kant and Schopenhauer, the historical conjectures of Hegel and Marx, which he studied so thoroughly in years gone by, receded into the background, as the prophets' pathos and the Messianic idea came increasingly to the fore.

As Stern reacquainted himself with his ancestral faith, he also joined a new Zionist youth group—*Habonim*. This wasn't particularly unusual. In 1933, many previously uncommitted Jews suddenly flocked to Zionist groups, and started to prepare for *aliyah*, or emigration to British controlled Palestine. But religious Jews were seldom among them. Stern's Zionist friends were mostly baffled by his new found piety, which they associated with a ghetto mentality, and regarded as anachronistic or positively unhelpful to their cause. Conversely, his orthodox Jewish friends at Synagogue regarded most Zionists as heretics and apostates, who were trying to force God's hand by hastening the arrival of the Messiah. The one thing that orthodox Jews and secular Zionists of that era shared was contempt for Reform Judaism, which promoted Jewish assimilation into the cultural mainstream, despite the galloping Nazification of Germany. Having embraced the promises of emancipation and equality put forward by the German Enlightenment a century before, Reform Jews tended to be very lax in observance, and quite bourgeois in their attitudes and aspirations. By contrast, orthodox Jews and secular Zionists in Weimar era were quite emphatic about their distinctive cultural identities, and regarded the Enlightenment's promises of emancipation and integration as completely hollow.

Meanwhile, the Nazis were ambivalent about Zionism, sometimes aiding and abetting efforts to transport Jews out of Germany, sometimes hindering them with a view to eventual genocide (Kaplan, 1998). Stern's memoir suggests that while he himself dabbled with Zionism, only to reject it by 1935, his younger brother Ludwig became deeply engaged, and despite his youth, became a prominent leader in the local chapter of *Habonim*. Indeed, Ludwig remained an ardent Zionist for the remainder of his life, while Karl Stern embraced Catholicism a decade later.

That being so, note that after Karl's conversion, Ludwig and he remained close, despite the vast (cultural and geographical) distances separating the bustling metropolis of Montreal, where Karl landed, and rustic Kfar Szold, the kibbutz where Ludwig and his family settled. This fact is amply attested to by their personal correspondence, and the recollections of family members (on both sides.) Still, reading *The Pillar of Fire*, especially the last chapter, "Letter to my brother," it is apparent that Karl's decision to reject Zionism was far from casual. Despite adolescent quarrels with his mother, when he defended the Zionist cause, Karl's rejection of Zionism as an adult was an integral part of the process that culminated in his conversion—or psychologically speaking, his assumption of a Catholic identity.

But much as he deplored the nationalist aspirations of the Zionist movement, Stern always praised the courage, idealism and communitarian socialism of kibbutzniks. Indeed, toward the end of his life, many colleagues recall him saying how proud he was of Ludwig! But these developments lay far in the future. In the meantime, he put out his first tentative feelers toward Christian friends at the Institute—Frau Flamm and the Yamagiwas—and sought counsel from Martin Buber (1878–1965), a prominent Zionist who tried to restore to aspiring *halutzim* (or would be settlers in Palestine) a real sense of their cultural and religious heritage.

One of the great Jewish philosophers of the twentieth century, Martin Buber was born in Vienna in 1878. His grandfather Solomon was steeped in Rabbinic Judaism, while his grandmother, Adele, was devoted to Moses Mendelsohnn, and efforts to modernize European Jewry. So from the outset, Buber's childhood environment tugged him in two different directions—back towards the medieval sensibilities of his grandfather, and forwards, into modernity and the Zionist milieu. When Buber's university career came to an end in 1900, Theodor Herzl invited him to edit the Zionist weekly, *Die Welt*, which he managed from 1901 to 1916. That same year, Buber became acquainted with another Zionist leader, Asher Ginsberg (1858–1927), known to his followers as Achad Ha'Am. Unlike Herzl, Ginsberg laid considerable emphasis on the need to be mindful and engaged with Judaism's spiritual heritage, and stressed the need for Zionists to develop a respectful Arab/Jewish dialogue prior to seeking any sort of statehood (Schaeder, 1973).

In 1916, Buber broke with Herzl, and founded a new weekly journal, *Der Jude*, which promoted Arab–Jewish reconciliation and the creation of a bi-national Israeli/Palestinian state. In 1923, Buber published his most famous book *I and Thou* (Buber, 1970). It gained a wide and sympathetic audience among liberal Protestant theologians like Paul Tillich, and a handful of Catholic philosophers, notably Gabriel Marcel and Emmanuel Mounier. Indeed, Marcel, who became an intimate friend of Stern's, wove lengthy reflections on Buber's theistic personalism into his "Existential diary" (Marcel, 1976).

Stern met Buber several times prior to Buber's emigration to Palestine in 1936. He found him to be a forceful and fascinating presence, and eventually confided his spiritual doubts and perplexities to him. To put their exchanges in context, however, remember that from 1932 to 1935, Stern was also very friendly with a lab technician named Frau Flamm, a devout Catholic widow who worked full time, raised a family, and despite her many challenges in life, radiated calm compassion. Many of the Institute staff, especially younger women, confided in her. Stern also spent many hours with a devout Protestant couple from Japan, the Yamagiwas. Unlike Buber, a more distant figure who provoked ambivalent feelings, Stern described these three friends lovingly. He was deeply grateful for their spiritual support, and the fact that they never attempted to convert him, but urged him to embrace prophetic Judaism and the idea of the Messiah whole-heartedly. The problem, he soon realized, was that discussions of scripture with them were at least as inspiring as those he had with his synagogue study group—so much so, in fact that when his beloved Dr. Frankel asked him to lead a local chapter of young Mizrahi Jews, who were both religious *and* Zionist, Stern demurred. Worse still, he could not bring himself to tell Frankel the real reason for his reluctance—a growing (though still somewhat tentative) sense that his Christian friends were right, and that Jesus is indeed the Messiah.

Then, one evening in December of 1933, Stern came upon a leaflet announcing Cardinal Faulhaber's forthcoming Advent sermon on the theme of "Jewry and Christianity." Stern was not in the habit of heeding such advertisements, but was so wracked with dread over the mounting persecution of Jews and Catholics that he decided to attend this event on December 17th, 1933. As Stern recalled, the crowd were quite conscious of the growing tension between the Nazi brass and the Catholic hierarchy, and were waiting in breathless anticipation for the Cardinal's remarks. What impact did Faulhaber's sermon have on Stern personally? He wrote:

> The sermon came as if it had been timed and written for my personal consumption. It had a profound and irrevocable influence on me. [...] I felt like a child who had known its own house from inside and from the garden, and who is now, for the first time, shown it from far away as part of the landscape. (Stern, 1951, p. 158)

Despite the tremendous impact of Faulhaber's sermon, Stern was not quite ready to take his leave of the Jewish community. Shortly after this event, Stern went to see Buber one last time. He told Buber that he had been studying the Epistles of St. John, and "found there the spirit of Judaism with such purity and in such overwhelming intensity that I could not understand why we did not accept the New Testament." Evidently, Buber agreed that St. John's Epistles reflected "Judaism at its highest," but went on to point out that to be truly Christian required more than this. One also had to believe in the Virgin Birth and the Resurrection of Christ from the dead. And these things are extremely difficult to believe, said Buber (Stern, 1951, pp. 161–163).

Buber's stress on the spiritual kinship between Judaism and Christianity, combined with skepticism with regard to the supernatural elements in the Bible are fairly typical of modernist Jews, for whom faith consists chiefly in the cultivation of justice, mercy and a truth loving disposition—i.e., the ethical dimension, rather than ritualism or belief in miracles. For Jews like these, giving credence to the supernatural elements of the Bible is optional, not essential, to the cultivation of a Jewish identity. So at first, heeding Buber, Stern felt slightly ashamed at his own credulity. But with the passage of time, Buber's reluctance to credit miracles came as a profound disappointment to Stern, who persuaded himself that the Voice at Sinai, for example, was not merely a metaphor, but an actual event, "a true physical phenomenon." And this, no doubt, is what Frau Flamm and the Yamawigas believed. As he himself put it:

> I emerged from the synagogue [...] and [...] met non-Jews who thought my thoughts and felt my feelings, who seemed to glow under the radiation of *shekinah*, the very seat of the Word. Somewhere deep down I felt that all of us Jews who reacted to nationalism around us with national vigor were closer to the Nazis than these people who believed in the God of Abraham, Isaac and Jacob.
>
> There was no getting away from it. If this German woman and that Japanese couple were right, then I was wrong. For if the Messiah had come nineteen hundred years ago then Revelation was no longer enclosed in the precious vessel of *am ha'amim*, the people of peoples. The true bond between the four of us was beyond the blood of the nation; it must have been provided by Him. (Stern, 1951, p. 167)

Stern's growing reservations about Zionism suggest that, consciously or otherwise, he was embracing his mother's objections to it. But rather than seeking a purely philosophical alternative, like the one she had embraced, he needed one that gave him certainty *and* an abiding sense of mystery—the "metaphysical sense" he praised so lavishly in his later work. Was Laudenheimer, his analyst, privy to these spiritual agonies? Probably so, because Stern acknowledges that in the midst of his crisis, he often feared for his sanity, and wondered if his leanings toward Christianity were not abetted by unconscious motives and a need for self-deception. But we'll never know for certain how often or intensively Stern addressed these issues in analysis, because he managed to talk about these contemporaneous events in his life as in they were quite separate, somehow.

Meanwhile, Stern's spiritual torment may have taken a physical (as well as emotional) toll. In January of 1934, he succumbed to the flu, was sent for X-rays, and abruptly informed that he had an advanced case of miliary tuberculosis—usually a fatal disorder. He spent the remainder of that year in a sanatorium in the Black Forest, and made what, by all accounts, was a nearly miraculous recovery (Goldstein, 1999). At the level of self-reflection, we will never know what crossed his mind during the enforced idleness of the sanatorium—though he met some very interesting patients, and admits that, as a result, he was "thinking constantly." However, we do know that he returned to Munich in December of 1934, and that a few months later, his patron and protector, Professor Spielmeyer, was dead of pulmonary tuberculosis. As soon as he could, Stern booked passage to London, where a new life awaited him.

One scene was indelibly inscribed in his memory just before Stern's departure for London: a meeting of Jewish youth groups—religious and Zionist—in Munich. They assembled to hear Buber expound on the Book of Jonah. Buber gave his personal interpretation of the text—one that was brilliant, in Stern's view, but also manifestly at odds with the traditional *midrashim* favored by the orthodox. Heated arguments between the Zionist and the orthodox youth ensued, but Stern was inspired by the energy and commitment of all concerned. And yet, significantly, this was the last communal event that Stern spent in close company with Jews, religious and otherwise. As he later recalled:

How could I forget those two days? We hardly stopped to eat. Everyone had the keenest feeling of concentration. Everyone knew that "in the coming year" he would be "in Jerusalem" or in some strange land. Some, I fear, were deported to concentration camps or and killed.

"Should I ever forget thee, oh Jerusalem [...]." Oh, how I should like to be able to see them all once more, my friends of those days, and tell them a story of a journey which seemed to have taken me infinitely far away from them, but in reality has led me right in their midst. (Stern, 1951, p. 189)

CHAPTER THREE

London to Montreal: 1935–1949

London and Liselotte

Much has been written about the experience of refugees fleeing Europe on the eve of World War II. While brief, Stern's account of his arrival in London is masterful, conveying the sense of isolation, vulnerability, strangeness and insignificance that enveloped him and his contemporaries on all sides. He wrote that:

> [...] we settled imperceptibly, like dust, in the huge cities of the Western world. Then there were corners where the dust tended to collect, and in which it was easily seen. There were streets full of us: Greencroft Gardens, London N.W.; Washington Heights, New York City. Many, however, settled like dispersed particles in Paddington, Ealing or Hendon. Each of us carried an invisible wall of strangeness around him because those summer evenings of our childhood in Konigstein or in Starnburg were incommunicable. (Stern, 1951, pp. 190–191)

If Jewish refugees felt like dust particles driven into inconspicuous corners by the prevailing winds, said Stern, their neighbors experienced them not as individuals, but as the incarnations of an abstract category, as "[…] the German Jewish refugee next door, part of that penetrating anonymity of the city, like the fog." Dust and fog; these are apt metaphors (Stern, 1951, Chapter Twenty-one). After all, both of them are insubstantial, have no permanent residence, and do not travel of their own volition, at the time or to a destination of their own choosing. And they are nuisances, potential hazards—not the sort of thing one welcomes into one's home or on the streets.

A similar sense of alienation blighted occasions that should have been joyous. When friends and relatives, parents and grandparents arrived by boat, Stern recalled, it was a not a genuine home coming, but a reunion accompanied by what he called "the joy of escape," or relief from desperation. But even this feeling soon evaporated, as everyone was now dependent on the anonymous generosity of the new host country, and in circumstances like these "[…] Generosity was no mother. It was a nurse with the odor of antisepsis" (Stern, 1951, p. 191). Moreover, and more to the point, for many, the friends and relatives, parents and grandparents they longed to see did *not* arrive, and the joy of freedom, such as it was, was stifled by their own inability—in the face of bureaucratic indifference and overwhelming odds—to help their loved ones to safety.

In an effort to overcome the crushing anonymity and helplessness of their position, to adapt and "make their way" in these strange new surroundings, Jewish refugees—Stern among them—tried to master the English language. But in so doing, Stern noted, their whole relationship to language changed. Moses Mendelsohnn, the leader of the Jewish Enlightenment or *haskalah*, had persuaded several generations of European Jews that German was the language of Jewish emancipation, and induced his followers to take great pride in the language of Herder, Lessing, Humboldt, Goethe, and Kant (Elon, 2002). But now their native language, once a prized medium of expression, a source of comfort and delight, became the "language of the Enemy," associated— in their own minds, and those of their neighbors—with "that thing behind us, that monstrous Anti-Mother, that dark and demoniac crater from which we had come." The lonely journey from the suffocating embrace of an annihilating anti-Mother to the indifferent ministrations of the "antiseptic nurse" was a step in the right direction, obviously. But it was hardly cause for celebration, and not likely to undo an irreversible sense of loss.

That said, Stern was luckier than most. And he knew it, too. Thanks to a scholarship established by a wealthy Jewish family, he quickly found a position at a neurological institute in Queen's Square. His task was to investigate tumors in the thalamus and the Red Nucleus—a portion of the motor cortex—in the human brain. Though plagued by worry about the friends and family he left behind, Stern flourished professionally. And though he made no attempt to "blend in"—to speak or dress like an Englishman, for example—he did create a fairly comfortable niche for himself while he was there.

One thing that worked in his favor was that, in many ways, Stern found his new work environment a welcome change from the world he left behind. As he later recalled, he admired that mixture "of sobriety and pragmatism, dryness and brilliant lucidity which is so characteristic of Anglo-Saxon science." He also delighted in the English fondness for eccentricity, for unusual and self-taught men, and was fascinated by the lively exchanges among doctors and technicians of different ranks and religious and political persuasions as they performed their intricate, research-related tasks. While acknowledging the "invisible walls" that surrounded members of different social classes, he was also impressed by the sense of solidarity among them, especially in the face of adversity. Even in the absence of a common faith or political ideology, communal rituals like tea and choral singing pervaded the work place, imparting a sense of civility and belonging quite unlike the rigid hierarchies he experienced in Frankfurt, Munich and Berlin (Stern, 1951, Chapter Twenty-one).

One non-Jewish refugee whose arrival preceded his by two years was Erich von Baeyer's remarkable sister, Liselotte. The Nazis dismissed her father from his faculty position, ostensibly because he was fifty percent Jewish, but really, thought Stern, because he was openly anti-Nazi. In any case, Erich and Liselotte's parents had left their lovely home in Heidelberg, and the Professor set up a private practice in some industrial town in the Rhineland. Disgusted and dismayed by developments in Germany, Liselotte went to London, where a friend of her father's, a Harley Street surgeon, put her up in luxury for three weeks at the Savoy Hotel. Then she decided to rent a small room by the Thames, and worked as a local guide for German tourists, a model for magazines and an actress in a short film advertisement for the Savoy Hotel, and finally, as a bookbinder at the Warburg Institute.

Figure 14. Stern and colleagues in London.

When Stern caught up with Liselotte over tea at the Cumberland Hotel, she was living in a rooming house near Primrose Hill. It must have been a strange meeting. Events at home had provoked a deep aversion to most things German. As a result, Liselotte still read Goethe and Nietzsche from time to time, but now claimed to be able to *smell* Germans at a distance, just as Hitler claimed in *Mein Kampf* (1925) that he could smell Jews. Her vehemence was hardly surprising. If Germans were odious to her, it was because the Nazis had robbed Liselotte of her trust in her ancestral homeland, and to a certain extent, in her ancestral faith. It also heightened her respect for Judaism. Stern recalled her saying that: "Compared with the power and the grandeur of the Old Testament, the Gospel was just sugary lemonade and Saint Paul a travelling salesman." To fill the gaping void inside, she did not embrace religion "in any formal sense," but took to reading the Psalms and the Book of Jonah, which gave her consolation in her darkest hours. She also kept a rosary given to her by Kati Huber, and declared that if she ever embraced a religion again, it would be Catholicism (Stern, 1951, Chapter Twenty-two).

Given her state of mind prior to Stern's arrival, her initial responses to Karl's declaration of faith in Jesus were quite understandable. Having nothing left to lose, presumably, Stern now declared openly that the differences between Judaism and Christianity were superficial, a matter of "public school terminology"; that once you understood the Messianic spirit "there was an organic transition, a transition of growth into the Gospel." For her part, Liselotte wondered why Karl would abandon his beautiful Jewish heritage, and interpreted his remarks as a kind of temporary insanity induced by the hardship of exile; one that was likely to wear off in in time. He admired her blunt honesty. As he later recalled:

> We had both been instilled with Goethean humanism, but our revolts against the bourgeois tradition had taken entirely different routes. We had both known the life of "freedom," the perfect libertinism of European youth in the twenties, and the hangover and nothingness of spiritual despair. No matter what our views were, her indomitable courage and her straightness of action expressed reality much more deeply than all my talk. (Stern, 1951, p. 203)

Contemporaneous photos of Liselotte prove that she was a great beauty, but if there was a deep erotic attraction between Karl and Liselotte at this juncture, it is not evident from *The Pillar of Fire*. Indeed, it is impossible to disentangle Stern's account of their courtship from their earnest conversations about faith in dark times. Nevertheless, they must have exchanged signs of mutual trust and affection, because they decided to marry one clear, moonlit night in St John's Wood. "Race mixing" or interfaith marriages were now a capital offence back home, and knowing that the Nazis might use any pretext to injure or harass their respective families, Karl and Liselotte kept their marriage secret and maintained separate residences for a while, just to insure the safety of their relatives.

Primrose Hill: Ludwig leaves; Felix to the rescue

With encouragement from Liselotte, the newly wed Karl Stern moved into a rooming house on Oppidans Road run by a generous and welcoming landlady named Mrs. Silk. It was a temporary home, but one he recalled with exceptional fondness. Indeed, Stern felt as if he and the other boarders—with all their quirks and eccentricities—had somehow been absorbed into a single, harmonious family. The landlady's son Claude, an Anglican clergyman, had lost his wife as a medical missionary overseas, and now wore a cassock and crossed himself when saying grace. Evelyn Cooke, a ship's captain, studied Bach's "Well tempered clavichord" while ashore. But even in this Dickensian atmosphere of charity, tolerance and fellowship, Stern was haunted by loneliness and worry about friends and relatives in Germany, and a persistent sense of alienation from the bustling, anonymous and indifferent city that enveloped the Silk's house on all sides (Stern, 1951, Chapter Twenty-three).

While struggling with these conflicting feelings, Stern began studying Thomistic philosophy and "Christian anthropology." Specifically, he read a book entitled *On Hope* by a German Catholic named Joseph Pieper, who drew on the early Church Fathers and modern existentialism as well as on Aquinas. While Stern's memoir seldom stressed the formative influence of books, this one was an exception. Pieper's book gripped Stern with the same intensity as Henri Barbusse's book *Le Feu* had at age fourteen, but with precisely the opposite effect. Both books engendered a sense of sudden illumination—of the proverbial scales falling from one's eyes. But instead of underscoring the horrors of war, man's inhumanity to man, and so on, Pieper's book gave Stern hope, and elicited a sense of calm exaltation and relief from doubt about the fundamentals of life. Awaiting the arrival of his first child, with Europe teetering on the edge of the abyss, Stern found much solace and inspiration in Pieper's work, and even experienced an episode of ecstatic illumination that lasted for two days. Why? The world, with all its chaos and suffering, suddenly *made sense*. As Stern recalled:

> I used to sit on a bench in Primrose Hill and look over all the City of London. If it were true, I used to think, that God had become man, and that His life and death had a personal meaning to every single person among all those millions of existences spent in the stench of slums, in a horizonless world, in the suffocating anguish of enmities, sickness and dying—if it were true, it would be something tremendously worth living for. To think that someone knocked on all those millions of dark doors, beckoning and promising to each in an altogether unique way. Christ challenged not only the apparent chaos of history but the meaninglessness of personal existence. (Stern, 1951, p. 208)

The claim that history is incoherent or unintelligible, and that existence is meaningless without Jesus would become *leitmotifs* in Stern's work, and are central to the last chapter of his memoir, Letter to my Brother. While he may have entertained ideas like these before this point, it seems likely that they only became settled convictions after reading Pieper, while living with the Silks on Oppidans Road.

At that point, apparently, Stern drafted several long letters to Jacques Maritain (1882–1973)—letters that, by his own admission, were never actually sent. This is somewhat puzzling, because Stern possessed enough confidence to write to Thomas Mann a decade previously, and even to write to Freud in 1935. So it is not at all clear what deterred him now; why the letters where not sent; and why the unsent drafts were not saved for posterity, among the many other drafts and notebooks he kept. After all, in many ways, Maritain was the perfect philosophical role model for Stern. He was well versed in all the literary and philosophical currents in which Stern was immersed, and like Mann, deeply opposed the virulent irrationalism embraced by Ludwig Klages and the Nazis, albeit for somewhat different reasons. Beyond that, Maritain was philo-Semitic, by the standards of his day. He was an outspoken critic of fascism and just as importantly, of unfettered capitalism (Michener, 1955). And last but not least—again, like Mann—Maritain was sympathetic toward Freud and psychoanalysis (e.g., Maritain, 1957)—a trait common enough among artists and writers of that era, but still quite rare among Catholic theologians.

Meanwhile, on July 3rd, 1937, Karl and Liselotte greeted the arrival of their first child, Antony. Photographs of the family's first years in London suggest a warm and intense rapport between mother and son. Stern himself never looked happier, although from this point onwards, most of the photos we have of Stern—including publicity photos—show him looking at the camera with a somewhat detached, sad or somber expression. Then, on November 7th, 1938, all hell broke loose. A distraught Jewish teenager named Herschel Grynzspan, whose parents and sister were trapped in German internment camps, killed a minor Nazi official named Ernst vom Rath in Paris. Hitler had been looking for a pretext like this to justify more brutal measures against German Jews, and treated Grynzspan's desperate act as a "declaration of war" on Germany and Austria, authorizing a massive pogrom known to posterity as *Kristallnacht*. In accordance with Hitler's instructions, Göring and Goebbels ordered thousands of SS and SA in plain clothes onto the streets at around midnight on November 9th, where they were joined by many thousands of civilians who commenced to riot. In the course of the next twenty-four hours, nearly one hundred Jews were murdered, and thousands more were beaten and maimed. Almost all the synagogues in Germany and Austria were destroyed, and 30,000 Jewish males were rounded up and sent to concentration camps (Gilbert, 2006). Among them was Karl's brother Ludwig and uncle Julius, who landed in Buchenwald.

Two days later, on November 12th, Hermann Göring fined German Jews one billion marks, or $400 million, to pay for the damage that the Jews had supposedly caused through Herschel Grynzspan's desperate provocation. This extortionist measure was paid for through the confiscation of Jewish homes and businesses. On that same day, November 12th, Göring also declared that Jews would have to wear a yellow star on their clothing; a policy that was only implemented a few years

Figure 15. Ludwig Stern.

later (Kaplan, 1998). Meanwhile, in the days that followed, laws were enacted that criminalized any and all forms of social contact between Jews and non-Jews. The penalties for Jews were heaviest, of course, but even ordinary Germans could be jailed and "rehabilitated" through special indoctrination programs just for having a friendly conversation with a Jewish neighbor (Gilbert, 2006).

So in retrospect, for most of Europe's Jews, the period from November 7 to November 12, 1938 marked the beginning of the end; the first, unmistakable intimation of the horror and depravity yet to come. In response to unfolding developments, hundreds of German Jews committed suicide (Kaplan, 1998; Kertzer, 2014). Newspaper headlines and radio bulletins announced these horrific events to the international community, and on receiving this news, Stern prayed for his family at a local Church run by Dominicans. His baptism and conversion were still five years away, so the fact that he went to Church and not to synagogue to pray for his family on this occasion was significant, particularly given the Vatican's muted response to these developments, which expressed far greater dismay and disapproval of Herschel Grynzpan's utterly desperate (but completely isolated) act than the carefully concerted carnage that followed (Kertzer, 2014).

Six weeks later, toward the end of 1938, Ludwig was freed, and asked to visit Karl before immigrating to Palestine. So on New Year's Eve, 1939, Karl left Liselotte and Antony in the care of friends in Cambridge, and returned alone to his London flat. Ludwig arrived late that evening looking gaunt, his skull completely shaven. His first words to Karl were "Play me some Schubert," and Ludwig listened intently while wolfing down two boxes of cornflakes. Then, his appetite assuaged, the brothers talked till dawn (Stern, 1951, Chapter Twenty-four).

Ludwig, then twenty-three years old, was merely twenty-two when he was apprehended by thugs from the SA. Conditions in Buchenwald were abominable, but the camp was not yet designed to kill Jews *systematically*. It was still a work and detention center—a brutal, filthy, chaotic place where many died from starvation, exposure, and lack of hygiene. Ludwig's unexpected release occurred because the Nazis discovered that, as a Zionist leader, Ludwig could organize large groups of Jews to leave Germany permanently, to emigrate to Palestine—something the Nazis still permitted, even encouraged, despite mounting objections from the Mufti of Jerusalem (Wistrich, 2010, Chapter Twenty).

Figure 16. Karl Stern at the piano.

Later that year, 1939, Uncle Felix in Chicago used his formidable legal skills and his personal wealth to extricate Karl's father and stepmother from Germany. The details of this process are not relevant here, but by all accounts, Felix's triumph was a near miracle. Karl's father and step-mother arrived in London dazed and relieved, but penniless, extremely sad, and uncertain about their future. They had made arrangements to transport their belongings to England, only to discover that all of their furniture, clothing and personal effects were stolen *en route*. A proud, elderly couple that had worked diligently their entire lives were now destitute, and completely dependent on the charity of others.

Meanwhile, Stern's grant was running out. Fortunately for all concerned, he'd made inquiries about employment abroad. A new acquaintance, Dr. Herbert Hyland (1900–1977), a Canadian neurologist, put him in touch with Dr. Wilder Penfield in Montreal, who had heard of Stern's work some years earlier from Spielmeyer. To his great relief, with Penfield's help, he secured a position at the Verdun Protestant Hospital on the outskirts of Montreal, then at the Hôpital de Nôtre Dame (Stahnisch, 2010). Shortly after that, he was appointed Lecturer in Neuropathology and Assistant Neuropathologist at the Montreal Neurological Institute, where he worked alongside Penfield, one of the great neurologists and neurosurgeons of the twentieth century, a position he held till 1944.

A new world: Montreal

Karl, Liselotte, and Antony Stern arrived in Montreal on Saturday June 24th, Sainte Jean Baptiste Day, 1939. As Stern recalled, there were parades in all the major thoroughfares, and the church bells rang incessantly. They spent their first day in a room at the Queen's Hotel, when a Catholic couple, the Langdons, invited them to stay in their apartment for a few days while they vacationed in the countryside. Mrs. Langdon was instrumental in arranging for a meeting between Stern and Maritain some months later, but meanwhile, Karl and Liselotte made their first tentative forays into Montreal from the Langdons' tastefully furnished home. They were not impressed (Stern, 1951, Chapter Twenty-five). As Stern recalled, they were actually quite demoralized by the:

> [...] monotonous infinity of houses, ugliness insistent and threatening by the very fact of its seemingly limitless multiplication. The houses were jerry-built, rows after rows, creeping along like fungi mass cultured by wealthy people who lived in cool stone buildings, far away from us. The houses were filled with settees; moonlit lake scenes with moose; mahogany radios; Jesus the Good Shepherd [...] and so on. With insignificant variations the same uniformity prevailed on all sides. Thoughts were channeled into all this by radio and newspapers, as if an ocean were artificially aerated. It was as though the mystery of human existence itself were replaced by a Prefabricated Life. (Stern, 1951, pp. 217–218)

The Sterns' discomfort and sense of cultural dislocation was compounded by another more immediate and pressing problem—poverty. For many months after their arrival, half of Stern's salary went to support his parents in England. And until he was naturalized, he could not legally augment his modest salary with a private practice. Fortunately, Liselotte had escaped from Germany with some of her family's furniture—hand crafted items from eighteenth century Franconia. The couple cherished these pieces for the remainder of their lives, faithfully transporting them from one home to the next as their family fortunes grew.

Another factor contributing to their initial unease was the tension among Montreal's ethnic enclaves. In Stern's own words: "[…] everywhere there are frontiers of mistrust" (Stern, 1951, p. 219). This was not chiefly a matter of social class, as it was in England, but of language, nationality and faith. The Francophone population, said Stern, possessed a rural-village culture not unlike early eighteenth century France. Even city-dwelling Francophones were unusually pious, traditional, and therefore wary (if not actually contemptuous) of finance and industrialization—and by implication, of the English and Scots and, of course, the Jews. By contrast, Montreal's Anglophones, were more modern and successful, but often smug, complacent and disdainful of their French neighbors—and toward the Irish, who also settled in Montreal in large numbers, often intermarrying with the Francophones. So, far from being a melting pot, a truly cosmopolitan city, Montreal (as Stern experienced it) merely reproduced and perpetuated all the old rivalries and antagonisms of Europe on a miniature scale "in the form of preciously preserved resentments of bygone times."

Though Stern did not mention them specifically, perhaps, contemporaneous developments in Europe were exacerbating Montreal's ethnic divides. Montreal's Jewish population was openly and emphatically anti-Fascist, and therefore supportive of the Republican side in the Spanish Civil War (1936–1939). By contrast, many Catholic Québecois were rooting for Franco and were openly anti-Semitic. This pro-fascist, anti-Semitic stance was not peculiar to Québec, of course. On January 9th, 1939, Father Agostino Gemelli, a Franciscan priest and confidante of Pope Pius XI, who founded the Catholic University of Milan, remarked:

> Tragic and painful without a doubt, is the situation of those who cannot be a part, for their blood and for their religion, of this magnificent nation. Tragic situation where we see again, just like in the past centuries, that terrible sentence that the deicide population has brought upon themselves, and for that reason they wander the world aimlessly, unable to find the peace of a nation, while the results of a horrible crime continue to follow them everywhere and all the time. (Foschi, Giannone, & Giuliani, 2013, p. 135)

L'Avennire d'Italia, Italy's most influential Catholic newspaper, gave Gemelli's remarks considerable notice, informing readers that his speech was:

[...] an authorized and solemn illustration of this Catholic doctrine that is professed and taught by all in the Church hierarchy from the top to the bottom and by the sovereign Pontiff in the infallibility of his magisterium. (Kertzer, 2014)

Several months after this chilling statement, and one month before the Sterns arrived in Canada, the Spanish Republicans finally surrendered to General Franco after a long and bitter struggle. Franco was a brutal dictator who enjoyed vigorous support from the Vatican—and, indeed, from Hitler—and his victory was greeted as cause for celebration, or at least relief, in the eyes of many French Catholics. As historian Robert Schwartzwald points out, the pre-existing antipathies between the French speaking Catholics and the mostly Yiddish-speaking Jewish community were intensified by these events, and played out rather nastily in the popular press. And they foreshadowed future trends, as many Québecois would soon greet the Vichy regime in France, which was also fiercely anti-Semitic, with great enthusiasm too (Marrus & Paxton, 1983; Delisle, 1998; Schwartzwald, 2009).

So consider Stern's predicament. He was still nominally Jewish, but married to a German speaking Protestant. This state of affairs was already a little awkward, rendering smooth integration into either the Jewish or the Anglophone communities in Montreal slightly complicated. He was also moving slowly but steadily toward conversion, but unlike many Catholics in Québec, was deeply opposed to Franco and Hitler. Considering the mood of the city then, it is no surprise that even after many months: "We had no feeling of 'belonging.' We felt like rabbits who turn up accidentally in the middle of a fox hunt" (Stern, 1951, p. 219).

Stern's feelings of being vulnerable and out of place are interesting from another point of view. Whether he knew it or not, Stern was one of merely 5,000 Jews fleeing the Nazis who were actually admitted to Canada. Many more were turned down or turned away on arrival. In *None is Too Many: Canada and the Jews of Europe 1933–1948* (Abella & Troper, 1983), Irving Abella and Harold Troper documented the Canadian government's response to the refugee crisis engendered by Hitler's rise to power. And as they point out, Canada did substantially *less* than other Western allies to accommodate Jewish refugees—despite the fact that Canada was a vast and under-populated country, very much in need of educated immigrants. Abella and Troper lay most of the blame for this shameful episode in Canadian history on Prime Minister McKenzie King, on Vincent Massey, the high commissioner to Britain, and minister of immigration, Frederick Charles Blair. But with that said, they also acknowledge that Canada's Protestant (Anglophone) elite were thoroughly complicit in this state of affairs. The notable exception—and the only hero in this piece, really—was Canada's ambassador to Paris, Georges Vanier, a native of Montreal, who would become a universally respected Governor-General under John Diefenbaker in 1959. Vanier made a brave, determined and eloquent effort to persuade McKenzie King and his cabinet to reverse course and admit more Jews on humanitarian grounds, all to no avail.

Another feature of Montreal that took the Sterns aback were the frank and frequent expressions of anti-Semitism among the city's (English and French speaking) Catholics. As he himself put it:

> Some Catholic people let us feel anti-Semitism for the first time since leaving Germany. In Germany we had been subject to the cruel precision of a huge, anonymous machine; here for the first time, we experienced anti-Semitism from person to person [...] the spirit of Catholicity we knew in Europe seemed lost [...]. (Stern, 1951, p. 219)

In Europe, Stern had grown accustomed to thinking of the Catholic Church as the earthly embodiment of supernatural grace; an institution that transcended the petty vagaries of nation and race. In Québec, to his dismay, he found that many Catholics had fused their religiosity with nationalist sentiments—sentiments that, in Stern's estimation, had no place in a Christ-centered cosmology. In *The Pillar of Fire*, Stern recalled a vigorous exchange between himself and a French-Canadian priest, who

> In spite of his spirituality [...] was not free from that resentment that which always seems to diminish the stature of a man. In the course of our conversation I pointed out to him how deep the traces of persecution and anti-Semitism are in every one of us, and that I could not believe that Christ would demand of me to join the ranks of those who, on the natural plane, are our persecutors. Everything in me, I said, revolted against the idea. He looked long and pensively at me, and said: "Yes, if following Christ would require me

to become British, I must say this would be a terrible demand." [...]
He continued to be silent for a while [...] and I knew that he understood. (Stern, 1951, p. 259)

In all probability, the nationalistic priest that Stern spoke of was a follower of Abbé Lionel-Adolphe Groulx (1878–1967). Groulx considered French Canadians to be a distinct race whose "blood" was contaminated by intermarriage; something to be avoided at all costs. Groulx also admired Charles Maurras, Mussolini, Franco, and Marshal Philippe Pétain (Delisle, 1993). But Québec nationalists were not the only source of anti-Semitic sentiments. Unlike Groulx, Adrien Arcand, who called himself "the Canadian Führer" was not a Québec nationalist, but an anglophile and a federalist with ties to the Tories, as well as to fascist groups elsewhere in Canada. All through the thirties, he gave thundering anti-Semitic speeches, many from the balcony of his own home in Montreal (Nadeau, 2011).

Fortunately, when he finally converted, Stern identified and aligned himself with prominent French Catholics who were philo-Semitic and anti-fascist, among them Jacques Maritain (1882–1973) and Father Marie Alain-Couturier (1897–1954). Indeed, without their encouragement and example, a man as sensitive and conflicted as Stern would probably never have crossed that threshold. Why? Maritain was a convert from Protestantism, and a follower of the idiosyncratic Catholic philosopher Léon Bloy. But his wife Raissa Oussmanoff was a convert from Judaism, and Maritain cherished his connection (by marriage) to the Jewish faith, and considered himself a kind of honorary Jew. Unlike Groulx and his followers, Maritain supported the Republican cause in the Spanish Civil War, and vigorously opposed the Vichy regime all through World War II. Indeed, after World War II, Maritain served briefly as de Gaulle's ambassador to the Vatican, and was a prominent participant in the committee that drafted the United Nations "Declaration of human rights" in 1948.

Maritain, in turn, introduced Stern and Liselotte to Father Marie-Alain Couturier (1897–1954). Couturier had arrived in New York at the invitation of the French Catholic Church to preach during the Lenten season in January, 1940, and later lectured at the *École des Beaux-Arts* in Montreal. Until his return to France in 1945, Couturier divided his time between these two cities, helping Jewish refugees and their families settle in the new world (Schwartzwald, 1990). An expert on sacred art, Stern described Couturier simply as a "priest-artist," and a tall, slender man of odd but imposing appearance. But Stern's brief, sidelong glances at Couturier's artistic side did not begin to do him justice. A French nationalist himself, Couturier was more sympathetic to the nationalism of Québec's French speaking majority than either Maritain or Stern were. But unlike many Québec nationalists of that era (e.g., Lionel Groulx, Roger Duhamel), he was publicly opposed to Marshal Pétain, Vichy France, and anti-Semitism. In an article entitled "Father Marie-Alain Couturier, O. P., and the refutation of anti-Semitism in Vichy France," Robert Schwartzwald cites a letter Couturier wrote to his brother on April 5th, 1942, as follows:

> As concerns the Jews, I beg of you, remember that you are Christians, that charity tolerates no anti-Semitism, and that even if certain measures seem politically inevitable among those who have been conquered, at least let us maintain the integrity of our hearts. Justice and clarity first of all—but anti-Semitism offends them both. I know very well that these ideas are not fashionable in the world today, but Christianity is Christianity [...] As for me, I have admirable Jewish friends and fully intend to be loyal to them. (Quoted in Schwartzwald, 2004, p. 149)

Baptism

Meanwhile, on August 26th, 1940, a daughter, Katherine, was born to Karl and Liselotte. Though Stern does not say so in *The Pillar of Fire*, there is reason to think that the interval that preceded and followed on the arrival of their second child was one of inner turmoil and indecision for him. Several factors may have contributed to Stern's troubled state of mind. One was his burgeoning friendship with Hugo Simons, a prominent Montreal lawyer whose portrait, painted by Otto Dix in 1929, hangs in Montreal's Fine Arts Museum. Simons was an Anthroposophist, a follower of Rudolph Steiner, and one of the few living representatives of "Goethean humanism" available to Stern in his new, North American milieu. Stern only references Steiner in his published work once, in *The Flight from Woman* (1965, pp. 293–294, ff, 9), but in a letter to Dorothy Day, dated January 15th, 1957, he admitted that: "[...] he (Steiner) [...] has influenced me a lot." That being so, it seems likely that Stern's attraction toward Anthroposophy and Hugo Simons' circle was probably a minor stumbling block to his conversion. After all, in his first letter to Dorothy Day, dated September 1st, 1945, i.e., a year and half after his conversion, he wrote:

> [...] some of my friends here belong to a peculiar originally German Gnostic group who believe in everything (they have retained the Eucharistic principle) but the hierarchy. They have gone back to biodynamic principles of farming and the ancient, well integrated principles of cultural life—and they keep on pestering me! Since they have many excellent cultural ideas their religious ideas are very tempting. (Stern, 1945, DD-CWC, Series D-1, Box 21, Folder 4)

Another, more insistent preoccupation that may have delayed that final leap of faith was something Stern referred to several times as his "traitor complex." As noted previously, Stern was astonished at the intensity of anti-Semitic sentiments among the citizens of Québec. Indeed, in Stern's estimation, open expressions of anti-Semitic sentiments were more prevalent there in the 1930s than they were among Catholics in his native Germany during the 1920s. Reflecting on this sorry state of affairs probably revived earlier fears that his desire to convert was merely a result of disloyalty and self-deception—an issue that re-surfaced in his dialogue with Maritain.

Another factor that may have deterred Stern from converting were the occasional letters from Ludwig, who settled in Kfar Szold—a kibbutz named after Henrietta Szold, an early and important Zionist leader. Ludwig's letters contain vivid descriptions of kibbutz life, which elicited Stern's heartfelt admiration. But reading between the lines, so to speak, they may also have provoked a diffuse spiritual longing and a sense of guilt, because the kibbutzniks' collectivism, i.e., their emphasis on perfect equality, the absence of private property and a hard-working, agrarian life-style, all appealed deeply to Stern, and seemed more consistent with the ideals he'd cherished as a youth than his own (increasingly comfortable, middle class) *modus vivdendi*. Indeed, one almost gets the impression that if Ludwig had abandoned his secular-socialist Zionist mindset, and furnished Karl with a satisfying religious-metaphysical rationale for resettling Palestine—one that included Jesus and Rudolph Steiner—he might actually have persuaded Karl to join him there.

While he wasn't about to uproot his family, in the circumstances, Stern admitted that the values and life style of the average kibbutznik were much closer to the spirit of the Gospels than those of "individualistic" Catholics who flourished in urban settings. Whether they knew it or not, he observed, many Catholics had effectively divorced their piety from their political and economic lives. Though he never used the word "hypocrisy" in this context, Stern was clearly troubled by gaping disparities between the theory (theology and devotional practices) and practice (daily life) among many well-to-do Catholics, who seemed to compartmentalize their piety, keeping it separate from their political and economic lives. In *Pillar of Fire*, for example, Stern spoke of many religious people who live "an individualistic sort of Christian life [...]." They often achieve a high degree of piety, said Stern, but:

> [...] the notion that the Negro problem, or the clearing of the slums, or problems of strikes in the coal-mining area has anything to do with religion is foreign to them. (Stern, 1951, p. 233)

Even after his conversion, unease on this point haunted him intermittently, prompting his generous support for Dorothy Day (1897–1980) and *The Catholic Worker*; a weekly newspaper which combined Catholic social teaching with militant non-violence, and with anti-racist, anti-nuclear, anti-war and pro-immigrant reportage and advocacy of various kinds, alongside rather traditional religious meditations. Day was a former Communist who converted to Catholicism on December 18th, 1927 and founded *The Catholic Worker* movement together with an itinerant Catholic philosopher named Peter Maurin in 1933. She and her followers led a life of voluntary poverty and service to society's marginalized and down-trodden—derelicts, prostitutes, lost souls—and demanded social justice for the working poor (Day, 1952; Fisher, 1989, Chapter 1).

Meanwhile, however, Stern confided his doubts and misgivings to a local nun, who advised him that re-building Israel on "the natural plane" was not sufficient, and not nearly as significant in God's eyes as the suffering he was experiencing as a result of his longing for true sanctity in the world. She also implied that his suffering on this score actually benefited Jews everywhere more than anything he might accomplish at his brother's side, and admonished him that if he failed to understand this, he should forget about Catholicism and the spiritual life and just pursue his natural inclinations.

While Stern listened attentively, perhaps, her words were evidently not what he needed to hear in order to decide the issue. However, through Mrs. Langdon, Stern now learned that Maritain was to visit Montreal, and she arranged for a private audience with the great man at the home of a mutual friend. When finally left to themselves, Stern recalled, Maritain and he spoke in whispers, and "I had from the first moment the deep impression of a strange and pleasant form of personal directness which was the result of great charity and humility" (Stern, 1951, p. 226). They spoke about the different denominations of Judaism, of Stern's yearning for sanctity, about Dostoyevsky's "Grand Inquisitor" and the problem of "iniquity in the visible Church." Maritain openly acknowledged these problems, but advised Stern not to be deterred by these "wounds" upon the Church, and above all

> [...] not to allow the precious fruit of my spiritual experiences to be corroded by my psychological self-analysis, to believe in the genuineness of these insights which occur on a plane quite apart from that of primitive motivations. (Stern, 1951, p. 226)

Given Stern's history to this point, this last bit of advice is ambiguous, and can be interpreted in several ways. To begin with, Maritain must have been advising Stern to trust himself and by implication, to trust Jesus; to stop devaluing or distorting what Maritain said was a genuine religious impulse by dwelling excessively on his "traitor complex." Then again, Maritain may have been urging Stern to abandon his critical faculties altogether and just surrender to his yearning for faith. And on some level, these messages, though quite different in emphasis, are not actually contradictory, so he may have intended to convey *both* these things by these remarks.

However we interpret Maritain's remarks, the fact remains that Stern's exchange with him did clinch the issue—though Stern did not *act* on his decision immediately. For reasons that are unclear, Liselotte decided to take the first decisive step toward baptism, so Stern arranged a meeting with her and Father Couturier, which he describes in *The Pillar of Fire*. Couturier baptized Liselotte and Antony on Whitsunday (the last day of Pentecost) on 1941. A short time later, he heard Dorothy Day speak for the first time at Montreal's Institute Pédagogiques. This too had a riveting effect. But even so, Stern himself was not baptized until December 21st, 1943—many months after the birth of their third child, Michael on June 10th, 1942.

Another mystery. Why this last delay? Again, we don't have enough information to know for certain, because Stern kept these things shrouded in secrecy. But apparently, the long (and perplexing) delay did not dim his enthusiasm. *The Pillar of Fire* concludes, fittingly enough, with a description of Stern's first communion at an early morning Mass on December 22nd, 1943, in the Church of the Franciscan Fathers in Montreal. Stern recalled that when he arrived at the Church it was still dark outside, and that in addition to himself, his wife, and his (much younger) godfather Victorin Voyer, the majority of those present in Church that morning were people on their way to or from work in local factories or hospitals. Most were perfect strangers. Nevertheless, Stern experienced the event as a transformative moment; a kind of spiritual homecoming. He felt:

> [...] as if others were there; my parents, and Kaspar Russ, and the Kohen family, the Jews from the Canal synagogue, and Jacques Maritain and Dorothy Day [...]. And there was no doubt about it—towards Him we had been running, or from Him we had been running away, but all the time He had been at the center of things. (Stern, 1951, p. 271)

Stern's longing to include so many Jews at his baptism ceremony may seem odd, but was perfectly in keeping with his hybrid religious identity. Though he had embarked on a new and different path, he still cherished all these people in his heart, and the gratitude he felt for their kindness and concern overflowed on this occasion. Even so, the fact remains that his parents, the Kohens and the Jews from the Canal synagogue would *not* have celebrated his decision to convert, nor have been present at his first Communion, even if they could have been; quite the contrary. Still, his desire to share his happiness and excitement with them, and his wish that they welcome his conversion to Catholicism is noteworthy. How many Jewish converts to Catholicism entertain similar thoughts about their Jewish friends and relatives as they enter the Church? And why? Sadly, we have no reliable estimates on matters like these. One thing we do know for sure, however, is that from this point onwards, the vast majority of Montreal's Jewish community shunned him, and that this fact caused Stern considerable anguish with the passage of time.

McGill, a miscarriage, Hiroshima, and Dorothy Day

In addition to being the year Stern was baptized, 1943 was the year that McGill University established its department of psychiatry under the chairmanship of Donald Ewen Cameron (1901–1967), then a professor of neurology and psychiatry at Albany Medical School in New York. A naturalized American (and native of Scotland), Cameron had studied psychiatry at the Burghölzli Clinic in Zürich, and later, under Adolf Meyer, at the Phipps Clinic at Johns Hopkins in Baltomore (Cleghorn, 1984). Wilder Penfield, who was instrumental in bringing Cameron to Montreal, advised him to hire Stern. He also advised Cameron to learn French and to integrate with the local French culture—something Cameron stubbornly refused to do. Cameron even refused to become a Canadian citizen, maintaining a residence in the United States.

Though he never warmed to Canada or Québec, Cameron was a tremendously ambitious and competitive man, an empire builder who, until his return to Albany in 1964, was often referred to as "the godfather of Canadian psychiatry." Though he leaned strongly toward biological (or Kraepelinian) psychiatry himself, Cameron was also the driving force behind the creation of the Canadian Psychoanalytic Society, which opened its first training program in Montreal in 1959. The fact that he did so is curious in itself, because Cameron regarded psychoanalysis as quasi-scientific at best. But Cameron was a pragmatist, and psychoanalysis was sweeping North America. He hoped to build McGill's psychiatry department to the point that it would rival the Menninger Clinic in Topeka, both in scale and prestige. If he succeeded, eventually, it was because he was the President of the American Psychiatric Association in 1953, the Canadian Psychiatric in 1958–1959, and the World Psychiatric Organization in 1961 (Cleghorn, 1990). As such, he had no difficulty finding and recruiting talent, and was prescient enough to bring some of the best psychoanalytic minds on the continent to Montreal at one time or another—Miguel Prados, Richard and Edith Sterba, Eric Witakower, Clifford Scott, and many others. At the time, the main reason given for creating a psychoanalytic institute in Montreal was to attract first-rate residents (Cleghorn, 1984), since most psychiatrists of that era needed to be analyzed if they wanted to advance through the ranks or maintain a private practice on the side.

In 1944, Stern was appointed a First Lecturer, and later as an Assistant Professor of Psychiatry at the Allan Memorial Institute of Psychiatry, a psychiatric teaching hospital affiliated with McGill University. In 1945 Stern was also given the leadership of the Geriatric unit, the first in North America, where he rubbed shoulders with Miguel Prados, a student of Cajal, Kraepelin and Mott who had strong interests in gerontology and in psychoanalysis (Cleghorn, 1984). In 1946, Prados started the Montreal Psychoanalytic Club with four members (including Stern), which by 1948, grew to a membership of forty. This organization formed the nucleus of the Canadian Psychoanalytic Society, which was founded in 1957. Meanwhile, Prados and Stern became friends as well as colleagues, and published many important articles together. By most accounts, Prados was also Stern's second psychoanalyst, from 1952–1953. Details concerning Stern's second analysis are even sketchier than those of his analysis with Laudenheimer, but given Prados' pronounced preference for Freud, there was probably no Jung in the mix, this time.

So by the end of 1944, as the tide turned against the Nazis, Stern was a father of three children, and making significant strides in his career. He had also brought his father and stepmother from London to Montreal, where they became devoted grandparents. Uncle Julius, the former entrepreneur and world traveler, had been released from Buchenwald some months after Ludwig, and made his way independently to Stamford, CT, where he worked in a factory, apparently content with his new life, his long letters to Karl still full of life and optimism, despite his diminished circumstances. The only personal tragedy that dimmed the Sterns' horizon at this point was the arrival of a fourth child, Johnny, who was born on November 27th 1943, and died of Spinobifida three days later—a month before Stern's baptism. There is no doubt that this experience took a toll on Liselotte. But by and large, in the mid-forties, things were "looking up."

Unfortunately, even in the best of times, world events have a way of catching up with us. On September 1st, 1945, five months after Germany's surrender, and five days after the USA dropped the A-bomb on Hiroshima, Stern sent his first letter to Dorothy Day, asking for spiritual advice. He began by reminding Day of their meeting in Montreal in 1941, several days after his wife's conversion. He described his intense enthusiasm for her work, saying "[...] there is nothing in the visible Church that I admire as much as your movement." He went on to lament the pitfalls of psychiatric materialism, and recalled a recent reunion with a woman from his *Habonim* circles in Germany, who was shocked at his "betrayal" i.e., his conversion; an experience which left him extremely shaken. Then he gets straight to the point:

> The more firmly and irrevocably I believe in the divinity of Our Lord the more serious become my doubts in the absoluteness of the Covenant of the Church [...]. I was horrified to see, for instance, that after the Atomic bomb the *Osserrvatore Romano* said that it had created "an unfavorable impression" (sic!) in the Vatican, and the next day the supplementary news that this statement was not authorized!! The vicars of Christ! I felt almost as if it was another crucifixion, and the curtain in the Temple was torn into two pieces [...]. I can no longer see any organic unity between the Hierarchy and those people who work as conscientious objectors in Mental Hospitals. (Stern, 1945, DD-CWC, Series D-1, Box 21, Folder 4)

Serious doubts, horror, and indignation; a second crucifixion; the Temple curtain torn in two. These feelings and figures of speech were not randomly chosen, nor were they the product of an untroubled mind. Stern then went on to condemn his own utterances as "terrible thoughts," and speculated that the main reason he was besieged by them was that he found anthroposophy "tempting" and that his "Gnostic" friends keep "pestering" him—or in other words, one imagines, inviting him to join their community. But while his attraction to Anthroposophy seemed genuine, there is something odd and contrived about this interpretation, which may be a complete red herring. Why? Because it appeared to imply that the horrors of Hiroshima and the Vatican's muffled commentary were not enough to provoke lively consternation all by themselves. Then, shifting gears, Stern noted that he is writing a book on "the Jewish question," but cannot make headway because of these "scruples and temptations," adding: "Please pray for me. Yours in Christ, (Dr.) Karl Stern."

Though probably the first, this was certainly not the last time Stern was assailed by doubt, or implored Dorothy Day to pray for him. Though he never disclosed this fact in public, for fear of damaging the Church—or perhaps, his standing within it—the fact remains that later in life, Stern was plagued by doubts about his faith, and that the politics of the Vatican sometimes contributed to his distress. One can sense this fact obliquely in an unpublished fragment from one of his notebooks, dated 15th March 1949:

> You think you are a traitor but you are not. If you are a traitor you are a traitor for Christ's sake. You think you have left Goethe behind, and Tolstoi, and Gandhi and Heine, Kant, etc. But there is nothing good and true in Kant or Goethe or Tolstoi which you cannot find again in the Church [...]. If you don't like Franco you can leave him alone. If you don't like Father Coughlin you can leave him alone. All you have to accept is Christ and his sacraments. (KSA, Series 7, Box 20, Folder 5)

General Franco needs no introduction, of course. But who was Father Coughlin, and why would potential converts be well advised to "leave him alone?" Father Charles E. Coughlin (1891–1979) is hardly known outside of North America, but was someone with a palpable impact on Stern's milieu on arrival in Montreal. A native of Hamilton, Ontario, Coughlin was educated at St Michael's College at the University of Toronto, and moved to Detroit in the late 1920s. After a brief period as a Roosevelt supporter, Coughlin became his tenacious adversary, and an open supporter of Mussolini during the 1930s. Indeed, his newspaper and radio broadcasts were wildly popular, and Father Coughlin used them to promote hatred of "Jewish bankers," alleging that Roosevelt was their pawn, and a budding Communist dictator (Fisher, 1989; Kertzer, 2014). So great was Coughlin's following that in October of 1936 Cardinal Eugenio Pacelli, later Pope Pius XII, visited Roosevelt in the White House to warn him of imminent the danger of America turning Communist. Roosevelt, mindful of Coughlin's appeal, countered bluntly that America was actually in far greater danger of turning Fascist (Kertzer, 2014, pp. 250–252).

Since this unpublished fragment on Franco and Coughlin is not embedded in a longer or more comprehensive discussion of religion and politics, it is difficult to discern whether Stern jotted this fragment down in an attempt to assuage his own inner doubts, or whether he was rehearsing a response to a potential convert who, like himself, was laboring under a "traitor complex." Fortunately, we are not obliged to choose between these two interpretations. They are not mutually exclusive. But the real point is that more than five years after his conversion, Stern was *still* troubled by the presence of powerful people in the Church who harbored pro-fascist and anti-Semitic sympathies. Indeed, one of the main points of Stern's book-in-progress was to develop a rationale for conversion *in spite* of these defects in "the visible Church."

Psychiatry, Freud, and the Devil

Parallel to Stern's lingering doubts and misgivings about politics and the Church, we find him expressing doubts and misgivings about the psychiatric profession toward the end of the forties. In a letter dated March 8th, 1947, Stern wrote to Republican Congresswoman Claire Boothe Luce, who had converted to Catholicism one year previously, thanking her for a recent article, and introducing himself as:

> A psychiatrist, and lecturer in psychiatry at McGill. I am a convert to Catholicism myself, after having gone through various stages of Marxism, left-wing Zionism, etc. I was trained in psychotherapy by a disciple of Jung, a disciple, however, who did not adhere to any "ism," was very eclectic, took in a tremendous amount of Freud and Adler, and was himself a Christian in a humanist Goethean sense.

With these introductions out of the way, Stern informed Claire Boothe Luce that:

> […] I feel, perhaps more strongly than you, that the many genuine observations of Freud must be integrated into a Christian anthropology. This is one of the most important tasks of Catholic scholars in the immediate future. (KSC, Series 2, Box 3, Folder 72)

These remarks were noteworthy, because they foreshadowed several later contributions, notably *The Third Revolution* (1954) and *The Flight From Woman* (1965a). But there is more, because Stern then went on to say that:

> Modern psychiatry has a horrible daemoniacal philosophical superstructure which can only with the greatest difficulty be removed from the basic, genuine intrinsic truth, or rather, truths.

> Many Freudians profess to be philosophically and religiously neutral. They may be sincere, but in that case they are deceiving themselves. Because in modern psychiatry there is in a disguised and implied form a philosophy of nihilism which, we shall see, will be as destructive to our Western culture as Nazism was. Here, however, I am probably saying things which you thought yourself. On the other hand, if I give you a prediction of what I am sure is going to happen on this continent in the wake of this new "psychologism," you would probably think I am crank. (KSC, Series 2, Box 3, Folder 72)

This last paragraph, with its reference to Nazism, recalls Stern's palpable unease with Kraepelinian psychiatry during his residency under Spielmeyer from 1932–1935. But it also foreshadows things Stern would write later—some through the musings of the fictional "Dr. Birnstam," an émigré-psychiatrist in his novel *Through Dooms of Love* (Stern, 1960). Meanwhile, however, let's be frank; this was a pretty dire assessment of the state of psychiatry and psychoanalysis—and a little puzzling, too, in light of his previous remarks about Freud. And was he really talking about psychiatry or psychoanalysis here—or was he *conflating* the two?

The answer is not clear, but either way, Stern concluded his letter by asking Claire Boothe Luce to keep his comments on this score confidential. His request is intriguing when we contrast his personal communications with her to his public pronouncements. Take the article entitled "Religion and psychiatry" published one year later in *The Commonweal* on July 23rd, 1948. Unlike his letter to Clare Boothe Luce, it addressed the "philosophical superstructure" of psychiatry and psychoanalysis with calm erudition and an admirable sense of proportion. Though quite critical of contemporary positivism and scientism, there was nothing shrill or alarmist about his tone, and no dire predictions about the long-term cultural consequences of these attitudes and beliefs in the population at large. The subject matter was the same in both cases. Why this obvious disparity in tone and emphasis?

There were probably several reasons for this. Perhaps Stern felt that if the general public or other psychiatrists guessed at the real depth or extent of his misgivings on this score some harm would result—whether to him or his profession is not entirely clear. Why did Stern feel this way? That is not hard to discern. Psychiatry's attitude toward religion has changed appreciably since the seventies. However, for the first half of the twentieth century, and well into the Cold War era, psychiatry and religion were still locked in a bitter adversarial struggle that started in the nineteenth century. In this climate of opinion, being religious and being a psychiatrist at the same time was inherently problematic. Let us recall two incidents Stern related to his readers. In a brief article entitled "Religion and psychiatry," Stern related the story from his student days concerning concerned an orthodox Russian Jew who was presented at a psychiatric case conference, and who talked at great length about the Messiah. As Stern recalled:

> Our teacher in psychiatry was a charming, very cultured professor who belongs to a school of psychiatry which thinks that it is able to explain everything in terms of localization in various areas of the brain. After our patient had been presented in conference, the professor called him back and said: "Incidentally, that idea about the Messiah, that is nonsense [...] forget about it!" (Stern, 1948b, p. 4)

Another pertinent anecdote from *The Pillar of Fire* concerns a chance meeting between Stern and a former research fellow from the German Institute for Psychiatric Research in the 1930s. The American psychiatrist remarked that: "The first thing we ought to do after the war is give people a rational outlook on life." Presumably, this entailed getting rid of all irrational fear and guilt inscribed in the collective psyche by centuries of religious indoctrination. Stern replied that World War II was unintelligible in the larger scheme of things unless it is seen in light of the passion of Christ. His American counterpart was astonished, and said: "If you really have come to believe stuff like that, you must be schizophrenic" (Stern, 1951, p. 228).

In any case, by now we have discerned a significant pattern in Stern's adult life; one not evident to most readers, perhaps, but fairly obvious from his correspondence. There is often a notable discrepancy between the attitudes and utterances of Karl Stern the public figure and Karl Stern the private individual. This was not a matter of him being hypocritical, "two faced" or histrionic in private—things Stern's critics might have said about him, had they guessed the true extent of his fears and misgivings. On the contrary, this discrepancy was probably due to the fact that he wanted to retain enough trust and credibility to be heard, and in due course, to make a difference. As a public intellectual, Karl Stern would be critical of mainstream Catholicism ("the visible

Church"), and of psychiatry and psychoanalysis. But he still hoped to play a *constructive* role in changing the climate of opinion (and prevailing modes of practice) in both his faith and his profession. He was therefore quite concerned about retaining the confidence of his peers in both these arenas, and so muted some of his criticisms to avoid the threat of ostracism, retaliation and marginalization.

Sometime in the mid 1940s, Stern started to take his family for summer vacations on Lake Mephremagog, where he spent many hours working on the book he wrote to Dorothy Day about in 1945. On March 2nd, 1947, he wrote to her again, asking her to review the chapters he'd produced over the preceding two years "in snatches in between work." And on May 26th, 1947, he wrote again, saying that his first visit to New York was "overwhelming"; that it was a "great thing" to visit her at 15 Mott Street. However, he hastened to add the visit was accompanied:

> [...] by a bad attack of bad conscience. I felt like a bourgeois going "slumming." I think that people constantly live on your mental bank account without ever paying anything into it. (Stern, 1947, DD-CWC, Series D-1, Box 21, Folder 4)

Figure 17. Karl, Liselotte and their children playing at Lake Memphremagog.

Clearly, Stern himself was determined not to be that way, and became a generous supporter of *The Catholic Worker* movement, and an occasional contributor to its newspaper, *The Catholic Worker*. He also gave Day a great deal of emotional support over the years. There is also considerable warmth and respect in the correspondence between Maritain and Stern. But the sheer number and length of the exchanges between them is paltry by comparison, and they lack the intimacy and reciprocity that Stern and Day developed over the years, and which lasted for the remainder of his life (Day, who was born in 1897, outlived him by five years, dying in 1980).

For example, in a letter written just before Christmas in 1948, Stern wrote to Day, indicating that in a previous communication of theirs she was despondent about the Church hierarchy's lukewarm response to her work. To cheer her up, Stern cited several examples of her impact on ordinary priests and nuns in Québec.

> For example, I often meet French-Canadian priests, little curés or monks, and it is amazing to see how these people who come often from such a narrow and parochial-nationalist atmosphere know you and Peter's name, and are intimately familiar with your personalist philosophy. (Stern, 1948, DD-CWC, Series D-1, Box 21, Folder 4)

Stern then went on to reference "a friend of mine, a Spanish physician who fled Franco-Spain as a Loyalist, very anti-clerical"—doubtless a reference to Miguel Prados. In any case, Stern continued, his friend's daughters were now pupils in a convent school, where the nuns were reading and discussing Day's memoir, *From Union Square to Rome* (Day, 1938). Stern concluded his letter as follows:

> I don't mean to say that personal fame is any true moral value but the fact that your work has become rooted in the Church must give you a measure of feeling justified satisfaction. Never mind the [...] Hierarchy. Most of them have always been like that. (Stern, 1948, DD-CWC, Series D-1, Box 21, Folder 4)

So on reflection, Stern's correspondence with Day reveals that as the forties unfolded, he wrestled with some curious and complex feelings about his faith. In his first letter to her, written five days after

Hiroshima, he confessed his profound disappointment in the Church hierarchy—and then, without intending to, perhaps, his simultaneous reluctance to own or express it openly, evidenced in his attempt to explain his anguish and uncertainty as the result of extraneous "temptations." On the other hand, he was so moved and impressed by Day's piety that, as the first draft of *The Pillar of Fire* was nearing completion, he advised her not to heed the hierarchy's "lukewarm" stance toward her—though in truth, the hierarchy's lukewarm public posture masked a highly *ambivalent* attitude toward Day and Peter Maurin (Fisher, 1989). And on some level, one suspects, both of them already knew that to be the case.

On December 2nd, 1949, Stern wrote to Day again. This time, however, he was not seeking advice, but offered his sympathy and support for the heartaches she was experiencing with her deeply estranged daughter and son-in-law. Letters like these were exchanged all through the remainder of Stern's life. So despite the plaintive tone of his first letter, the relationship between Stern and Day was really not one sided, but one of mutual sympathy and support. However, the aforementioned letter is also quite notable because in it, Stern admitted that he suffers from "the most acute, fatal depressions, a hereditary burden from my mother, I think." While they do not occur often, he said, the interference they create is "paradoxical" because:

> [...] I am in [...] conflict because all of my work takes place within the atmosphere of a most belligerent materialism in which "problems of human behavior" are regarded as it they were questions of broken down machines, this is the very antithesis [...] of a Christian Personalism. At times I feel perhaps Providence has allowed me to be stranded within this set-up because I have the heaviest teaching schedule of all the staff, and naturally I am able to get my 2 cents worth in with the medical undergraduates, the nurses and the social workers. At times I think I am fooling myself, and I ought to be doing something entirely different. Thus far, the Holy Ghost has not given a clear cut answer. (Stern, 1949, DD-CWC, Series D-1, Box 21, Folder 4)

Another striking ambiguity! To begin with, Stern attributed his "fatal" depressions to a genetic predisposition he acquired from his mother, and in the next breath, he explains it as the result of current conflicts surrounding his profession, and a sense of futility or a missed vocation—music, to be sure. In fairness to Stern, however, there is no real contradiction here. Both hereditary and environmental tendencies could have been in play, contributing to his bouts of mental paralysis. Meanwhile, despite his moods, Stern's stance toward modern psychiatry was becoming less passive, more confrontational, as he took advantage of his position as chief lecturer at the Allan Memorial Institute to give psychiatric students "his 2 cents worth."

Altogether, the cumulative impression one gets is that despite (and because of) some acute inner conflicts, Stern was striving to strike a balance between being brutally honest and being somewhat effective with his psychiatric peers, and between instilling confidence and the capacity for doubt and critical thinking in his students. Conscientious people in the mental health professions often struggle with ethical dilemmas like these, but strive to keep the extent or severity of their struggles concealed from public view (and really, who can blame them?).

The question that emerges at this juncture is: Did Stern only confide his misgivings about the "belligerent" materialism in psychiatric circles, and his fears of being ineffectual as a teacher, to strong Catholic women—and fellow converts, at that? Or did he confide his concerns to Catholic men like his young friend (and former student) Victorin Voyer, or novelist Graham Greene, whom he befriended the following decade?

Though we lack the documentary evidence to prove it, perhaps, it is certain that he confided in Voyer, Greene, and perhaps a handful of others about these issues as well. Moreover, as the sixties commenced, he would confide many doubts about psychiatry to Dr. Noel Walsh, a former student and friend from Ireland. So, in perusing his correspondence, we have stumbled willy-nilly on another significant pattern in his adult life. Stern confided his deepest doubts and misgivings about his profession to fellow Catholics, but the reverse was seldom true. He would not confide any of his doubts or misgivings about his chosen faith to psychiatrists (or other mental health professionals)—unless they happened to be Catholic. What we make of this state of affairs will depend on how we understand or interpret the rest of his life.

CHAPTER FOUR

The Pillar of Fire: 1950–1955

The Christopher Award

On January 29th, 1951, Father James Keller, director of The Christopher Award committee, sent Stern a brief letter asking him to attend an award ceremony at New York's Astor Hotel on February 15th. The Christopher Awards were created by Father Keller in 1949 to salute authors who "affirm the highest values of the human spirit." While Stern was merely one of five recipients that year, the excitement surrounding *The Pillar of Fire*, was extraordinary, and the book's publisher, Harcourt & Brace, was already touting it as a worthy successor and companion to Thomas Merton's *The Seven Story Mountain*, published three years earlier, in 1948. Evidently, Merton agreed with this appraisal of Stern's book. In fact, on reading *The Pillar of Fire,* Merton wrote to Robert Giroux as follows:

> It is a fascinating book. Karl Stern's conversion would be the death of the nineteenth century myth that science and religion are incompatible, if that myth had not already died. He shows that a scientist who is fully aware of the implications of his science is bound to accept faith. At the same time, he does not make

> the mistake of trying to give a purely "scientific" account of his conversion. The thinly disguised Messianism of Marx has hitherto offered the promise of a religious satisfaction which Communism itself must necessarily refuse them. Some day, I think, many people are going to follow the road that Dr. Stern has followed. (KSA, Series 10, Box 25, Folder 1)

Did many people, including erstwhile Communists, follow in Stern's footsteps and embrace the Catholic faith, as Merton predicted? While we might cite sales figures, if we wanted to, it is really impossible to *quantify* the spiritual response to Stern's book. Later that year, and for many years to come, Stern was inundated with letters from grateful converts and potential converts—some, like himself, from Jewish backgrounds. Many non-Catholic Christians—including C. S. Lewis and Reinhold Niebuhr—also wrote to say how moved they were by his memoir, indicating that the "buzz" the book created was not merely a Catholic affair. Hugh McLellan, author of *Two Solitudes* (1945), a classic of Canadian literature, wrote Stern, saying:

> I can only agree with what the reviewers have all said—at least, all the reviewers I have read. How you can write so well in another language completely floors me. You have a feeling for the texture of English which is amazing. I could feel the grit in the air that first hot day you spent in Montreal. (KSA, Series 2, Box 4, Folder 4)

While all the letters Stern received—or saved, at any rate—probably had emotional resonance for him, letters from fellow Catholics he befriended before his newfound fame surely meant the most. Stern's beloved friend Dorothy Day, wrote: "The book has a tremendous impact—and so gently written—so much with the long view, the view point of eternity. It is truly great." Writing somewhat belatedly because of illness, Jacques Maritain sent his hearty congratulations for the Christopher Award, and was extremely enthusiastic about the book's prospects.

Some scholars compare *The Pillar of Fire* to the narratives of two other converts from Judaism, notably the phenomenological philosopher Edith Stein (Stein, 1933) and Eugenio (Israel) Zolli, formerly chief Rabbi of Rome (Zolli, 1954) (see, e.g., Neuhaus, 1988). But in some ways, the *The Pillar of Fire* also resembles Dorothy Day's book *From Union Square to Rome*, which was published in 1938. Day's book sought to explain her conversion to Catholicism to her younger brother John, who had joined his sister in her activist life, but unlike her, was still a Communist (Fisher, 1989). Similarly, Stern's final chapter, addressed to his younger brother, was entitled "Letter to my brother." Though ostensibly written for younger brothers who were still steadfastly secular in outlook, both books—or portions thereof—were really intended for a much wider audience, inviting them to become vicariously acquainted a brand of Catholicism that integrates spirituality with intense concern for social justice and activism on behalf of the poor and victims of racial and ethnic prejudice.

Nevertheless, in *The Pillar of Fire* Stern distanced himself slightly from Dorothy Day's perspective, situating her work and ideas within the context of two different Catholic responses to the malaise of modernity. According to Stern, there was:

> [...] one large group of people who feel that industrialization and Western urbanization in themselves are neither good nor bad, and that it is a duty of Christians to penetrate the city and the factory with the salt of the gospel. They are careful not to discard the impulse of justice immanent in Marxism and the Labor Movement. They feel that even our present day technology can be spiritualized [...].
>
> On the other hand, there are those who feel that technocracy and industrialism have reached a stage at which they can no longer be reconciled with Christian principles. They are people who reject industrialization as such and attempt to bypass it. [...] They feel that the de-humanizing forces immanent in technocratic society are too strong to be overcome in any way but by de-centralization or by the principle of voluntary poverty. (1951, pp. 231–232)

Stern located Dorothy Day in the second group, but did not embrace either approach himself, arguing that in future, *both* will be necessary to transform society, nevertheless adding that:

> [...] even if Dorothy Day and her followers were wrong on every single point, her merit will always remain the fact that she has transferred that peculiar immediate social consciousness of the early

> Communists right into the Center of the Church, that is to say she has made innumerable Christians deeply aware of the social injustice right in our midst, Christians of the highest aim who otherwise would never have been aware of the urgency of the social question. (1951, p. 232)

Just how does an ancient faith produce highly spiritual people who lack awareness of "the social question?" Stern suggested that during the Middle Ages the "visible Church" was woven into the pattern of a caste-based society, and that the great spiritual leaders of that time did not address the issue of social justice "in a way that can be transferred immediately to our time." With the demise of feudalism, secular and progressive thinkers dismissed or vilified the Church because they identified it with the old order, and it was not until the nineteenth century that the Church began to address these issues.

Meanwhile, said Stern, at the dawn of the twentieth century, two secular ideologies, Capitalism and Communism, became locked in an adversarial struggle for world domination—a struggle whose outcome seemed quite uncertain at the time. At the dawn of the Cold War era, when this rivalry threatened nuclear annihilation, most North American Catholics were ferociously anti-Communist (Fisher, 1989). But Stern took a different approach, and suggested that:

> [...] there are actually two Karl Marxes. One of them was full of truly religious fury. He hurled curses at the capitalists of the nineteenth century and he uncovered the lack of justice and charity inherent in industrialist civilization—very much in the manner of an Old Testament Prophet. His attempt to interpret history was in its motives much more spiritual than he realized. I suppose that an attempt to interpret history with the methods he used is better than no attempt at interpreting history at all. Many of the early communists were followers of this Karl Marx, and their materialism was only a historical costume the dress of the nineteenth century. (Stern, 1951, p. 260)

The other Karl Marx, said Stern was a "streamlined Hegelian absolutist" and a strategist of class warfare, and it was this second Karl Marx who was "successful," leading to horrors equaled only by National Socialism. Therefore, said Stern, it is no coincidence:

> That precisely at this moment the Church reclaims all that has been diffused into these secular currents; that she is re-assimilating the elements of the social gospel which has been disguised, for instance, in Marxism; that hundreds of young priests adopt the social teaching of the Church and become "radicals"; that the two poles of the gospel, the mystery of personality and the mystery of the multitude, begin to fuse again in the consciousness of the people. (Stern, 1951, p. 234)

In Stern's estimation, the ferment that was taking place within the Catholic Church might yet provide a viable alternative to the arid, oppressive materialisms of Capitalism and Communism and truly humanize Western society. Was Stern's optimism on this score actually warranted? In retrospect, probably not. In the mid-eighties, Pope John Paul II's militant anti-Communism prompted him and Cardinal Ratzinger, later Benedict XVI, to stigmatize liberation theology, which grew out of precisely the kinds of spiritual currents that Stern was addressing here. And despite stunning advances in technology, poverty and ethnic strife (including genocide) has increased at a frightening pace globally since the Berlin Wall came down. Even so, there is no doubt that at the time, Stern's hopefulness on this score struck a deep chord in many hearts, and that Pope Francis has rekindled similar hopes that have long lain dormant in the Catholic world.

Christianity and Freud: "The truth shall make you free"

Another interesting feature of the book, which differentiates it from other conversion narratives, is Stern's attitude toward psychoanalysis, which was hardly typical among Catholics of that era. As Paula Kane, Marous Chair of Contemporary Catholic Studies at the University of Pittsburgh, points out:

> [...] the Catholic argument against Freudianism as expressed by the Church involved four issues: 1. that Freudianism expressed a dangerous eroticism in its probing of the intimate lives of clients; 2. that analysis usurped the role of the priest; 3. that it undermined the training of the will necessary to create the "whole" person; 4. that it functioned as false or ersatz religion which tried to replace the sacrament of confession with something inferior. (Kane, 2014, p. 7)

That being so, Kane continues:

> [...] the Church's moral-philosophical critique was always intervening, and always tried to trump psychoanalysis with the *a priori* assumption that the goal of human existence was salvation, not happiness in this life. (ibid.)

Undeterred by the prevailing climate of opinion, Stern depicted Freud as a great humanist whose positivist leanings obscured the latent Christian meaning of his work. In his own words:

> Psychoanalysis with its detailed care for the history of each individual and its emphasis on psychic injuries, reaffirms, more than any other discipline in psychiatry or psychology, the dignity of the human person. This is, in the end, one of the reasons why psychoanalysis has been rejected by Communists and Nazis alike. Freud's atheistic philosophy is a tragic historical accident, but it *is* an accident. His philosophical statements are amateurish and contradictory, and they can easily be separated from his psychology without doing harm to the latter. (Stern, 1951, p. 249)

Accurate or not, this too was a timely message. For as Stern's correspondence attests, at mid-century, many Catholic intellectuals were becoming receptive to psychoanalysis. Indeed, during the 1950s, many of them—including Thomas Merton, Clare Boothe Luce, and Graham Greene—asked him to recommend reading material so that they could become better informed on this subject.

As novel as Stern's ideas seemed to many readers, he was not the first to argue that psychoanalysis is compatible with Christian teaching. That honor goes to the Reverend Oscar Pfister (1873–1956), a friend and follower of Freud, who wrote a spirited rejoinder to *The Future of An Illusion* called "The illusion of a future" (Freud, 1927c; Pfister, 1928). Pfister said that science and religion converge in their belief in the emancipatory power of truth; the belief that "the truth will make you free." Of course, the logical upshot is the corollary assertion is that errors and illusions enslave or mislead us. And according to Pfister, this renders the injunction to practice inner honesty and to root out self-deception a religious as well as a scientific duty (Pfister, 1928). Though he believed in the emancipatory power of truth as fervently as Pfister did, Stern approached this issue a little differently. He argued that there is no intrinsic conflict between science and faith, and therefore, that the effort to embrace the two simultaneously need not occasion any inner conflicts in the believer. As he put it:

> Some time ago I read that Pascal's early death was caused by the inner tortures he endured resulting from the conflict between Science and Religion. It is quite possible that Pascal suffered inner conflicts, but there is no indication that this was one of them. I presume that de Broglie is a Christian and that Planck was a Christian. Pascal and Newton were Christians. It is possible that they were Christians *besides* being Scientists or *on account* of being Scientists, but why should they have been Christians *in spite of* being Scientists?

After all, he said:

> There can be no incongruity between Science and Religion, at least not in a sense of a First Cause, a Creator. As far as that first step is concerned, Newton and Pascal not only cannot have labored under any painful conflicts, but on the contrary—whatever great discoveries they made in their Natural Sciences must have confirmed the first basis of their belief. Their belief, in turn, helped them to integrate their discoveries. Those discoveries would have remained amorphous chunks if the scientists had not in the back of their minds continuously carried the idea of a meaningful Universe. (Stern, 1951, p. 251)

Not surprisingly, like Stern, Pfister laid considerable emphasis on the fact many great scientists were believers. But despite the obvious kinship between the two men, there was also a significant difference between Pfister and Stern. Pfister was a liberal Protestant, and was therefore quite skeptical of the supernatural elements of the Bible, which he tended to interpret ethically or allegorically—like many Reform Jews. He also accepted the Darwinian theory of evolution, and placed considerable emphasis on the idea that a sound religious education requires Christians to think critically and historically about Biblical texts—again, like Reform Jews.

By contrast, Stern valorized the simple and unvarnished faith of farmers, tradesmen, and servants, and tried to link this kind of unquestioning faith to an evolving metaphysical framework that combined elements of Aristotle, Aquinas, Bergson, Scheler, Marcel, Maritain, and other specifically Catholic philosophers. He rejected Darwin's theory of evolution, and was skeptical of evolutionary theorists within the Church (e.g., Teilhard de Chardin). All things considered, Stern's attempt to reconcile Freudian theory with a faith that includes belief in miracles was fraught with many more problems than Pfister's Protestant approach was.

Still, Stern's emphasis on a Catholicism that embraces science *and* social justice had deep resonance for many Christians outside the Catholic orbit, prompting C. S. Lewis to write the following.

> Magdalen College
> Oxford
> Dec 25, 1951
>
> Dear Dr. Stern,
> A copy of [...] *Pillar of Fire* has reached me this morning sent, I understand, at your order. I value this personal present not less, but more, because I already have the book, have read it with unusual interest and pleasure, and recommended it to others who agreed with my high opinion of it. Indeed, it is nearly ripe for re-reading: that second reading which is, in a good book, so much better than the first [...]. The theme of *The Pillar* interested me as well because I have been in close correspondence with a talented Jewess [...] now going through a process of conversion to Christianity, and it was of great value to me to see the same transition in your more mature and scholarly mind. Of course you do a great many other things in *The Pillar*, and introduce me to quite a new atmosphere [...] a rare achievement, for in general biography lacks the immediate convincingness of a good novel [...]. I very much hope you will write more. If you should ever be in these parts I hope I may have the pleasure of meeting you.
> With many thanks and good wishes,
>
> Yours sincerely,
> *C. S. Lewis*
> (KSA Series 2, Box 3, Folder 65)

Stern could not have known it at the time, but the "talented Jewess" Lewis was referring to here was probably Helen Joy Davidman, a novelist and former communist who converted to Christianity, and married Lewis five years later.

Another buoyant letter came from Gregory Zilboorg, the world's most celebrated Catholic psychiatrist and psychoanalyst at the time.

> Gregory Zilboorg, MD
> 33 East 70tth St.
> New York 21, NY
> February 1, 1951
>
> My dear Stern,
>
> Our paths have not crossed for several years—although I have thought of you many times.
>
> [...] last summer I had the pleasure of renewing my acquaintance with Father Couturier whom I visited in Paris. As a matter of fact, he and a couple of friends came to the airport upon our arrival. It was the first time I saw him in his Dominican garb.
>
> However, this writing is prompted by something else. I just finished reading the page proofs of your *Pillar of Fire* [...].
>
> There are many, many beautiful things in your book. Many I would like to discuss with you. To write about them in a letter would be both presumptuous and anemic. We will talk about them. To your spiritual road you have a very clear, simple, design; that is why it has such an immense impact.
>
> If and when you are in New York please let me know. I will advise you when I am in Montreal.
>
> With kindest remembrances and best wishes,
>
> Yours cordially,
> *Gregory Zilboorg*
> (KSA, Series Box 5, Folder 58)

Encouraging letters like these poured in from all sides, and many letters from fellow Jewish converts were even more effusive. But *The Pillar of Fire* provoked anger and shock among Stern's Jewish readers, whose letters bristle with indignation. One example, from George Edelman of New York City, reads as follows:

> Dear Dr. Stern
>
> Yielding to the counsel of a Catholic cleric, I've picked up your "Pillar of Fire" for earnest Jewish study.

> I've read the jacket and your own foreword, and pause to communicate the incommunicable. You were a Poalei-Zion adherent and turned Catholic? I am entering into the jungle of ideas that your book, at this early juncture, promises, and wonder how I will emerge.
>
> During the war, when I here in New York City was so excruciatingly beset by the horrors in Christian Europe, I one day visited a Catholic Church not far from my home. I thought some clue there I might find to the moral collapse of an entire continent.
>
> The Church was empty; it was a weekday afternoon. Directly under the priest's rostrum, on the left of the pulpit-altar, I saw a horrifying sculptured scene, a black bearded Jew lay prostrate and bleeding, pale as death itself, and the priest's feet in the rostrum atop this, before the assembled worshippers, standing atop the dying Jew.
>
> In a flash, though I was frightened by what I saw—for this is humanity loving America—but in a flash I thought I knew the clue to our appalling experience in Christendom. It tallied with the history of our people in Catholic Christendom almost everywhere.
>
> But you became a Catholic—from a Jew. You speak of electricity in the foreword, and of even inanimate objects being affected—and you're a psychiatrist. What can have happened? [...] in your mind or heart, an imperceptible, as yet little understood, electrical transformation?
>
> I'll risk and read. Meanwhile I invite word from you.
>
> Faithfully, etc.
> (KSA, Series 2, Box 2, Folder 73)

While Stern kept this letter among his personal papers, there is no indication whether he replied to it. And on reflection, what could he possibly say? Clearly, Mr. Edelman's remarks were not only intended to express his own confusion and incredulity, but to elicit feelings of guilt and doubt; to trigger Stern's "traitor complex." Even so, Edelman's letter was comparatively civil in comparison with one from a former member of the Canal Street synagogue in Munich. The author of this letter was Gottfried Neuburger, one of the orthodox Jews Stern met in Munich while living with Frau Kohen. In a scathing letter dated October 5th, 1951, this childhood acquaintance remembered Stern as someone

[...] who knew all the semi-Hebrew expressions, that formed the jargon of the cattle-dealers, but who had trouble in reading even the simplest daily prayers. (KSA, Series 2, Box 2, Folder 44)

Similarly, Neuburger said: "[...] from childhood on you have celebrated Chanuko and Christmas together, making both empty formalities." And as an adult, Neuburger complained: "You have gone from Leibnecht to Herzl to Freud to Buber, all on the outer fringes of Jewry, all thorough agnostics or atheists [...]."

Then, in a final fit of indignation, Neuburger added:

> The Karl Stern I knew was a very ambitious and intelligent boy. I am trying to figure out what mental change, if any, he has undergone. He now believes that a Jewish illegitimate [...] child was a god, that a Jewish young man, crucified by the Roman occupation authorities—as were thousands of others—as a subversive character and a persistent demagogue, was a god, that a Jewish bachelor who [...] had not the faintest idea that he was or would become a god, was a god. [...] Would the Karl Stern I knew seriously believe in the divinity of someone whose godlike nature was decided on in a council by a majority vote centuries after his death? (KSA, Series 2, Box 2, Folder 44)

Toward the end of his letter, Neuburger taunted Stern by lumping him together with converts such as Thomas Merton or Scholem Ash "who know the trick of turning spiritual experiences into hard cash." Unlike Edelman, Neuburger did not invite Stern to attempt an explanation or even a reply, saying: "I [...] have no time for further correspondence. I just thought you might be slightly amused to know how the simple Canal Street Jews feel about your book."

Did Stern anticipate such indignation from former acquaintances he hoped might remember him fondly? Perhaps so, but one can only imagine that this letter—and others like it—hurt him, because on March 9th, 1951 Dorothy Day wrote:

> You must suffer terribly over the controversy among the Jews. I do feel for you. But thank God you wrote it. You had to. You were inspired I know. It is a beautiful book of calm and peace. Everyone

I meet is reading it. My love to your dear family [...]. (KSC, Series 2, Box 2, Folder 63)

Given that the Jewish community were furious or scornful, Stern was extremely fortunate that his extended family were more accepting of his decision to convert. We'll never know what they said or thought in private, but the letters he received from his uncles, aunts and cousins at this time were far less angry and confrontational. Many members of his extended family wished him well, and greeted his conversion with curiosity, perplexity, but also warmth and amusement. Above all, note that even after *The Pillar of Fire* was published, Karl's correspondence with Ludwig continued to flourish. And despite having renounced his German name for a Hebrew one—Ludwig Stern became Shimon Shavit—he still signed letters to Karl as "your Ludwig"; an obvious sign of affection.

All in all, given the immense success of his first book, 1951 may have been the happiest year of Stern's adult life. We get a glimpse into his domestic situation in an article called "Meet the Karl Sterns" in *The Catholic World* in March of 1951, written by James Shaw. The premise of this whimsical portrait was that despite his scientific and literary accomplishments, Stern was *really* a musical genius—at least in the eyes of fellow musicians. Feigning an inability to discern his true vocation, Mr Shaw took readers on a guided tour of the Stern household, ostensibly to get a better sense of the man. On first encounter, he finds the celebrated Dr. Stern on all fours in the living room horsing around with Antony, aged thirteen, Katherine, aged eleven, and Michael, aged seven, and their dog Maxie. Not only is Dr. Stern vigorously involved in the action, but he is giving a rapid, blow by blow commentary on everything that ensues when the ball is loosed, as if he were a radio announcer and this were a real sporting event—complete with commercial interruptions for Armour's dog food.

Shaw's description of this spirited romp is followed by an account of an annual household event known as "Upside down day," when the Stern children boss their parents around, and Karl and Weibi—the family's nickname for Liselotte—mimicked their children. Shaw's portrait of Liselotte, which followed next, was both searching and sympathetic, as he tried to discern something about the man by his choice of a spouse and vice versa (Shaw, 1951).

If we were to take our cue from the title of Shaw's playful character sketch, we could conclude that Karl Stern was actually several different people, all of whom were remarkably accomplished. And if we were following the lead of some influential theorists nowadays, we might even infer (quite seriously) that Stern had as many "selves"—or at the very least, identities—as he had social contexts. If asked, however, Stern himself would have rejected this interpretation as a concession to (or symptom of) a rationalist, mechanistic mind-set which promotes fragmentation, isolation, and abstraction, rather than a holistic understanding of the human person. If we take Stern's personalism seriously, then the effort to disentangle Stern the researcher from Stern the clinician and Stern the teacher, and so on, is utterly absurd. By the same token, it is impossible to cleave these professional "selves" from the literary, philosophical and musical Stern, and any of these from the stalwart man of faith. Stern a similar point in connection with Weimar music historian Wilhelm Schmid, to whom he devoted a chapter in *The Pillar of Fire*. Stern wrote that:

> The most remarkable feature of this man was [...] the perfectly homogeneous synthesis of artistic and spiritual or, better, of musical and religious values.
>
> The word "synthesis" is not quite correct, for it implies that these elements once existed separately. In his case, one could not conceive of them separately [...]. Music was religion, allegiance to something; and religion, on the other hand, was deeply interwoven with its modes of artistic expression. "*Musica sacra* penetrated and tempered *musica vulgaris*, the firstborn, with its creative breath," Schmid said. The profound organic relation was apparent everywhere [...]. (Stern, 1951, p. 183)

After the Christopher Award in 1951, Stern became a celebrity in Catholic circles, and was widely sought after on the Catholic lecture circuit in North America. Thanks to the efforts of Clare Boothe Luce, on April 21st, 1951, he was declared an Honorary Member of The International Mark Twain Society, an honor he shared with former Presidents, Prime Ministers, and generals, and many esteemed clergymen, scientists, novelists, poets, and playwrights of the day. Stern put his newfound celebrity status to good use, urging readers of *The Catholic Worker* to make donations to *L'Eau Vive* ("Living waters"). On page five of the

December, 1951 edition of *The Catholic Worker* ("From the mail bag"), Stern informed readers that he had recently visited a community by this name near Paris, which was:

> [...] initiated by Father Thomas Philippe, a Dominican [...] Male and female students of the university of Paris and the nearby seminary of the Dominican Fathers live in a cooperative community [...]. The agricultural work is done by the students themselves, the cooking and washing by the girl students. The liturgical life forms the center of the existence of these young laymen but the settlement is inter-denominational. I met there a young Lutheran from Norway and a Confucian from China. Perhaps the most interesting group is one of Christian-Arab students [...]. Of all things the European traveller can see today this experiment is one of the most encouraging [...]. (KSA, Series 9, Box 22, Folder 1)

Like Marie-Alain Couturier, Père Thomas Philippe was a French Dominican who combined deep spirituality with an open-minded, ecumenical outlook, long before ecumenism became official Church policy. He was the mentor and spiritual preceptor to the celebrated Canadian scholar and activist Jean Vanier, who lived at *L'Eau Vive* (in Soissy-sur-Seine) for a year before returning to Canada to complete his doctoral thesis. Stern's efforts to assist the young Jean Vanier came to the attention of his father George Vanier, then Canada's Ambassador in Paris, later Canada's most beloved Governor General, who sent Stern Christmas greetings on December 21st, 1951, saying:

> My wife and I feel that your book will be a success in France where it will do much good. Jean was very touched by your letter and I understand that your work on behalf of Eau Vive has borne fruit already.
>
> May 1952 be a year of health and happiness for you and those dear to you.
>
> Yours very sincerely,
Georges P. Vanier
(KSA, Series 2, Box 5, Folder 37)

The Third Revolution

If 1951 was a banner year, 1952 presented some complex challenges. Joseph Pieper was lecturing in Canada that year, and recalled a conversation with Stern in which he feverishly confided that:

> [...] it was no longer possible for him to continue to work in an atmosphere of a completely secularized Psychiatry that would be solely guided by the conviction that all the sources of mental illness had to be found in Religion which needed to be eliminated as a psychiatric "complex." Even at night, he was haunted by the perception that a radically nihilistic revolution was about to take its origin from the North American continent. This revolution had the sole promise of the socio-psychoanalytic-therapeutic creation of absolute happiness. (Cited in Stahnisch, 2010, p. 50)

In light of these misgivings, in September of 1952 Stern left the Allan Memorial Institute to become Chief of the Department of Psychiatry at the Ottawa General Hospital, a predominantly Catholic Hospital. He was followed there by a former student and close friend, Victorin Voyer (1917–1975), who helped Stern transform this new department into an important center for education and research. Later that same year, he became a Professor of Psychiatry at the University of Ottawa, where he remained a popular figure for the rest of his life. Needless to say, the move from McGill to the University of Ottawa had nothing to do with Stern's effectiveness in the classroom or the laboratory. As Frank Stahnisch points out:

> There are numerous local accounts highlighting Stern's ability as an academic teacher: he seemed to have interested a whole new generation of medical students in Montreal and later in Ottawa in the histological study of the brain, psychopathology and the anthropological perspective of psychiatry. These accounts attest to the value of a broad training which is often forgotten in the tunnel vision that lauds scientific excellence in a specific discipline, disregarding a solid education as the deep source of future innovations. (Stahnisch, 2010, pp. 50–51)

But according to Robert Cleghorn, who succeeded Ewen Cameron as the Director of the Allan Memorial Institute in 1964, Stern's departure from the Allen Memorial Institute had less to do with his holistic and humanistic leanings than it did with:

> [...] his religious convictions, which saw a denial of spirit and a hazard in the prevalence of the widespread agnosticism of science.
> (Cleghorn, 1984)

This is true as far as it goes. But on reflection, one wonders whether Stern's frequent questioning of the materialistic and deterministic underpinnings of mainstream psychiatric theory and practice, and his deep popularity among students annoyed or alarmed Ewen Cameron. After all, Stern now had a wide public following who were receptive to his evolving critique of psychiatry. This fact was not lost on Cameron, who was the very embodiment of the anti-religious, nihilistic tendencies Stern found so disconcerting. From Cameron's perspective, by contrast, Stern was probably a major nuisance who was threatening to become a genuine liability.

Whether Stern left voluntarily, whether he was pushed, or whether he read the proverbial writing on the wall and left *before* being pushed out, as seems likely, remains unclear. But to say that no love was lost between Cameron and Stern would be an understatement. As Stern confided to Noel Walsh, Cameron epitomized the "daemoniacal" side of psychiatry he'd complained about to Clare Boothe Luce in 1947. And in years to come, as Cameron's flagrant abuse of patients gradually came to light, many others came to see Cameron in a very similar light (Collins, 1988; Burston, 1996).

In the meantime, it is interesting to note that Stern's brief analysis with Miguel Prados commenced just prior to his departure from "the Allan." Was this sheer coincidence, or did the (inner and interpersonal) conflicts that culminated in Stern's departure prompt him to seek comfort and clarity in his colleague's analytic practice? Or did he just feel that his first analysis had been insufficient? We lack enough information to say for certain. Perhaps all these factors were in play. In any event, around the time he left "the Allan," Stern began working on a book in which he attempted to "baptize" Freud, integrating his ideas into a "Christian anthropology," just as he had said he would do in his letter of 1947 to Claire Booth Luce.

Stern's second book, *The Third Revolution: A Study of Psychiatry and Religion* was published in 1954. It explored the Freudian concepts of libido, psychosexual development and sublimation in the light of Catholic teaching. In many ways, *The Third Revolution* expanded on arguments already present in *The Pillar of Fire*, namely that Freud provided Christianity with an "embryology of love"; that *scientism*, not science itself, is the real enemy of religion; that the positivist underpinnings of Freudian metapsychology obscure the fact that Freud's greatest clinical discoveries were not the product of detached scientific reasoning, but of what St Thomas called "knowledge by co-naturality," i.e., empathy and intuition. This time, however, before addressing Freud specifically, Stern prefaced his discussion with a thoughtful critique of the de-humanizing tendencies that bedeviled the mental health field, and more specifically, Kraepelinian psychiatry, behaviorism, cybernetics, and communications theory. And to that end, he also borrowed freely from existentialism and phenomenology.

Another intriguing dimension of *The Third Revolution* was Stern's reflections on the similarities between faith and paranoia. He began the final chapter of this book by noting that in a rationalist society, all faith is suspect. To believe in events that run contrary to natural law is folly so long as empirical evidence and experimentation are deemed to be the sole criteria of truth. The tendency to interpret religious ideation in psychopathological terms makes good sense, from a rationalist standpoint, especially when you consider the phenomenological resemblance between paranoia and faith. This resemblance resides in the fact that the fundamental premise of the paranoid personality—i.e., that Freemasons, or Jews, or the Vatican, are conspiring against them in some hidden fashion—is unproven and extremely unlikely on the face of it. Nevertheless, the paranoid person "sees" things and attributes motives and intentions to others that are profoundly counter-intuitive to those who do not share his fundamental premise, and clings tenaciously to his interpretation of events, even when there is abundant evidence to the contrary.

Similarly, said Stern, believers assume the existence of a kind of benign conspiracy orchestrated behind the scenes for our benefit by God, and are apt to maintain that faith even when the evidence does not appear to support that conclusion. But whereas paranoia is rooted in a fundamental mistrust of others and the world, and is apt to produce hatred and aggression, faith is rooted in abundant trust, and tends to produce love. Consequently, Stern concluded that:

> Paranoia is the mirror image of faith in an ugly distortion. Just as the saint has no difficulty in recognizing other persons as

> ambassadors of Christ, so the paranoid patient easily sees other people as ambassadors of the hated adversary. This is most significant for the psychology of the masses; in times of political restlessness, paranoid personalities (blatant clinical and milder subclinical cases) come to the front. They have an extraordinary power to mobilize latent paranoid tendencies in the population. Vigilance turns into distrust. And in the end hatred becomes a strange bond of union. In totalitarian countries that strange Gift of Distrust, the readiness to see machinations behind events, is systematically mobilized and channeled. (Stern, 1954, pp. 280–281)

Though he did not mention names here, there is no doubt that when he composed these lines, Stern was describing Hitler, Stalin, and Joseph McCarthy, paranoid politicians who were skilled at demagoguery (see, e.g., Stern, 1965b). But a moment's reflection discloses a problem with this line of argument. After all, if history is any indication, paranoid personalities who mobilize the latent paranoia of the masses are as apt to flourish in religious communities as they are in political movements. And in such cases the line between religious and political beliefs and motives is quite blurry or non-existent.

In light of pious hate mongers like Father Coughlin, for example, the only way to justify Stern's characterization of faith as the opposite of paranoia is to stipulate in advance that movements that bind people together in hatred or mistrust are not really religious, but *pseudo-religious*, no matter what kind of elevated rhetoric they use to get followers. Stern would likely have endorsed this caveat, because like Maritain, he was apt to differentiate between the visible and the invisible Church; the former being encrusted with layers of mediocrity and sin, the latter being pure, and endowed with abundant reserves of piety and grace. But if so, then what of the cruel slaughter of Jews that preceded the Crusades in Germany, or the Inquisition that destroyed or dispersed so many Jewish communities under the leadership of Tomas de Torquemada in the Iberian peninsula? Were these movements that convulsed entire societies religious, or merely pseudo-religious? And who gets to make that determination—clergymen, historians, sociologists, the victims or their lineal descendants? Though it ended on a very upbeat note, *The Third Revolution* did not address, much less answer, these disturbing questions.

Nevertheless, like *The Pillar of Fire*, *The Third Revolution* struck a very upbeat and responsive chord in Catholic readers. On November 22nd, 1954, for example, Thomas Merton wrote to Stern, saying:

> I have just finished reading *The Third Revolution* [...] you have said something that needs to be said, and you have said it clearly and well. I fully agree that a defensive attitude toward psychoanalysis, on the part of the clergy and the faithful, would be "destructive" [...].
>
> It seems to me that, for myself, one of the graces of the Marian year has been the rediscovery of psychoanalysis. Last December I ran into a review of some books of Karen Horney, and since then I have read most of what she has written. I find her immensely valuable [...]. Through her I have also run into Erich Fromm. Although he says things in a way which I would never say them, as a Catholic, I see his general trend and am in full sympathy with it. And his background is more or less religious, too.
>
> [...] As a result of all this, I see that it is going to be important for me to keep on reading about psychoanalysis [...] [and] to keep in contact with someone like you. I hope you will someday come down to Gethsemani and visit us. I should like very much to have a talk with you about all these things. Please consider yourself invited down here at any time. And Mrs Stern too—we have a ladies Guest House. (KSA, Series 2, Box 4, Folder 26)

Focused as it was on psychoanalysis and Christianity, *The Third Revolution* lacked the broad appeal of *The Pillar of Fire*. But though it did not sell as well, *The Third Revolution* made a strong impression on the Catholic intelligentsia, prompting Henry Luce, the publisher of *TIME magazine*, the American ambassador to Italy, and a good friend of Pope Pius XXII, to commission an interview with Karl Stern that appeared in *TIME* on August 1st, 1955. The interview did not cover any new ground, but it helped to boost Stern's public profile in the United States and by implication, no doubt, in Canada as well.

Meanwhile, to make his case compelling to Catholic readers, Stern sought the imprimatur of M. J. Lemieux, O. P., Archbishop of Ottawa, which appeared on the flyleaf at the back of the book. While this gesture attested to the strength of Stern's religious convictions, and his determination to reach Catholic audiences, it undermined his

Figure 18. Karl Stern circa 1955.

credibility *outside* the Catholic orbit. After all, Freud's animus toward the Roman Catholic Church was well known, and one can only imagine how Freud himself would have greeted this development, had he lived long enough to witness it. Freud tolerated Oscar Pfister's religiosity quite happily. But Pfister was born a Protestant, had embraced Darwin, and had no use for supernaturalism, interpreting it analogically when circumstances required. Stern, by contrast, was born Jewish and had converted to Catholicism, and never addressed—or even acknowledged—the stigma that Freud and his circle attached to conversion to Christianity; at least, not in print. Moreover, Pfister's allegiances were clear-cut. When the rupture between Freud and Jung took place, he sided firmly with Freud. Stern, by contrast, was far more receptive to Jung's ideas than Pfister was, a fact that Jung gratefully acknowledged. On April 26th of 1960, Jung wrote to Stern as follows:

April 30, 1960

Most honored Herr Doctor!

I've just finished reading your book. I read it from start to finish with the greatest interest, as it was always my wish to span the divide between—or at least to attempt to connect—the two disciplines which assume practical responsibility for the cura animarum, thus theology on the one hand and medical psychology on the other. As different as their respective point de départ may be, they fuse in the empirical soul of the human individual. On the Protestant side I succeeded with the Bernese Professor Hans Schär; on the Catholic I've found in you an extraordinary understanding, for which I thank you warmly. You've happily avoided the epistemological reefs, thereby creating a place for empirical psychology within Catholic spirituality, in gratifying contrast to Anglo-Saxon and French theologians, who in their ignorance of the epistemological problem deny all justification to an empirical psychology. It is a merit of your work, one which cannot be too highly prized, that it permits us to go a stretch of distance together, and I trust to mutual profit. We are both convinced that our imperiled age needs psychological illumination, and that someone must take the first step, which however he cannot do alone. Your positive approach is thus a great encouragement not alone for me, but first and foremost for the good cause, as well as an important step forwards.

The cleft separating our point de départ as well as those of our clients and their spiritual demands imposes the external divergence in our aims. Your theological orientation is aligned along ecclesiastical axes, whereas I find myself obliged to follow the unbreakable paths of individuation and its symbolisms; i.e. whereas you speak more determinately of Christ, I, as mere empiricist must more prudently employ the term ἄνθρωπος, as this archetype comports a 5000 year old, more or less conscious phenomenological history. This usage is as idea less determinate, and thus more appropriate.

I am principally occupied with persons who have either lost their Christianity, never had any, or indeed represent other religions even while still belonging to the human family. I can hardly take the stance of a theologian friend who said: "the Buddhists don't matter to us." In the context of a medical consultation they indeed do matter and deserve to be addressed in a humane manner.

I thus entirely understand that the individuation process and its imagery need less be treated by you than by me.

One more question! Was it with soft reproach that you said (with respect to "Answer to Job") that I don't bother with "biblical theology"? Had I done so, I would have written from a theological perspective and you might justly accuse me of blasphemy. The Protestants similarly accused me of not taking higher exegetics into consideration. Why then didn't these gentlemen issue a Job edited in accordance with their convictions? I'm a layman and as such am confronted with a Job translated for a lay public cum consensu auctoritatis. And it is this Job that the layman ponders over, not over exegetic speculations which he in any case never comes across and which moreover add nothing relevant to the book's spirit.

This neither here nor there! I am frankly pleased by the resonance owed your book, and I wish it a maximum dissemination.

With most obliged thanks

Your very devoted
C. J. Jung
(KSA, Series 2, Box 3, Folder 47; translated by Stephen Stern)

Given the length of time that probably transpired between the time Stern sent Jung his book and the time Jung replied, Stern was probably quite relieved to receive a response as cordial and generous as this one. After all, *The Third Revolution* was not uncritical of Jung. Toward the end of Chapter Ten, Stern had warned Catholic audiences:

Many people wonder how Jung's theory can be reconciled with Christianity, since there are many archetypes and only some of them are Christian [...]. In Jung's papers the primeval images of the great religions of the East often seem to play a greater role that those of the Hebrew-Christian religion. So do American Indian, Germanic and other types. Indeed, in Jung's writings and in those of his school one frequently finds the atmosphere of a Museum of Comparative

> Religion, an air of detachment and condescension, which deprives matters of the spirit of their devouring fire. By studying religion on the same plane as psychology, the Jungian analyst is apt to acquire the benevolent neutrality which characterizes many of our sociology professors [...]. Matters of the spirit are part of a noncommittal therapeutic method; Jacob no longer wrestles with the Angel in a horrible grip which leaves him forever limping—instead he takes his daily hour of gymnastics. (Stern, 1954, pp. 265–266)

Moreover, Stern continued:

> The Jungian school frequently fell in with the neo-Gnostic movements which were fashionable in Europe between the two wars, and which were profoundly dissociated from the spirit of Christianity. It is probably all this which kept Catholic scholars away from the Jungian movement for a long time [...]. (Stern, 1954, p. 266)

Nevertheless, Stern hastened to reassure readers that when all was said and done:

> The reality of non-Christian archetypes does not have to have a neutralizing or killing effect. When Saint Paul speaks of "God who, at sundry times and in divers manners, spoke in times past to the fathers by the prophets" many hold that he does not hold to the Hebrew tradition alone. The prefiguration of the Incarnation can be traced in all people; in the Hebrew people it can be traced in a special way. (Stern, 1954, p. 266)

Given the tone of his letter to Stern, Jung must have read these lines with equanimity, because the only hint of reproach in his letter surfaces with reference to *An Answer to Job* (Jung, 1952). This strange book prompted Father Victor White, an English Dominican who corresponded with Jung for many years, to break with Jung some months before his reply to Stern (Lammers, 1994). This fact might account for the inordinate length of time it took Jung to respond to Stern's book. It certainly explains the relief Jung expressed that Stern had not followed in the footsteps of certain "Anglo-Saxon and French theologians," and the absence of any mention of Father White in his letter. Indeed, reading between the lines, it almost appears as if Jung was recruiting

Stern to replace White, who died that same year, as his principal partner in dialogue "on the Catholic side." In the wake of the furious exchanges between Jung and Father White, Stern's calm reflections on the theory of archetypes must have been a balm to Jung, who realized that this was the best compromise a conscientious Catholic scholar could now offer an a-typical Protestant with Gnostic leanings like himself. The complex mix of gratitude, enthusiasm, and hints of wariness evident in Jung's reply probably reflect this realization.

CHAPTER FIVE

Through dooms of love: 1955–1967

Family woes

In 1955, Stern and his family returned from Ottawa to Montreal, where he became an Associate Professor of Psychiatry at the University of Montreal and the Psychiatrist in Chief at the Institut Albert Prévost at Hôpital de Sacré-Coeur, both French language institutions. Stern still commuted to Ottawa to lecture weekly, and continued doing so until 1968. But on his return to Montreal, Stern had sufficient leisure to become active musically again, and began to host frequent *soirées*. Prior to his Ottawa interlude, musical evenings at the Stern home tended to feature solo performances by Stern himself (Stahnisch, 2010, p. 24). Now, however, Stern reached out to a group of amateur and professional musicians to host evenings devoted to chamber music. Israel Libman, a recent graduate of McGill medical school, and a gifted violinist, became a regular member of Stern's chamber music ensemble, which met at Stern's home on 4137 Marlowe Avenue As Dr. Libman recalls, Stern was deeply appreciative of his musical skill, and developed a warm interest in his career. Moreover, Dr. Libman says, Stern expressed great pride in the courage and accomplishments of his brother Ludwig, who had since changed his name to Shimon (Simon)

Shavit to shed his "ghetto identity"; a common practice among Zionists in those days (Libman, 2010).

After two years of intense musical collaboration, Dr. Libman invited Stern to deliver a talk on psychoanalysis and literature to a fraternity of Jewish physicians and residents at McGill. This is a theme Stern excelled in, and Libman hoped that this evening would be the first of many. The talk took place sometime in 1957 or 1958, as Libman recalls, and went extremely well. The fraternity's members were moved and impressed by Stern's mastery of the material, by his erudition and enthusiasm. But sadly, despite the warm applause that followed, there was no return engagement. Stern was still *persona non grata* as far as Montreal's Jewish community was concerned, and no amount of good will or lively erudition were going to change that fact.

Though no public record exists of this event, notes Libman, the mere fact that it took place is noteworthy, because the all-Jewish fraternity of physicians and residents that Stern addressed—which no longer exists—was a product of *de facto* segregation. In that era, Jews were not admitted to Canadian medical fraternities, and there was even a freeze on the hiring of Jews at McGill, which lasted from 1952–1962. Being an Anglophone and Protestant institution, the cultural and theological odium attached to being Jewish at McGill were probably a little different than those that still lingered among the French Catholic majority in Québec. But the fact that these blatantly discriminatory practices persisted more than a decade after the Allies liberated the concentration camps is astonishing. These reflections provide the context for Libman's recollection of Stern saying to him, on more than occasion: "Israel, don't forget, if any of the Jewish boys (at McGill) have a problem, tell them to come and see me."

Clearly, says Libman, Stern meant it. And so, one wonders, did Jewish students facing discrimination actually seek out Stern when they ran into problems? As Libman recalls, they did not. But the story reveals much about McGill University and Montreal's Jewish community at that time, and the "knock on" effects of anti-Semitism for Stern and his family. For in addition to being anti-Semitic, McGill University was (more covertly) anti-Catholic as well. Being a Jew who converted to Catholicism, Stern was likely the target of both kinds of prejudice, and therefore, perhaps, doubly ineffectual at his previous place of employment. One wonders if this fact ever dawned on Stern, and whether he hoped that, despite all, his efforts on behalf of Jewish students might diminish the stigma attached to him by the wider Jewish community.

While Stern's musical life flourished as never before, the atmosphere at home was becoming increasingly difficult. From a distance, the cumulative impression one gets is that as he approached his fiftieth birthday, the relationship between Karl and Liselotte became more conflicted. Moreover, as he became more famous, the engaged, accessible and fun loving parent James Shaw depicted in "Meet the Karl Sterns" gradually gave way to an increasingly remote and demanding father, at least where Antony and Michael were concerned. Stern remained close to (and relaxed with) his daughter Katherine—largely, she says, because he did not expect her to achieve much, career-wise. Not that the old (or rather, younger) fun loving father ever disappeared entirely. Stern still made his children laugh, particularly at the piano. Like the Danish comedian Victor Borge, whose performances and recordings Stern relished, he had a remarkable ability to improvise lyrics and melodies, and to mangle musical scores creatively, with uncanny precision, on the spot. But music and humor aside, a driven, demanding quality now entered into his relations with his sons, who were burdened by his dynastic ambitions, and were expected to follow in his footsteps, becoming doctors or scientists as well. So as Stern's fiftieth birthday came and went, a new, somewhat awkward domestic equilibrium was taking shape—one that was punctuated by periods of dramatic instability.

One fact that contributed to this new state of affairs was that on November 27th, 1943, the Sterns welcomed their fourth child, Johnny, into the world. He died a few days later of spinobifida. This heart wrenching experience was followed by at least two more miscarriages for Liselotte during the early to mid-fifties. Now in her mid-forties, Liselotte must have dreaded the prospect of another failed pregnancy, and since birth control was out of the question, their love life probably sputtered to an abrupt halt. To complicate matters further, at some point in the late 1940s or early 1950s, Liselotte underwent a series of hospitalizations, some lasting several months, during which time Antony, Katherine and Michael were often separated from their parents and one another, and cared for by priests and nuns in local boarding schools. Whether (or to what extent) these episodes were exacerbated by her miscarriages is unknown, but Liselotte's diagnosis was manic depression, or what is nowadays called bipolar disorder, a fact that never registers directly in Stern's personal correspondence. In his letters to

Dorothy Day, Stern merely alluded to Liselotte's "bad phases," noting that they invariably started in the late fall or early winter. One letter to Day, written shortly before Christmas, 1956, indicates that Lislotte was doing unexpectedly well that season, suggesting a pattern of "bad phases" in the years immediately preceding. Meanwhile, Stern himself suffered from occasional episodes of severe depression and long, debilitating bouts of insomnia, which prompted him to seek refuge in a sound proofed room every evening to shut out all external noise. Liselotte slept in her own room, and often drank in secret (except for an occasional beer with meals, Karl seldom drank, and then, very sparingly).

Finally, Liselotte was severely disappointed that neither Karl nor her children supported her growing desire to create a rural retreat for handicapped people and mental patients outside of Montreal. On March 28th, 1956, eleven days before Karl turned fifty, she wrote to Dorothy Day, begging to see and speak with her about her evolving plans, saying:

> I *have* to discuss something with you—I am day dreaming more and more intensely about the Farmatorim (farm-sanatorium) for crippled and mental patients. I have a big number of patients and staff who would work right in. What we need is a rich sick person who would supply us with an old French Canadian farmhouse near here! Karl is not quite ready yet, and that is my stumbling block! (KSA, Series 5, Box 20, Folder 8)

Details of her plan are somewhat sketchy, but the therapeutic community Liselotte envisaged sounded like a cross between Dorothy Day's Peter Maurin Farm in New York, and Jean Vanier's L'Arche community in France. An undated, type-written pamphlet found among Stern's paper gives a fair description of what she had in mind.

> A large house in the country, within commuting distance of the city, pleasantly situated by water, with land available for light farming, will be called La Relue, or the Farmatorium. For it will attempt to combine the care of mentally and physically handicapped persons in one house. It will be for those who are not able to live a normal life in society yet are not in need of hospitalization. It is believed that the beauty and the peace of a life close to the land, in the loving

atmosphere of a home [...] should create the kind of environment where rehabilitation is most likely to occur.

To keep the spirit of a family, the household will not number more than twenty to twenty-five persons, patients and staff inclusive. And in that spirit, each will be asked to do what he can to help the others and contribute to the running of the place. "From each according to his ability, to each according to his need" will be the living principle here, and will hold good not only on the physical and mental plane but on the financial as well. No distinction will be made between staff and patients.

The work of house and farm, all manner of handicrafts and a book-binding shop will be carried on at La Relue.

The best qualified nurses will be in charge of the Farmatorium and these will be adequately paid. However, formal training is not necessary for all personnel; able-bodied volunteers will also be welcomed. In fact the co-operation of many persons who are interested in the work will be needed—physicians, psychiatrists, psychologists, dentists, nurses and so on [...].

Does this idea sound Utopian, unpractical, unrealizable? Well, a few level-headed persons in the medical, psychological and religious fields have been asked their opinion about it and have been encouraging. The need for such a place is obvious. Many of the trained personnel are ready and available. The patients to fill it are always with us. Only more voluntary help is still needed to make La Relue a reality. Anyone interested in any aspect of this new, worthwhile work may contact. [...]

(KSA, Series 5, Box 20, Folder 8)

Dorothy Day, a frequent visitor to their home, could not travel to Montreal that spring, so Liselotte flew to see her in New York from Saturday May 5th to Tuesday May 8th, 1956—a journey she chronicled in her diary (KSA, Series 5, Box 20, Folder 8). It is not known what advice Dorothy Day offered on this occasion, but it is clear from subsequent events that Liselotte's own family regarded her plan as "Utopian, unpractical, unrealizable." Undaunted, Liselotte pursued this idea vigorously all through 1956 and 1957. In fact, when psychiatrist (and former student) Noel Walsh joined Stern at St. Mary's Hospital in 1964, the Farmatorium issue was a still a source lingering tension between Karl and Liselotte. Her family's reasons for opposing the

Farmatorium scheme are not documented, to my knowledge, but we might reasonably suppose that her pursuit of this project would have interfered considerably with their domestic lives, and in view of her frequent hospitalizations, exposed Liselotte (and perhaps some patients) to some new and unforeseen risks.

In the midst of the Farmatorium controversy, another crisis emerged; one which had lasting reverberations for the entire family. In 1955, Antony Stern enrolled at McGill University, with a view to following in his father's footsteps. But in October of that year, he met a talented sophomore named Daryl Hine (1936–2012). Hine was a native of Burnaby, British Columbia, and a budding poet who in due course, would become a celebrated and award-winning translator and classics scholar. Despite his Protestant upbringing, and his father's fervent wishes, Hine converted to Catholicism during his first year at McGill, and spent some time in a monastery in the summer of 1954, before resuming his university studies. It is unclear to what extent Hine was still committed to Catholicism when he and Antony Stern met. In 1975, the year of Stern's death, Hine privately published a lightly fictionalized account of his relationship with the Stern family in a book called *In and Out: A Confessional Poem*. Hine dedicated this volume—reissued by Alfred Knopf in 1989—to Antony Maurice Stern and Liselotte von Baeyer Stern, leaving no doubt whatsoever about whom he was referring to in his text. But in the poem itself, Hine furnished the Stern family with pseudonyms. Karl was named Immanuel Star (Stern, of course, means Star, in German), Liselotte was called Charlotte, and Antony named Hyacinth. If the account in *In & Out* is accurate, then when Hine met Antony/Hyacinth, he was already wavering in his faith, but unable to make a clean break with the Church. Indeed, as Hine tells it, his relationship with the Stern family, and Karl in particular, contributed to his deepening disenchantment with Catholicism (Hine, 1989).

In one telling passage, Hine recalled a conversation he had with "Charlotte," and that "when she broached her idea of teaching the derelict practical crafts such as weaving and bookbinding, Hyacinth caught my incredulous eye and suppressed an unfilial giggle" (Hine, 1989, p. 140). In all likelihood, this was an oblique reference to Liselotte's Farmatorium idea. And if Liselotte did not actually share her plan with Hine at that particular juncture, she would have done so when she brought Daryl and Antony to meet Dorothy Day on her pilgrimage to New York City in May of 1956, an experience which Hine did not relish much, but chronicled from his own perspective.

In any case, over a period of two years, Daryl Hine became quite familiar with the Stern family. Much as he liked Liselotte, Hine despised Karl, who had no redeeming qualities, in Hine's estimation. He parodied the book that made Karl famous, calling it *The Pillar of Salt*, and was astonished that Antony—who resembled his mother, physically—consciously tried to emulate his father. Becoming a psychiatrist, Hine noted, was an odd ambition for someone like Antony. And Hine had a point there. Antony was a very gifted artist, and might have flourished in this profession. But becoming a psychiatrist would put Antony in a position where he would have to identify and/or compete with his famous father, which would only turn out well if his identification with his father was uncomplicated by less filial feelings.

Meanwhile, at some point in their relationship, Antony and Daryl became lovers—as Hine told it, on Antony's initiative. Remember, the year was 1956, and the stigma attached to homosexuality was still quite severe. Rightly or wrongly, Hine believed that Liselotte gave her tacit approval to their affair, turning a blind eye to their intimacies (Hine, 1989, p. 264). While not likely, on the face of it, if that was indeed the case, then any suspicions Karl harbored about this state of affairs—whether at the time, or retroactively—would only have intensified the growing estrangement between him and his wife.

Either way, when the affair finally came to light, Karl insisted that Antony enter analysis, and strongly recommended that Hine do likewise (he even recommended an analyst for him!). Antony complied, and in relatively short order, disappointed his erstwhile lover by pronouncing himself "cured" and getting married three years later. Hine resolutely refused to be analyzed—an extremely courageous move, given the temper of the times. But Hine's unwillingness to be analyzed at the time did not prevent him from "psychoanalyzing" Karl, Liselotte and Antony subsequently, under the guise of pseudonyms, and very much after the fact. For better or worse, *In and Out* is saturated with psychoanalytic allusions and interpretations. Indeed, on reflection, it is the longest (and perhaps *only*) psychoanalytic poem of the twentieth century that is truly of epic proportions.

All in all, 1956 was a difficult year for Karl and Liselotte. The high points, such as they were, were few and far between. In a letter dated May 11th, 1956, a few days after her pilgrimage to New York City,

Liselotte wrote to thank Day, and informed her that Karl was revising his forthcoming novel with the assistance of Graham Greene, who was a frequent house guest during the late 1950s. Greene had developed a lively interest in psychoanalysis, and read *The Third Revolution* with considerable admiration and interest. But Liselotte was not privy to their exchanges in the room next door. "I wonder what they talk about," she wrote.

A letter from Karl to Dorothy Day, dated January 7th, 1957, gives us some indication of the exchanges between Stern and Green at that time. Stern noted that Greene liked the book—"At least so he said [...]"—but that he himself was concerned about the longer term repercussions of a practicing psychiatrist writing such vivid descriptions of hospitals and physicians (DD-CWC, Series D-1, Box 21, Folder 4). The novel was set in Chicago in 1949, and while not exactly a *roman a clef*, drew extensively on his recent experiences of psychiatric politics at the Allan Memorial Institute and the Institut Albert-Prévost.

Meanwhile, on July 5th, 1956, Liselotte wrote to Dorothy Day, informing her that she, Karl and Michael, now fourteen years old, would be in New York City again on August 11th, when Stern delivered a talk entitled "Dying yet we live" to the annual communion breakfast of the Edith Stein Guild in New York. Katherine was unable to join them, because she was attending the von Trapp family's summer camp—the first, but by no means the last reference to the Sterns' warm relationship with the musical von Trapp family. Stern's talk to the Edith Stein Guild that August was published in two parts in the September and October issues of *The Catholic Worker* (Stern, 1956a; Stern, 1956b). He took this opportunity to explore the character and circumstances of Catholic clergy and lay people in Germany and Austria who resisted Hitler, and told many tales of courage in the face of mind-boggling brutality.

In early October of 1957, Stern went to Europe on a trip for UNESCO, and after a visit with Ludwig and family, paused in Rome to attend the World Congress of the Lay Apostolate, where he delivered a paper on "Group Psychology in the atomic era in light of Christian philosophy" (1959a). It must have been a memorable occasion, because in *Group Psychology and the Analysis of the Ego* (1921c), Freud had written that religions based on love extend that love only to members of their own faith, and are naturally inclined to hate and persecute outsiders, especially Jews. Commenting on Freud's critique of Christianity, Stern wrote:

> I do not think [...] that this was an intentionally malicious distortion. This prejudice [...] is unfortunately widespread among those who are outside the Church, that it actually belongs to the very doctrine of the Church that the love of Christ extends only to its members and that the love of the members for one another only extends to the actual border of the visible Church. This is not a testimony against Freud or something to show off his complete ignorance, but [...] a testimony against the faith of the people as it is actually lived. It is a great shame that from history people get the impression as though the Church were herself containing a unit that guarantees love of the members for one another and implies hatred and persecution for those outside it. (Stern, 1975, p. 8)

Put differently, Stern was calling attention to a profound gap between theory and practice, noting that many believers failed to live up to the basic precepts of their faith. In so doing, of course, he also implied that if they were really honest with themselves, Catholics would give Freud the benefit of the doubt, because he provided an accurate description of how many Catholics *behave*, regardless of what they believe, or what the Church actually teaches.

Was his Roman audience receptive to Stern's defense of Freud? We'll probably never know. But he was acutely disappointed with the conference as a whole. In fact, he wrote to Dorothy Day (October 29th, 1957) complaining that the layman's conference was dominated by the clergy. As a result, lay Catholics who had travelled from all over the world had few unscripted opportunities to speak *to each other*, except in the halls, or during breaks, and so on. The cumulative impression Stern conveyed is that the priests and bishops present were controlling and condescending toward the laity; an attitude Stern found quite offensive. So once again, Stern was complaining about the Catholic hierarchy to Day. But there was nothing plaintive here, and no hint of perplexity, as there was in the wake of Hiroshima. This time, Stern's irritation was palpable (Stern, 1957, DD-WCW, Series D-1, Box 21, Folder 4).

Around the time that Stern was in Rome, Antony met his future wife, Lilian Wilker in a biology lab at McGill. Lilian was born in Paris to highly assimilated Viennese Jewish parents who were trying to escape the Nazi menace. When the Nazis invaded France, her parents fled to the French countryside, and sought to blend in and invent new (non-Jewish) identities. Her father soon left the country to join the French

Foreign Legion, but before doing so, he made a bargain with a local nun that in exchange for "cover" and protection in a local convent, Lilian would be raised Catholic. And so she was until 1952, when the family immigrated to Montreal, and her parents attempted to integrate into the local Jewish community. Like most Jewish teenagers of that era, Lilian was sent to an English language high school for the express purpose of preparing her to study at McGill. A multilingual European of Jewish ancestry, Lilian had hybrid strains that enabled her understand many of the attitudes and experiences of the Sterns, and did not harbor any of the prejudices and preconceptions that divided the far more homogeneous cultures of French and English communities, respectively. Moreover, and just as importantly, from Antony's standpoint, she was not particularly religious, despite her decided preference for Catholic culture.

As Lilian recalls, she and Antony dated for three to four months before she actually met Karl and Liselotte. She found Liselotte to be warm and welcoming, a free spirit, and good company. By contrast, Karl was somewhat severe and emotionally withdrawn. She concluded that Karl was a good therapist, but completely at a loss in family matters, and that Karl and Lisellote led "parallel lives." She later discovered that Liselotte was hospitalized frequently for manic-depression, and drank a great deal in secret.

While Antony and Lilian were preparing to make their marriage vows, in 1958, another student at McGill named Olaf Skorzewski met and courted Katherine Stern. Olaf's family hailed from Zbonzsyn in Poland, though when Katherine and Olaf met, he had an engineering degree from McGill University and had travelled widely in Europe and Latin America. Like Lilian, Olaf was a transplanted European, and found his future father-in-law quite aloof. He claims to have never seen Karl touch, never mind embrace, Liselotte, in the entire time he knew them! His future wife Katherine was a promising cellist, and well on her way to a professional career. But after her marriage to Olaf, she interrupted her studies to raise their children, and only went back to her cello when her youngest child was six years old. She graduated in 1975, the year her father died, and became a member of the Orchèstre Métropolitain, performing chamber music till her retirement in 2010.

But these developments lay far in the future. Meanwhile, in 1957, family matters, though fraught with difficulty, were not the only source of stress in Stern's life. Toward the end of 1957, Stern left the Institut

Albert-Prévost to found the department of psychiatry at St. Mary's Hospital, a position he held for ten years, from 1958 till 1968. Stern had quarreled with members of the Institute's board, and in due course, was replaced by Dr. Camille Laurin (1922–1999), a protégé of Lionel Groulx, who would later become a leading figure in Québec's separatist movement. In 1957, however, Laurin was not a politician, but an energetic young psychiatrist who sought to transform Albert-Prévost into a more Menninger-like Institution, with a stronger emphasis on the provision of psychoanalytic therapy. Though he wrote and lectured knowledgeably about Freud, was analyzed by Miguel Prados, and offered analytically oriented psychotherapy to many of his patients, Stern was not accredited by the International Psychoanalytical Association (IPA) to practice psychoanalysis, and was therefore deemed unqualified to spearhead the kind of initiative Laurin and the Board of Trustees evidently had in mind (Desgroseilliers, 2001).

However, Stern *was* superbly qualified to lead St. Mary's psychiatry department. St. Mary's was a predominantly Catholic hospital, and in addition to serving Montreal's Francophone population, it served immigrants from other countries, including refugees who had fled to the West from Hungary, Yugoslavia and other Iron Curtain countries. It also served many Holocaust survivors, who were not welcome at Verdun, Albert Prévost or the Montreal General Hospital. Because of prevailing prejudices, many of them landed in Stern's lap.

While Stern was better suited to his new position at St. Mary's, the stress and aggravation of the preceding decade, Liselotte's frequent hospitalizations, and the domestic problems that preceded or ensued from them, eventually took a toll on Karl's health. For in January of 1959, mere months after Antony and Lilian were married, Karl experienced his first heart attack. He was only fifty-three when this calamity took place—not unheard of, certainly, but still quite young to be so ill. On February 2nd, 1959, Liselotte wrote to Dorothy Day, informing her that Karl was recovering from an unspecified illness and from mental and emotional distress, noting that he was attended by three special nurses—whether at home or hospital is not clear. Her next letter to Day—on February 9th—indicates that the nurses' services were no longer required, and that during the preceding days Karl and she had recovered a lost feeling of intimacy that was brought on by his critical illness. Her letters to Day on February 21st and April 3rd describe Stern's gradual recovery, and his growing excitement about the publication of his forthcoming novel, *Through Dooms of Love*.

Meanwhile, in the Fall of 1959, Noel Walsh, a native of County Mayo in Ireland, came to St. Mary's to do a residency in psychiatry. He joined Stern on hospital rounds, and eagerly soaked up as much of Stern's clinical acumen as he could. After a brief stint a St. Mary's, Walsh completed his diploma in psychiatry under Cameron at McGill, and returned home, to Dublin. But he rejoined Stern at St. Mary's in 1964, initially as a student, but increasingly as a colleague, friend and confidante.

As the sixties commenced, Karl and Liselotte welcomed a lively procession of grandchildren, who arrived in rapid succession. Phillip Stern, Antony and Lilian's eldest, was born in 1959, while Anna Skorzewska, Katherine and Olaf's first child arrived in mid-1960. Stephen Stern and Jan Skorzewski both arrived in 1961, while Matthew Stern and Andrew Skorzewski arrived in 1962. After a three year hiatus, Eva-Marie Stern and Peter Skorzewski arrived in 1965, while Daniel Skorzewski and David Stern—the first child of Michael Stern and Elizabeth Fodor, who married in 1965—arrived two years later in 1967.

Liselotte greeted these new arrivals with warmth and enthusiasm. And though they never suspected this fact, of course, the grandchildren's fondness for their Oma, as she was called, probably helped Liselotte manage her ups and downs more effectively, and in so doing, avoid hospitalization during the sixties. But not everything was rosy. Karl, or Opa, as his grandchildren called him, was a less palpable presence in their lives. He could be engaged and entertaining at times, but after his heart attack, he was frequently inaccessible or simply too aloof and preoccupied to spend time with them.

In retrospect, and by her own admission, it was Katherine's children who benefited the most from Liselotte's tender ministrations. After all, when her own children started to arrive, Katherine simply shelved her musical career for a decade and half, and moved nearer her parents' home to facilitate regular visits between them and her own growing family. The situation with Antony and Lilian was quite different. After graduating from McGill, Antony interned at the Montreal General Hospital and the Allan Memorial Institute from 1961 to 1963. After a brief, uncomfortable interlude living in Karl and Liselotte's basement, Antony and Lilian decided to rent a flat that was quite far from his parents' home. They did not own a car, and public transport was often not available. To make matters worse, Antony was hospitalized during

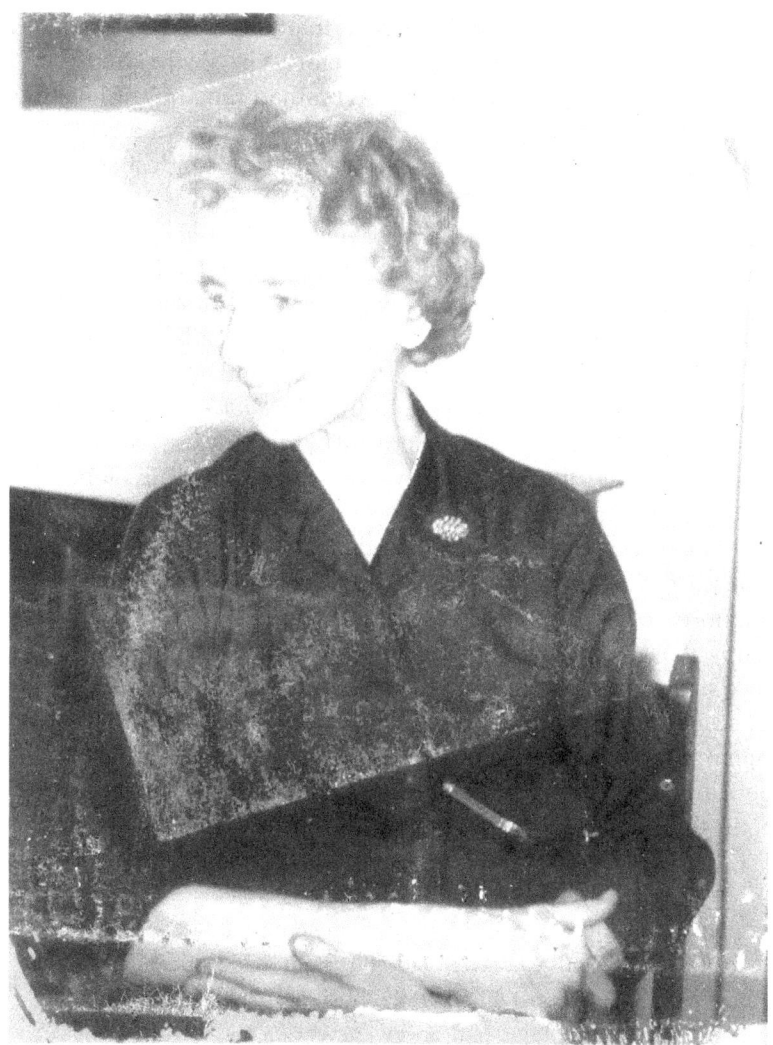

Figure 19. Liselotte circa 1962.

this period, and diagnosed with manic-depression, like his mother. By all accounts, both before and after his hospitalization, Antony was pretty fragile and self-absorbed, and not much of a "family man." Lilian quickly became Antony's main emotional support. Like Daryl Hine, she felt that Antony was living in his father's shadow, and noticed that he became more anxious and disturbed than usual when he spent too much time in his father's presence. Therefore, visits with Oma and Opa for Philip and Stephen were less frequent than they might have been. The fact that neither Antony nor Lilian were religious anymore also added to the emotional distance between Karl, his eldest son and his daughter-in-law—at least where Karl was concerned.

Meanwhile, in 1960, Karl's novel, *Through Dooms of Love*, was finally published. In a letter to Dorothy Day, Stern fretted that his novel might provoke his abrupt expulsion from the psychiatric profession. These fears might have been justified in the preceding decade, but by the early sixties, they were somewhat exaggerated. After all, much younger psychiatrists were now publishing books like *The Divided Self* and *The Myth of Mental Illness* that were sharply critical of their profession, which only seemed to enhance their popularity—outside of the profession itself, of course (e.g., Laing, 1960; Szasz, 1961).

But Laing and Szasz, who authored these books, provoked vigorous responses from their colleagues, while the psychiatric establishment just ignored Stern's novel, and treated its appearance as a non-event. Perhaps it is mere coincidence, but one could easily argue that the silence surrounding Stern's novel in psychiatric circles is foreshadowed by a scene in the book itself, when Dr. Joseph Birnstam, a Viennese psychiatrist who is culturally dislocated, and often at variance with his American colleagues, addresses them at staff party, when he tries to explain the recent suicide of an ex-patient at the mental hospital they all work at, the Holy Jordan. After a few stiff drinks, Birnstam exclaims:

> "For every soul which is incarnated, the entire universe is preparing itself. *The entire universe*, see?" Birnstam held forth. "This is the meaning of the constellations, the position of the stars. See, how people in olden times had an awareness of the dignity of man? Everything had to be in a state of readiness when the baby is born. Now on the lowest storey, I mean … I don't know if you know what I mean […]." He laughed […], "Let us say on the closest level where the flesh is, love must be. No? You don't understand? The constellations and the universe, all that is for nothing if a baby is not received into a world by loving souls […]."
>
> "Could you try to say it all again without bringing in the souls and stars? Try."
>
> "No. *Prosit*."

He took a big gulp [...], "That's what's wrong with all of us. Man in the mid-twentieth century is estranged from the *Reich der Mütter*, we're all cut off from the cosmic maternity, you don't seem to know what I am talking about." He laughed about himself, and the way they all watched him, talking. "Nor do I, for that matter," he added. (Stern, 1960, pp. 130–131)

Cosmic maternity, the dignity of man, the alignment of the stars; these themes were hardly the stuff of science, though they vaguely foreshadow ideas Stern expressed in a more cogent and articulate fashion five years later, in *The Flight From Woman*. Meanwhile, Stern seems to set up this scene such that poor Birnstam does not really expect to be understood, and on reflection, is amazed at himself for expecting a more favorable reception from his uncomprehending peers.

While psychiatrists greeted the book with indifference, many lay people found Stern's descriptions of mental hospitals, and the people who work in them, extremely illuminating. On April 3rd, 1960, novelist Anne Fremantle summarized the book's plot in *The New York Times Review of Books*, as follows:

Basically it is the story of the Radberts, Marianne and her father Leonhard, who escaped to the United States from Czechoslovakia [...] in 1939. Leonhard's wife had already left him and died in England, so there is nothing and no one to interrupt the father–daughter dialogue. Dr. Stern details it meticulously.

Radbert, the erstwhile millionaire owner of Bavarian glassworks, is now reduced to a flatful of photos and souvenirs, a dog and a daughter, yet by her love, he is meted out his daily dose of security, adulation, self-importance, even power. Marianne models; in the evenings, Radbert gives lectures on glass-making and music to small groups of no significance. Marianne is desired by her boss, an attractive, self-made mother's boy named Barney. But at 26, Marianne has fled from passion; she loves only children and old men, wishing she could produce the former by some sort of Virgin Birth.

Later her father has a [...] peculiar kind of stroke that makes him not only sick but psychotic. Marianne has to put him into Holy Jordan, one of the biggest and best "institutions" in the country.

> Dr. Stern is superb in his handling of the men who man this ship of the ship-wrecked [...].
>
> The intrigues at Holy Jordan are fascinatingly described, the shuffling for position, the status seeking, the half-smothered, half articulate *rancunes* [...]. That no one can become a psychiatrist unless he himself is crazy seems one conclusion; that we *all* are, more or less, is another. (KSA, Series 8, Box 22, Folder 2)

Fremantle's brief review deliberately juxtaposed the awkward and uneven romance between Marianne and her boss, which she found implausible, and Stern's vivid and descriptions of the political machinations within the mental hospital (and the wider psychiatric world) that she thought were excellent. While she was right, her review did not do justice to Stern's soulful evocation of the sense of homelessness and uprooting experienced by émigrés fleeing Hitler, which contributed significantly to Leonhard Radbert's rapid decline, obligating Marianne to adapt, strike out on her own, and finally leave her tragic past behind. Indeed, Stern's depiction of how two generations cope differently with the memory of a world that is irrevocably lost was one of his novel's greatest strengths. In a Catholic journal called *The Tablet*, under the heading "A Great Novel," Peregrine Walker wrote on the following January 7th, 1961:

> The novel is a brilliant piece of documentation. Here, accurately described, is the closed world of hospitals, with all their rivalries and inflated trivialities: and the central tragedy of Radbert is a statement of the refugee's plight in a world that prefers to forget. We have had too many "psychological" novels, and perhaps never before one in which a trained intelligence, allied to such discernment, has re-stated a theme that is so much older and more enduring than case histories. A fundamental honesty illuminates the whole story; nurses, garment workers, nuns, tycoons are all seen with the co-ordinating sympathy of a writer who uses his professional skill but who knows its limitations too. (KSA, Series 8, Box 22, Folder 2)

Was *Through Dooms of Love* a great novel, as Peregrine Walker declared? No, decidedly not. Though quite engaging in places, *Through Dooms of Love* was too sprawling and ambitious to be a literary masterpiece.

The book's pervasive themes include the squalor and the horror of old-fashioned mental hospitals; the impact of class differences on the delivery of mental health services; the conflict between Kraepelinian and psychodynamic psychiatry; the ubiquity of familial conflict and estrangement; the intergenerational transmission of mental disorder; the inheritance of family dramas or "scripts" that get re-enacted afresh like a proverbial "repetition compulsion"; the inescapable impact of suffering and loneliness, the curious relationship between madness and the sacred.

Stern's effort to address these issues was commendable, often illuminating, and even prescient at times. But to really do justice to them all in a single novel is an *extremely* tall order, even for a latter day Dickens or Balzac. Successful novels that explore the process of psychiatric hospitalization usually focus narrowly on the experience of the patient as it is lived, and less on the patient's developmental history, social context, or the special circumstances surrounding the patient's hospitalization and the subsequent ramifications of this event for other family members, etc. In fairness to Stern, these topics *were* commonplace concerns for psychodynamic clinicians of that era, but not for the "average reader" in search of a satisfying read, no matter how well informed they might be about mental hospitals. Finally, as Fremantle noted, Stern wove some worthwhile reflections about psychiatric politics and the human condition around a somewhat tepid romance between Marianne Radbert and her erstwhile employer, and the result was an alternation between occasional profundities, articulately expressed, and some contrived situations and awkward clichés. Stern was a brilliant essayist and an accomplished non-fiction author, but his talents as a novelist were more modest, and really not up to a project this ambitious.

Capitalism, Communism, and Kennedy's assassination

In the Fall of 1961, Father Adrian van Kaam (1920–2010) who chaired the Psychology Department of Duquesne University in Pittsburgh, invited Stern to join a panel of distinguished speakers at the annual conference of the American Association of Existential Psychology and Psychiatry. The conference was in honor of Gabriel Marcel, who delivered a paper called "My death and myself" on November 12th, 1961 at the Carnegie Endowment International Center in the UN Plaza on 46th

Street. The other panelists at this event included Father van Kaam, Paul Tillich and Leslie Farber.

Despite his familiarity with existentialism and phenomenology, Stern was not involved with the American Association of Existential Psychology and Psychiatry prior to this point, and on reflection, his attitude toward Freud probably had something to do with this state of affairs. After all, Stern was on a mission to save Freud from his followers, and in certain sense, from himself, arguing that there was a lucid, intelligible core to Freud's theories of human development that are compatible with existentialism, phenomenology, and the kind of theocentric humanism he shared with Maritain and Marcel. By contrast, Rollo May, Leslie Farber, and several of the AAEPP's leading members were actually trained psychoanalysts who had become severely disenchanted with Freud and his followers. The exception was Father van Kaam, who never trained as an analyst. Rather than addressing Freud's faults and failings, or rejecting him outright, like Agostino Gemelli, Father van Kaam, a prolific author, simply never mentioned Freud in his books and articles, acting as if Freud was irrelevant, or had never existed—a curious attitude for a priest/psychologist at mid-century!

That being so, the idea to involve Stern in this event probably came directly from Marcel, who was a frequent visitor to Stern's home in Montreal. But regardless of where it originated, in the first instance, this invitation proved timely, because the theme of dying and becoming—and of "dying with" a beloved person—were very much on Stern's mind. After all, this had been a pivotal theme in the lives of his fictional characters Leonhard and Marianne Radbert in *Through Dooms of Love*. Moreover, and more importantly, he himself was still recovering from a near-fatal heart attack. His novel approached this topic in an indirect, literary manner. But Stern's conference paper, called "Death within life," was couched in existential idioms, and for those versed in this brand of philosophy, was quite pithy and direct. Stern's contribution, along with those of Marcel and his fellow panelists, were published in a special issue of *The Review of Existential Psychology and Psychiatry*, which van Kaam edited at the time (Stern, 1961).

Stern's contribution to the Marcel symposium had another interesting upshot. In the concluding paragraph of "Death within life," Stern observed that:

> [...] it is interesting to see how the godless civilizations of today "handle" anxiety for, after all, our way of facing anxiety is our way of facing death. We have two materialistic climates of life in the world today, the one which surrounds us here, and the one which prevails behind the Iron Curtain. Our brand of materialism is largely hedonistic and pragmatic, the Marxist one is more ascetic and future oriented. In that sense, Marxism, as Maritain, Berdyaev and others have pointed out, resembles a Christian heresy, while our Western materialism is more pagan in character. Our hedonistic pragmatic civilization drowns out anxiety by noise, as it were. The entire world of the "entertainment industry," of advertisement (in the largest sense of that word) is gauged for distraction, to drown our Silence, the great message of death. This is a world in which Heidegger's *Neugierde* (curiosity) and *das Gerede* ("talk" as contrasted to speech) *das Man* (the common denominator) serve to combat anxiety. In the Marxist society man achieves a false sense of immortality by his membership in a collective to which is allotted (in spite of dialectical materialism) a pseudo-transcendental reality. (Stern, 1961, p. 144)

This brief comparison between Capitalism and Communism is striking, because despite the virulence of anti-Soviet propaganda in popular culture, Stern seemed inclined to put the two forms of materialist culture on a par. Elsewhere, Stern even played devil's advocate sometimes, noting that though based on false premises, dialectical materialism was at least a *coherent* system with a specific philosophy of history; one inspired, in the first instance, by a Prophetic indignation at social injustice. And needless to say, Stern admired idealism, asceticism, and self-sacrifice, of which there was plenty in the history of Communism. By contrast, said Stern, Capitalism is based on crass hedonism and unbridled individualism. It lacks a single, unifying idea or a coherent philosophy of history (Stern, 1975, p. 241).

So, on a purely philosophical dimension, Stern sometimes appeared to suggest that Communism was actually the *lesser* of two evils, albeit by a very narrow margin. This appraisal obviously reflected Stern's preference for coherent systems of thought, for a clear conception of the goal of history and human development, and for idealism and self-sacrifice; traditional and religious values that were secularized under

Communism, and which were manifestly at odds with the sprawling, anarchic marketplace of ideas found in the West. Though he shared this somewhat "countercultural" perspective on Marxism with Maritain and Dorothy Day, who saw Communism as a kind of Christian heresy, this was not the attitude of most Catholic intellectuals in North America in the Cold War era.

Nevertheless, at a pragmatic level, Stern's *personal* loyalties and priorities were somewhat at variance with his public pronouncements. For example, in 1958, in a letter to Dorothy Day, Stern gently criticized her for underestimating the brutal, repressive, and mendacious quality of Communist regimes. As one point, he even cited Arthur Koestler, who admonished ex-Communists (like Stern and Day) that they had a special duty not to idealize Communism, or to minimize the potential threat it posed to basic human freedoms. By Koestler's reckoning, Capitalism, for all its faults, is the lesser of two evils, and by a *considerable* margin (Koestler, in Crossman, 1949). And again, without saying so in quite so many words, Stern concurred.

So the cumulative impression one gets is that despite his unconventional perspective on Soviet Communism, and his willingness to criticize Western capitalism, Stern wanted Kennedy to succeed in defeating Khruschev's designs in Cuba and Latin America. But nuclear war was on the horizon, and despite the Church hierarchy's cryptic silence after Hiroshima, many Catholics intellectuals of that era could not countenance the prevailing rhetoric about pre-emptive nuclear strikes against Russia, or "acceptable loses" in the event of an all-out nuclear war. Stern was no exception. In a front page article in *The Catholic Worker* dated April, 1962, called "The case for Christian pacifism," Stern wrote:

> As is well known, St. Thomas' teaching on the morality of war is based on the so-called principle of the double effect. According to this principle, an act leading to both good and evil results is permissible if a) the act in itself is good or indifferent and b) the good effect must be proportionate to the evil effect and must follow as immediately as that evil. Moreover, the perpetrator must not do the evil effect for itself. From all of this it is evident that nuclear war cannot be justified under any circumstances. Entire concepts such as a "just war," "defensive war," so neat and reasonable when it comes to the chessboard pictures of walled cities with bow and arrow mercenaries become meaningless when instead, two soulless

machines for the killing of innocents are ticking away for the time of the trigger. (KSA, Series 8, Box 22, Folder 2)

These words were published six months before the Cuban missile crisis (October 15–28th), and while we have no record of Stern's thoughts and feelings during the crisis itself, it is certain that he hoped Kennedy would prevail. Like most Catholics, Stern was touched by the Kennedy mystique, and the belief that America's first Catholic president was leading the country toward greater justice and equality. As a result, Kennedy's assassination on November, 22nd, 1963 disturbed him deeply. Carlos Placci, who was visiting Stern on the day of the assassination, says he talked of little else.

In the summer of 1963, some months before the crisis began, Antony, Lilian and their three children had left for Cincinnatti, where they lived till Antony completed his training as a psychiatrist. Carlos Placci had commenced a psychiatric residency there a year or two before, and had promised to "keep an eye" on Antony, becoming a close family friend, and playing a strong supportive role during Antony and Lilian's American sojourn. Like Montreal and Topeka, Kansas, Cincinnati was a major center for psychoanalytic training and research in those days. But Antony's departure from Québec was not motivated solely by the desire to further his career. Lilian had urged him to leave Montreal, hoping that by escaping Karl's immediate sphere of influence Antony's mental health would slowly improve. She even hoped that, once away, Antony would find the courage to drop psychiatry altogether and strike out on his own, possibly as an artist.

Sadly, that was not the case. Despite Lilian's urging, Antony remained determined to become a psychiatrist, and his psychiatric residency was conducted under the supervision of highly respected clinicians: Drs. Maurice Levine, Allan Ross, and William Powles. Antony's psychoanalyst during his American interlude was Dr. Paul Ornstein, who would later become a leading figure in Self Psychology, the psychoanalytic school founded by Heinz Kohut. Meanwhile, in the summer of 1964, Noel Walsh, now a fully credentialed psychiatrist, came to work as Stern's right hand man at St. Mary's. Walsh did most of the administrative work there in exchange for close and convivial mentoring, an arrangement that benefited both men. With his encyclopedic knowledge of the neurological and psychiatric literature, Stern helped Walsh to prepare lectures for residents and interns, and developed a course of personal study to address some of the lacunae in Walsh's education. Among other things, he insisted that Walsh read Shakespeare, Tolstoy, Dostoyevksy, and Ibsen, arguing that their character portraits were more deep and discerning than most psychoanalytic case studies. Walsh's reading under Stern's guidance was not strictly literary, however. It included Descartes, Kierkegaard, Schopenhauer, and Sartre—the same philosophers Stern was writing about in his forthcoming book, *The Flight From Woman*. Far from resenting these lengthy excursions into literature and philosophy, Walsh was deeply appreciative of the many hours Stern spent tutoring him in Western philosophy, and in particular, the work of Karl Jaspers. Often their discussions occurred during long walks, which were the only form of exercise that Stern took—and even then reluctantly, on the doctor's orders.

This mentoring arrangement lasted for roughly three years, during which time Stern supervised Walsh on a wide range of issues. For example, in 1946, many Holocaust survivors had flocked to Montreal's thriving Jewish community, and were initially seen at The Jewish General Hospital. Things changed in 1951, when West German Chancellor Konrad Adenauer announced a formal process of reparations to Israel, a process that widened to include survivors living elsewhere around the world. To expedite this process, the West German government even hired psychiatrists in Canada to assess whether Jews living there who claimed the right to compensation were actually entitled to do so, and Stern supervised Walsh in the assessment of many such cases. Walsh, who was a devout Catholic, was also entrusted with treating many of the priests who were sent to St. Mary's, Stern having tired of treating priests for two decades already.

By 1965, Walsh and his family were settled comfortably in Montreal. Unlike Stern, whose health was poor, and was increasingly reclusive, Walsh was extremely vigorous and outgoing, and continued to cultivate contacts with psychiatrists at "the Allan" and elsewhere. That being so, he started to arrange soirées at his home for small groups of psychiatrists and residents at the Allan Memorial Institute who listened to Stern talk about the convergences between psychoanalysis, philosophy and literature; something they were not likely to get in the course of their regular training. Towards the end of these informal talks, Stern would often go to the piano and play a piece by Beethoven, Mozart or Schubert and talk about its emotional tone and

Figure 20. Karl Stern, right, and Noel Walsh, seated, at St. Mary's Hospital.

potential therapeutic value for particular kinds of patients. But despite these evenings, and Walsh's ongoing efforts on behalf of Holocaust survivors, which were well known in the Jewish community, Jewish psychiatrists sedulously avoided Stern, because of lingering mistrust and outrage at his conversion to Catholicism more than two decades previously.

A public intellectual: anti-semitism, abortion, and the Quiet Revolution

Meanwhile, in 1964, Stern paid a second visit to Rome to witness the progress of the Second Vatican Council (Vatican II). Though he was too dutiful to criticize it publicly, to my knowledge, Stern could not muster any enthusiasm for the second Vatican Council. Indeed, he wrote that most of the "new theology" is phony and meretricious, although much of it was really quite consistent with his own theological leanings (Baum, 2011).

Fortunately, Stern's reservations about Vatican II did not prevent him from speaking out against anti-Semitism and other forms of collective hatred. Indeed, ever since *The Pillar of Fire* was published, Stern was in demand on the Catholic lecture circuit, and the evils of anti-Semitism was easily the most frequent topic of his talks to Catholic audiences. He even did a brief segment on the subject of racism and hate mongering on the Canadian Broadcasting Corporation's controversial news show, *This Hour Seven Days*. As a result, perhaps, on December 3rd, 1964, John Matheson a Liberal MP, and Parliamentary assistant to Prime Minister Lester Pearson, convened a Parliamentary committee on Bill C-21 concerning genocide, and Bill C-45, which sought to amend the Post Office Act in order to stem the flow of hate mail from the John Birch Society and kindred organizations in the United States. The first person to testify on these matters was Dr. Charles Hendry, who directed the Graduate School of Social work at the University of Toronto. The second person was Karl Stern, who appeared before the Parliamentary Committee on February 26th, 1965 (Stern, 1965b).

This was not Stern's first time on Parliament Hill, as it turns out. There is a letter from the Minister of Health and Welfare (and future Canadian Prime Minister) Paul Martin to Stern dated May 1st, 1953, thanking him warmly for his address to the Voluntary Health Committee of the House of Commons and Senate. But on this particular occasion, more than a decade later, the press was present, and as the *Montreal Gazette* reported, Stern "held the parliamentary committee spellbound for almost two hours as he reviewed the psychiatric conditions which form the basis of group hatred" (KSA, Series 9, Box 22, Folder 3).

Judging from the published proceedings, Stern gave a masterful summary of the psychoanalytic literature on racial, religious, and ethnic prejudice, instructing MPs on the meaning of terms like paranoia, projection, and inferiority feelings, and so on, using vivid anecdotes to illustrate his theoretical points. Stern was also quite critical of the "entertainment industry," which plays to the lowest common denominator, indulging people's taste for violent programming. He even criticized the CBC's decision to air an interview with American Nazi leader George Lincoln Rockwell on "This hour has seven days" (October 25th, 1964), arguing that many viewers who tuned in would sympathize with Rockwell, and that this effort to inform the public actually gave the Nazi ideologue a public platform to spread his poisonous ideas, as well as to offend the objects of his hatred (Stern, 1965b, pp. 1784–1785).

Impressed with Stern's outspokenness, perhaps, one parliamentarian asked Stern if psychiatry had a special role to play in drafting legislation to prevent hate crimes. Stern emphatically said "no." To explain his position, he told the story of a hot dog vendor who operated a cart outside the Bank of England. One day, the vendor was approached by a friend who asked to borrow five bob, to which the vendor replied: "I'd love to lend you five bob, but I have a strict contract with the Bank that I won't lend money if they won't sell any hot dogs." After the laughter subsided, Stern added: "This is what I always feel when I am asked to intrude in a field outside of psychiatry" (Stern, 1965b, pp. 1782–1783). Uttered unexpectedly in the midst of serious discussion, this humorous digression was a good way of poking fun at himself, as well as communicating his anxiety about overstepping the bounds of his professional competence. This combination of modesty, reticence, and puckish humor was vintage Stern. However, in private, he sometimes poked fun at his audiences, too. Take this little ditty composed later that year for the amusement of his devoted secretary, Christina Boland, called "The R.C. Circuit":

> Today I ask you, Dr. Stern,
> To speak in our hall,
> In April 1966
> I'm speaking for us all
>
> The Parish of the Sacred Heart
> West of Chicago's loop
> We may not be exceptionally smart
> But we *are* an eager group
>
> Do choose the subject for yourself
> Your choice will be tremendous
> The only snag: our parish priest
> Has power o'r the hall to lend us
>
> His name is Father McEntee,
> He just hates certain themes,

> Like group or race hostility,
> Or sex or Freudian dreams
>
> I am enclosing a list
> Of topics for your choice
> Non-controversial as they are
> They'll make us all rejoice
>
> "Novenas for the Couple Chimes"
> "A Pioneer in Marriage"
> "The Boon and Curse of Bubble Gums"
> "The Jet-pushed Baby Carriage"
>
> We follow you, dear Dr. Stern
> Whatever you may choose
> We come to you all set to learn
> You can't—can you?—refuse!
>
> (KSA, Series Box 1, Folder 11)

While Stern gently reproached Catholics for bowing to clerical pressure to avoid controversial topics, he himself was sometimes less than forthcoming on major issues of local, national, and international importance. Even in his private correspondence, there is a resounding silence on the Quiet Revolution, which changed Québec irrevocably, and which was now well underway. As the sixties unfolded, health care and education, which had been formerly provided by the Church under (Conservative) Premier Maurice Duplessis, were now provided and regulated by the new (Liberal) Provincial Government. There was a wave of unionization in the public sector, and massive hydro-electric projects which paved the way for a new economic order which, at long last, created a flourishing Francophone middle class. This in turn heralded a sharp decline in the Church's traditional authority—though not in the nationalistic sentiments the Church in Québec had once embraced (Gavreau, 2005). As a result, most of Québec's churches, even the most exquisite, are almost empty today, being little more than historic sites or tourist destinations. Indeed, thanks to the Quiet Revolution, Stern's earlier hopes of a resurgent Church humanizing the social order and mitigating the evils of materialism subsided. Nevertheless, in an unpublished fragment on the theme of modern alienation, he wrote:

There is a glimmer of hope: As Bergson once stated, after a long period of crisis in which the machine will have freed man from all drudgery latent creative forces will be mobilized. Moreover, it is possible that in a climate of scientism and technocracy, in spite of the impoverishment of faith, there may be awakened a greater longing for the transcendental as manifested in artistic values. Dostoyevsky, who prophesied the contemporary depletion of faith said at the same time: "The world will be saved by beauty." (KSA, Series 3, Box 11, Folder 25)

Another subject Stern might have been expected to say something about was abortion, which was a burning issue at the national level. Despite repeated requests from Noel Walsh, Stern steadfastly refused to take a public stand against abortion, fearing it could impair his effectiveness as a clinician. Condemning abortion outright, said Stern, prevents potential patients from trusting him, and when speaking with other clinicians, he always advised them not to be judgmental toward women who had undergone this procedure, for fear of exacerbating their suffering and ruining any chance of a achieving a genuine therapeutic rapport. In a talk entitled "The problem of guilt" at The First Annual Loyola University Summer Institute in Pastoral Psychology, later published in *Love and Success* (1975) Stern observed that the:

> [...] postulate of a "non-judgmental atmosphere" in the therapeutic situation is something which has preceded modern psychiatry for a long time. It is one of the oldest traditions, even outside of psychiatry, and even before Christianity [...]. If a girl came after a criminal abortion to a gynecologist, and he gave her a sermon it would be highly unethical from a medical point of view. (Stern, 1975, pp. 71–72)

Nevertheless, Stern conceded that in reality:

> [...] there are two forms of "judgment." Many writings in the social and psychological sciences imply, as you know, a certain moral relativism. Moral values depend on factors of social, cultural, historical, ethnic constellation. There may be one society is which adultery is regarded as normal, and another society in which it is regarded

as immoral. Therefore, there is no absolute moral value. If you adhere to such a philosophy you cannot possibly judge. If moral values are not anchored in something outside the system they do not transcend the natural condition. However, if you believe in moral values that are transcendental you cannot judge either but for an entirely different reason, namely the evangelic principle of the "judge not." These two forms of non-judgment are dynamically different [...] the patient, like a child, has a kind of sixth sense. And if you, in the very depths of your being, harbor a feeling of "thank God I am not like one of these" you will fail completely in the therapy. (Stern, 1975, pp. 72–73)

Another startling lacuna in Stern's work and correspondence from this era was any serious reflection on the Vietnam War. His motives here are harder to fathom. He could not plead ignorance or indifference, because scores of Catholic priests and nuns, including Father Daniel Berrigan, who edited *The Catholic Worker* for a time, were vigorously opposed to it. Then again, most of those who actively opposed the Vietnam War also welcomed Vatican II with considerable enthusiasm (Carroll, 1996).

The flight from woman and the feminist response

Given the striking omissions on the Quiet Revolution, abortion and the Vietnam War, it is intriguing to note that one issue on which Stern was not the least bit reticent was the emerging feminist movement. Many feminists in the sixties argued that Freud's ideas about sex and character were profoundly androcentric or patriarchal. Specifically, they argued that Freud's claim that female identity crystallizes in response to penis envy and an innate sense of inferiority, and therefore, that most women fail to develop a strong super-ego, is ludicrous and offensive. Stern agreed, and in *The Flight From Woman* (1965a), revised the libido theory on which the psychoanalytic theory of gender was based. According to Freud, libido or sexual desire is intrinsically active and masculine in character. It seeks a climactic or convulsive release. By Stern's reckoning, however, receiving, enfolding, and holding, which are not aggressive or orgiastic in character, and are more characteristic of women's sexual experience, are also libidinous activities and experiences. Moreover, Stern claimed, any human being who lacks a measure of *both* of these libidinal components or attitudes is clinically disturbed.

Stern used the technical phrase "contra-sexual *analage*" to refer to the feminine polarity in men, and the male polarity in women, and noted the resemblance between this idea and Jung's idea of the anima in men and the animus in women (Stern, 1965a, Chapter Two).

Stern did not stop here, however. In *The Future of An Illusion* (1927c), Freud contended that the child's desire for the father's protection soon supersedes its desire for maternal care. Moreover, he attempted to trace all religious longing and belief back to the yearning for (and fear of) the father (Freud, 1912–1913; Freud, 1927c). Without contradicting Freud in quite so many words, Stern turned Freud's patricentric (or father-centered) psychology on its head by emphasizing the primacy of the mother–child bond, and the idea that its impact on development is lifelong, and not just confined to early infancy.

While Stern's revisions of Freudian theory were quite timely, and entirely in keeping with the evolving feminist critique of Freud, in other respects, *The Flight from Woman* was a sharp rebuke to feminism, or a certain kind of feminism. Stern was an essentialist, who was committed to the notion that masculine and feminine attributes are rooted in nature, and are not merely social constructions. In a chapter devoted to the "metaphysics of the sexes," Stern cited convergent testimony from the *Tao Te Ching, The Upanishads, The Bible, The Zohar*, and Plato's *Symposium*, all on behalf of the idea that sexual polarity is rooted in nature. Stern expressed considerable alarm that:

> [...] today, for the first time in history, there occurs a trend which runs completely contrary to this. Not only is the metaphysics of sexual polarity regarded as a residuum of prescientific superstition, but even the belief that anatomical complementariness expresses psychological complementariness is no longer taken for granted. (Stern, 1965a, p. 12)

Stern then went on to cite the work of Margaret Mead and Simone de Beauvoir, who argued that male and female character traits or aptitudes are merely cultural artifacts, rather than the result of evolutionary or biological processes. Stern was slightly more sympathetic to Mead, because Mead did make some small allowance for innate gender differences. But he was severely critical of Simone de Beauvoir, whose erudition he admired, but whose book *The Second Sex* (1949) he interpreted as an attack on marriage and above all, on motherhood.

In fairness to Stern, he wasn't the only one to find de Beauvoir's rhetoric incendiary. In a review of a recent translation of *The Second Sex*, published in *The New York Times Review of Books* in May of 2010, Francine du Plessix Gray decried de Beauvoir's "truly paranoid hostility toward the institutions of marriage and motherhood." She notes, for example, that by de Beauvoir's account, conjugal love is really "a complex mixture of attachment, resentment, hatred, rules, resignation, laziness and hypocrisy." Similarly, she notes, throughout *The Second Sex* derogatory phrases like "the servitude of maternity," "woman's absurd fertility," the "exhausting servitude of breast-feeding," abound. Similarly, according to de Beauvoir, menstruation "inspires horror," and "signifies illness, suffering and death" while the pregnant woman, says de Beauvoir, experiences her fetus as a "parasite." Unsurprisingly, notes Plessix Gray, de Beauvoir goes on to add that: "There is nothing like an 'unnatural mother', since mother love has nothing natural about it." Instead, de Beauvoir says: "Maternity is a strange combination of narcissism, altruism, dream, sincerity, bad faith, devotion and cynicism" (du Plessix Gray, 2010, p. 7).

Having privileged the mother-infant relationship as the one most crucial for later psychosocial development, Stern was shocked and indignant at this kind of talk. And though she may have regretted it subsequently, when she wrote *The Second Sex*, de Beauvoir was obviously seething with contempt toward motherhood, and indeed, perhaps, the whole *bodily* dimension of female experience—menstruation, pregnancy, childbirth, lactation, and the sheer physicality of mothering small children to a wholesome maturity. But as Stern pointed out, whatever else men and women share in common, men simply do not have these bodily experiences, which are uniquely feminine. If you deliberately subtract the experiences of menstruation, pregnancy, childbirth, lactation, and so on from the lived experience of womanhood, it is not at all clear what kind of embodied experience or "being-in-the-world" that is still distinctively female is actually left. For his part, Stern acknowledged that:

> For millennia women have suffered atrocious forms of social and legal injustice. It is no exaggeration to say that they have been, and often still are, the victims of a kind of interior colonialism. However, since the French Revolution and the rise of the feminist

movement the cry for equality has changed into an assertion of sameness. Any view of dissimilarity smacked of injustice. [...] The idea that anatomical differences are nothing but a matter of accidental implements of the body, interchangeable, as it were, is a touch of Cartesianism [...]. In the end of the very idea of sexual polarity is regarded, in relation to the findings of the social sciences, as a pre-Copernican universe would be in relation to the findings of astronomy ... What began in feminism as a movement of liberation is bound to end in a slavery worse than the first. For if there really existed a world in which "sexual characteristics" are the mere "product of culture," in which Mark might as well have Martha's personality, and Antigone the personality of Achilles—persons would be reduced to fleshless ciphers, to mere intersection points in the graph of the social structure. (Stern, 1965a, pp. 14–15)

Stern's prediction that the feminist movement might result in a new form of slavery was not calculated to endear him to feminists in that (or any other) era. Nevertheless, it is instructive to note that *The Flight From Woman* elicited a positive response from feminist philosopher Susan Bordo. In "The Cartesian masculinization of thought" (1986), *The Flight to Objectivity: Essays on Cartesianism and Culture* (1987) and *Feminist Interpretations of Descartes* (1999), Bordo treated Stern's book as prescient and insightful, but eschewed his essentialist views on gender, downplaying the personal, biographical dimension of Descartes' life that Stern seized upon to explain his theory. In its place, Bordo offers an alternative perspective on modern misogyny—one which emphasizes the more encompassing cultural trends that presumably provoked Descartes radical bifurcation of existence into the mental and bodily realms (Bordo, 1986; Bordo, 1987; Bordo, 1999). Katherine Rudolph, Associate Professor of Philosophy and Media Studies at Rhode Island College, notes that:

> [...] with a nod toward Stern, (Bordo) suggests that Cartesian anxiety is a function of separation from the organic [...] universe of the Middle Ages and the Renaissance. The result is a supermasculinized model of knowledge that requires detachment (principally from the body) and the rebirth of nature as a machine. Unlike Bordo, (Stern) [...] does not invoke an impersonal historic

> episteme to make his point [...] but [...] does rely heavily, following a psychoanalytic model, on Descartes' personal history to suggest that the experience of maternal bereavement shattered Descartes' "certainty of being" [...]. (Rudolph, *Hypatia*, 2004, p. 190)

Like Bordo, then, Rudolph finds Stern's matricentric theory of human development too psychological to do justice to the complexity of the issues involved in the epistemic shift that took place in the wake of Descartes. She chides Stern for identifying women with nature in a way that "to a modern reader seems rather dated." At the same time, however, as recently as 2004, Rudolph freely acknowledges that "[...] many of (Stern's) claims are prescient in relation to later feminist discussions."

In addition to being a response to feminism, *The Flight from Woman* was a prolonged meditation on the whole malaise of modernity. According to Stern, the ascendancy of rationalism and positivism in modern times have contributed to a kind of hyper-masculine mentality, and an excessive emphasis on abstract thought and the rational, discursive intellect that shapes and disfigures contemporary culture. Our collective valorization of the masculine intellect leads to excessive mechanization and depersonalization, and a corollary devaluation of other, more personal ways of knowing and engaging with the world, above all, empathy and intuition. The resulting decline in "womanly values" is not only detrimental to women's welfare. It bodes ill for religious life, because faith is the highest expression of what Stern termed "the poetic mode of knowledge," which is rooted in a feminine-receptive orientation, even in the male of the species (Stern, 1965a).

The Flight from Woman elicited a flurry of reviews, among them a lavish and thoughtful appreciation from the celebrated Montreal poet, publisher, and journalist Louis Dudek. He hailed Stern's third book in the *Montreal Star* on September 18th, 1965 as "fascinating," "original," and "profound." Some months (and many reviews) later, Stern received the following letter from Graham Greene:

> 8 November 1965.
>
> My dear Karl,
>   I've just been reading *The Flight from Woman* with great admiration and pleasure. It's an extremely interesting book and I've

enjoyed it more than anything you have written since *The Pillar of Fire*. You have even made me want to read Goethe! What is happening to your book in England?

Affectionately,
Graham
(KSA, Series 2, Box 3, Folder 18)

And some years later, on February 2nd, 1968 another Catholic writer, poet Robert Lowell wrote to Stern as follows:

> I have been skipping about with fascination in your *Flight From Woman* [...]. You write without cliché or coarseness. What more can one say? You have a subtle sense of character, most with the women, but in a more rugged way with your famous men. Also, the theme is a deep one; I hadn't thought of the similarity in this of Faust and the Comedia. You give Christian solutions, and you give them well, without formula ... You are a gentle judge, and a just one, only gently tipping the scales. (KSA, Series 2, Box 3, Folder 70)

The fact that so many Catholic writers and poets hailed the book as a major accomplishment is not surprising. But others outside the Catholic orbit were also quite impressed. In a review entitled "Manicheanism and the denigration of woman," published in 1966 in *American Imago* (23(2): 184–186), American psychoanalyst Harry Slochower wrote that Stern "writes engagingly, breaks fresh ground and manages to create focused pictures in a few pages." He added that:

> Readers who cannot follow Stern's theological theses and their extrapolations will yet find his examination of the philosophical and literary figures highly rewarding. These chapters are psychoanalytically grounded and are written with literary skill. (Slochower, 1966, p. 185)

Finally, Slochower concluded: "While there are problems with *The Flight from Woman*, in many ways it was a prescient book, one which deserves continuing study and reflection." Agreed! Sadly, this was probably the most favorable review Stern ever received—or would receive—in a Freudian journal.

The family ordeal: suicide and aftermath

In 1966, Antony, Lilian and their four children returned from Cincinnatti to Montreal. Stern was still extremely anxious on Antony's behalf, and had harbored great hopes for Antony's treatment with Paul Ornstein. However, these hopes were completely dashed. Antony was hospitalized four times during his residency in Cleveland, and attempted suicide twice—in the summer of 1963, and the spring of 1964. Fortunately for all concerned, Lilian and the children weathered these storms with steadfast support of Carlos Placci, whose patience and generosity helped them manage these crises.

In addition to causing Stern considerable anxiety, Antony's illness was probably a source of considerable embarrassment. Even in correspondence with Dorothy Day, his closest confidante, allusions to Antony's illness were few and cryptic, referring to an anonymous "patient" who causes him anxiety rather than "my son." The third such letter, dated July 2nd, 1966, reads:

> Dear Dorothy,
> Just a brief note to tell you that the patient about whom I was so distressed last summer is back in Montreal with his wife and four children (the youngest, a sweet girl, was born during his illness). He is scheduled to begin his regular work in Montreal on August 1st.
> Although his illness is apt to occur again and although I work in this field and know too much about these things, you can imagine how happy I am. I simply cannot tell you how grateful I am to you for your great spiritual help, in prayer, in thought, in dialogue!
>
> (Stern, 1966, DD-CWC, Series D-1, Box 21, Folder 4)

Clearly, however an expert analyst and intercessory prayer were not sufficient, so Stern approached Heinz Lehmann (1911–1999), the Clinical Director of Psychiatry at the Douglas Hospital in Montreal. Nowadays, Lehman is chiefly remembered for introducing the use of chlorapromzine with schizophrenic patients. In fact, however, he was also a convert from Judaism, and on very friendly terms with Stern. Though he leaned more toward Kraepelin, Lehmann shared Stern's distaste for Cameron's grotesque "experiments," which he deemed to be pseudo-scientific (personal communication, Guttman,

2010). In the midst of this burgeoning crisis, Lehmann urged Stern to get Antony on lithium—the latest (and to that point, only) drug that was demonstrably effective in the treatment of manic depression. But lithium was still quite new in Canada, and the drug itself is exceedingly toxic, with numerous "side effects." Besides, despite his respect for Lehmann, Stern still placed more faith in psychoanalysis than in psychopharmacology—though Antony was taking injections of Largactyl from his psychiatrist, Manny Striker.

Since the Largactyl was not effective, and lithium was still new, Stern asked Noel Walsh to provide Antony with psychotherapy. Walsh was a few years older than Antony, and a very expressive and engaging fellow whom Stern thought would make an excellent role model for his son. But this was not to be. On the advice of his own analyst, Dr. Walsh wisely declined to analyze Antony.

In 1967, with the World's Fair (Expo '67) on his doorstep, Stern suffered from a multitude of health complaints, including another heart attack, which left him severely incapacitated. These health crises could not have come at a worse time. Ever since his return to Montreal, Antony's mental status had been precarious, provoking lively consternation among all who knew him. Finally, on May 24th, 1967, toward

Figure 21. Liselotte (left), Karl (center) and Antony (right), circa 1966.

midnight, Antony finally decided that he had suffered enough, and took a fatal overdose of barbiturates. Fearing the worst, Lilian summoned Katherine and shortly after, Noel Walsh to the house early the next morning. Walsh examined the body and certified that Antony was dead. Neither Katherine nor Lilian—Stern's daughter and daughter-in-law—felt able to break the news to Karl, so it remained to Walsh to inform Stern of his son's suicide. Aching with sadness, Walsh went to Stern's home, and found him sitting in a wheel chair listening to classical music on a tinny transistor radio. Walsh broke the news to Stern slowly, and did his best to console him, assisting him in the days leading up to the funeral, and indeed, in many ways, for months afterwards.

How did Karl and Liselotte cope with Antony's suicide? How does any parent cope in such harrowing circumstances? In the days immediately following his death, Liselotte secluded herself in her room and drank heavily. She emerged shaken and depleted, and in truth, never recovered completely. When you consider that she'd already lost little Johnny to spinobifida in 1943, and suffered at least two miscarriages subsequently, you realize that in the wake of Antony's suicide, she carried a very heavy burden into her final years. So did Karl, though as Lilian recalls, he was far less demonstrative in the days immediately following Antony's funeral.

Still, if Karl appeared more composed than Liselotte, if you consider his theoretical views, you realize after a moment's reflection that his mind *must* have been filled with deeply distressing thoughts at the time. After all, only two years previously, in his Parliamentary testimony, Stern had informed Matheson's inquiry on genocide and hate literature that suicide is often the result of repressed hostility. In his own words:

> You must remember that there is verbal hostility, quarrels, and what we call in psychiatry suppressed hostility, hostility of which we are conscious, but which we willfully hold back. There is also the field of repressed or unconscious hostility. For instance, something which a great number of people do not know is that much of anxiety and repression, which we deal with in our work, is due to poorly handled conflicts of hostility. Some psychoanalysts have said that every suicide is a backfiring homicide, that the suicidal

man has murderous impulses towards somebody else, and that his homicidal impulse is backfiring backwards against himself. Whether one can generalize to that extent I do not know, but there is no doubt—and that is my own clinical experience—that a great number of suicides are backfiring homicides. (Stern, 1965b, pp. 1773–1774)

If Antony's suicide *was* a "backfiring homicide," who was his unconscious hostility directed towards, if not toward own his father? Surely this thought occurred to Karl. Besides, actions speak louder than words, and even if the Freudian perspective on suicide is overly simplistic, suicidal people always communicate two emphatic messages to their family and loved ones by ending their own lives. The first can be summed up in the statement: "I see no future here for me," or more precisely, perhaps, no viable or desirable future. This "statement" may have a vindictive subtext, but in the end, it is really a product of despair. Whether it is explicitly stated or merely implied, this is simply an honest self-appraisal, a self-conscious acknowledgement of the suicidal person's state of mind at the moment of decision.

The second statement, by contrast, reflects the person's lived experience with significant others, past and present, with whom the suicidal person is in conscious communication or unconscious rapport, and can be summed up simply as: "You failed me." Whether friends and family members own up to receiving it consciously, for those left behind, a loved one's suicide is experienced and interpreted—consciously or unconsciously—as a standing reproach. As a rule, this message lingers long after the fact, no matter how hard those addressed in this way tried to buoy the spirits of departed person, to make their life tolerable and hopeful, while they were alive.

Karl saved few of the condolence letters that he and Liselotte received. This one, dated June 10th, from Graham Greene, is one of them. It reads:

G6 Albany
London W.1
June 10

My dear Karl,
 I have been away on a motoring holiday out of touch & have only just received the shocking news about Antony. I'm very very

sorry for all of you. I have very happy memories of him. Thank God we as Catholics don't have to feel that this is an end, but the blow is a horrible one for you, and you have received so very many of them during the last years. The *Pillar of Fire* (was) […] too often the *Pillar of Smoke* by day.

When you feel able do write and tell me a little of what happened and how you are.

Affectionately,
Graham
(KSA, Series 2, Box 3, Folder 18)

Though more Stoic than Liselotte, the suffering that Stern endured in the wake of Antony's suicide took its toll in several ways. In 1968, Stern suffered another heart attack and later, a stroke which left him partially paralyzed and aphasic. Sensing that something was imminent, perhaps, he asked Noel Walsh to replace him as Chief of Psychiatry at St. Mary's—a position Walsh held from 1968 till 1970, when he returned to Dublin. Meanwhile, Stern confided to Walsh that Antony's suicide had shaken his faith, not just in Catholicism, but in psychoanalysis as well. He began to ruminate about the past, and fretting that he should have heeded Lehmann's advice, and put Antony on lithium after all.

CHAPTER SIX

A legacy lost: 1968–1975

The final years

On May 8th, 1968, one year after Antony's suicide, Karl's step-mother Helene passed away. Her death was not unexpected, but Karl was exceedingly fond of his step-mother, and for him at least, this was another significant blow. Shortly after her death, he wrote to Dorothy Day mourning her passing, saying that she was such a saintly person that she would certainly go to heaven, despite her steadfast refusal to convert to Christianity. Though it is probably impossible to verify, many Jewish converts, like John Oesterreicher, probably harbored similar thoughts in relation to their parents at their time of death (Connelly, 2012).

Meanwhile, Karl's faith in Catholicism and psychoanalysis were both badly shaken, though you wouldn't have known it from his interview with Fernand Seguin on CBC television in June of 1968. Despite his physical infirmities, this superb interview (available in the CBC's online archive) shows Stern in excellent form, with his dry, self-deprecating humor and calm serenity remarkably intact—at least while he was on camera. No one who was watching a man this funny, articulate and composed would imagine that his faith was shaken, or that his health was now in a steep and irreversible decline.

Despite this bravura performance, two months after his television appearance, on August 30th 1968, Stern wrote to Dorothy Day, saying: "When I think of the events of the past few years I have so much of a sense of failure." Taken in context, this abject confession probably referred to his ineffectiveness as a spokesperson for Catholicism in Québec, rather than his conduct as a father. And in fairness to Stern, this was not the first time he had alluded to such feelings. In fact, over the years, he and Dorothy Day exchanged numerous letters in which they confessed to feelings of failure or inadequacy, and rallied to one another's support, offering prayer and encouragement of various kinds.

Was Stern a "failure"? That is a matter of perspective, I suppose, but as if to assert the contrary, on Oct 8th, 1969, Laval University, the oldest university in North America, bestowed an honorary doctorate on Stern, honoring him for his scholarship and contributions to Québec society. While this ceremony and the attendant publicity must have buoyed his spirits considerably, this handsome tribute probably did little to check his declining spirits in the long run. Reading between the lines of his letter to Day, one cannot escape the impression that his (mostly private) feelings about Antony's suicide were coloring his appraisal of his public role as a spokesman for Catholicism in Québec.

In early 1969, Stern wrote to Dorothy Day about a recent fall that caused him to break his hip and his arm. Some months later, on January 23rd, 1970, an enfeebled and demoralized Karl Stern wrote that: "I cannot write any more. I cannot walk anymore [...] I cannot dress." He noted that Liselotte was also very unwell, but nonetheless "very brave" (DD-CWC, Series D-1, Box 21, Folder 4). And brave she was, right up till her death in 1971.

Meanwhile, when Antony died in 1967, Lilian sought work teaching English at Concordia University, and later, as a translator for the Canadian Chamber of Commerce. Her income was quite modest at first, so between the Fall of 1967 and July of 1972, when Lilian remarried, Stern supplemented her income to support his grandchildren. To that end, he sustained a fairly brisk private practice in his home, where he was cared for by a lively and devoted Jamaican woman named Mrs. Alexander, who Katherine's children remember fondly to this day.

Despite his housekeeper's diligence and warmth, maintaining a practice in Stern's condition was not easy. Stern had been fluently trilingual before his stroke, but was now competent only in his mother tongue, German. While his comprehension of English and French was unimpaired, he now struggled to express himself in the languages that his patients spoke. Still, he managed somehow. In the midst of all these difficulties, Stern suffered another considerable setback. With one hand permanently paralyzed, he could no longer play the piano. Making music had been a source of solace and inspiration; a form of recreation, of therapy and of worship for Stern all through his adult life. Now, despite encouragement from friends and relatives, he declined to play even one-handed parts in compositions he knew well.

Despite his physical infirmities, Stern was *intellectually* active through much of this period. Shortly after his stroke, Stern asked friends and family members to help him assemble a final volume of essays, entitled *Love and Success*, which appeared several months before his death on November 6th, 1975. Judging from the title, one could imagine that it was an inspirational or self-help type of book. Thankfully, that is not the case. In addition to some innovative essays on psychoanalytic themes—child development, the problems of guilt, creativity, and a very thoughtful critique of Alfred Kinsey—it contained some splendid essays on Christian humanism, pacifism, and a searching, sympathetic portrait of his childhood heroes, Rosa Luxemburg and Karl Leibknecht. In addition to religious and politically oriented pieces, *Love and Success* contains some striking reflections on literary figures, including Dostoyevsky, Rilke, Tolstoy, and Alfred Doblin—a troubled Jewish convert to Roman Catholicism, and author of *Berlin Alexanderplatz*, the classic evocation of life in Weimar immortalized by Werner Maria Fassbinder in the sprawling film of that same name.

On July 19th, 1975, journalist Robert Fulford published a favorable review of *Love and Success* in the Ottawa Citizen, entitled "U of O's Stern mixes Freud, Catholicism" (p. 70). Fulford prefaced his review with reflections on several of Stern's earlier contributions, including *The Pillar of Fire*, *Flight from Woman*, and *Through Dooms of Love*, which he described as a "touching novel." Fulford described *Love and Success* as a somewhat uneven collection of essays centered around the fear of galloping dehumanization in medicine and modern society, and the desire for a deeper and richer human life. And while quite respectful of Stern's yearnings for wholeness and transcendence, he chided Stern for being prudish about the increasing prevalence of nudity in movies.

Further evidence of Stern's intellectual activity at this time is provided by Hector Warnes. Warnes, an Argentinian psychiatrist who replaced Noel Walsh as the Psychiatrist in Chief at St. Mary's when Walsh returned to Dublin in 1970. In a letter to the author, Warnes recalls:

> During my stay as Chief of Psychiatry at the St. Mary's I often visited Karl Stern and took him for a drive. We were preparing a paper on the Psychology of Money (the drive to amass wealth and the various interpretations of the fixation with money). Stern was lucid and brilliant and, in spite of his aphasia, we carried on long conversations. As far as I understood him he was deeply ecumenical. He was very fond of his brother who worked in Israel. I know that they had exciting correspondence on Society and Religion because Stern asked me to read some of those letters. For him the greatest psychologists were Dostoyevsky and Kierkegaard. He was conversant with the greatest philosophers, and was closer to C. G. Jung than to Freud […]. (Warnes, 2009)

Was Stern closer to Jung than to Freud, as Warnes alleged? Well, no—not in print, anyway. For example, we have an unpublished paper that Stern delivered to the Canadian Psychiatric Association's meeting in Ottawa on June 5th, 1959, called "The use of dream interpretation in short-term psychotherapy." It is Freudian through and through (Stern, 1959b). And when Noel Walsh asked Stern some years later whether he favored Freud or Jung, Stern replied that both Freud and Jung had considerable merit, but that Freudians were often the better clinicians. Finally, the motivation behind hoarding and the desire to accumulate money is typically a Freudian past time, which had already spawned a vast and varied literature by 1970. So what accounts for this curious claim of Warnes'? Was Stern recalling his first analysis with Laudenheimer in Warnes' presence at this penultimate phase of his life? Perhaps so, since old age is often a period of life review, as Erikson points out, and that period of his life in Germany prior to London, Montreal and his marriage to Liselotte seems to have occurred to him frequently at this time.

For example, in February of 1970, Stern published his last article in *The Catholic Worker*, entitled "Thoughts on the resurrection." In this article, Stern described the resurrection of Jesus as a scientifically unverifiable but nonetheless authentic event that changed an otherwise unremarkable occurrence—a brutal Roman execution in first century Palestine—into "the turning point of history." Reflecting on his experience at the Moabit Hospital, he wrote:

> I used to work in a mental hospital and had to perform autopsies, frequently of patients I had known in life. Many of these were anonymous, forgotten people who for years had lived demented and deteriorated in the dark corner of a ward. When their bodies and inner organs were laid out on an autopsy table it often did not seem to make much difference whether they were alive or dead. It certainly did not make any difference to society at large. In fact, in many cases no person ever turned up to claim the body.
>
> In such a situation you are faced with a simple alternative; either that which we see in the autopsy room is not the whole show and will be transfigured—or the whole of human existence is, as Sartre's hero Monsieur Rocquentin puts it, "one big mess that makes you vomit." These are the only two possibilities, and no matter how hard you try, you will find there is nothing in between. It is one of those formidable "either/or" situations of Kierkegaard. Either the whole of living nature, all Flesh has a glorious meaning which will be revealed, or else it is meaningless, or to quote Sartre again, it is "pure contingency."
>
> There is no cut and dried solution to this problem. Nevertheless, we may, as one does in Euclidean geometry, introduce some "tentative factors" (p. 2). We know that it is hate that desires death, and love that desires life. We can still visualize him as a baby in the arms of his mother, or at least someone who looked at him with maternal care. And whoever loved him would have been horrified to see him as a mass of dead flesh. He had been loved not as a disincarnate soul (a ghastly thought) but as a living being. His very existence had been brought about by love, or by that natural foreshadowing of love, namely desire […].
>
> If our limited human love, as lovers, mothers, desires the life of the flesh, and wishes it never to die—the same thing must be true of Infinite Love, only infinitely more. Hence, if the incarnation and the Death of Christ were the manifestation of Infinite Love, the Resurrection follows quite logically. Love demands life, and Infinite Love demands Infinite Life. (Stern, 1970, p. 2)

There are several striking things about this statement. First, in view of his enfeebled condition, Stern was doubtless thinking about his own death some years hence. And to redeem the memory of countless unfortunates who, unlike him, died in complete anonymity, his thoughts go immediately to the loving gaze and embrace of the recently bereft mother. Needless to say, we cannot discount the possibility that, on some level, he was thinking about Liselotte's inconsolable grief over Antony. But by the same token, the religious train of thought he was describing here antedates these troubling experiences by more than three decades.

That being so, in light of Warnes' comments, it is interesting to note that Stern's tendency to link death and resurrection with the maternal imago, rather than the father-figure, is more characteristic of Jungian depth psychology than it is of Freudian psychoanalysis. In Freud's writings, the themes of death and dismemberment are routinely associated with the father, and more specifically, with the fear of castration (Freud, 1912–1913; Hogenson, 1984). So Stern was basically a Freudian, though an unorthodox one, whose matricentric brand of psychoanalysis was linked to a distinctively love-centered Christian piety.

As regards his uncompromising either/or stance on the resurrection, several responses are possible, depending on your point of view. From the standpoint of a devout Christian, his logic is impeccable. But a Jew or a Muslim who does not take Jesus for the Messiah might reproach Stern for indulging in the kind of cheap religious rhetoric that makes genuine faith or spirituality hinge entirely on our adopting the doctrines of *his* personal faith, which by direct implication, if not in so many words, relegates all others to an inferior or perhaps utterly inconsequential position. From this perspective, perhaps, Stern seems to treat Judaism and Islam as having fragmentary or distorted premonitions of the truth—a stance that does not invite genuine dialogue with members of other faiths.

By contrast with the non-Christian believer, an agnostic or atheist might object that the stark choice Stern posed between a love-centered supernaturalism and an utterly meaningless universe is simply a false dichotomy, and reproach Stern for ignoring or dismissing other ethical and spiritual orientations that do not fit the procrustean bed of his preconceived schemata.

If you read Stern's last article in *The Catholic Worker* as an exhortation to all readers, and not merely to Catholics, both of these objections to Stern are completely intelligible. But if you read his statement as a personal confession, a more charitable interpretation quickly dawns on you. The old man who made this statement was once the teenager who was shocked by the scale and severity of human savagery during World War I, and who shortly thereafter felt a profound spiritual void that his ancestral faith did not entirely address. As he groped for a viable identity, and a sense of cosmological coherence, he felt the inadequacy of Marxism and Zionism, and sensed the dangers that lay dormant in the romantic irrationalism of Schopenhauer, Nietzsche, and Klages (among others). When faced, as a young man, with this hospital-housed spectacle of death, dismemberment and utter depersonalization, a latter day Golgotha on an industrial scale, Stern felt that he had simply run out of options; that he could not face the horror and enormity of death and human suffering in any other way.

Another reason I have seized on this particular statement of Stern's is because however it was actually intended, as an exhortation or a confession—or perhaps both, in some measure?—this statement is oddly revealing. While Slochower noted Stern's ability to "create focused pictures in a few pages," the fact remains that Stern seldom revealed *himself* openly in his work. Indeed, Stern's elusiveness even prompted Erich Fromm to reproach him with being secretive in his review of The Pillar of Fire (Fromm, 1951). What caused this zeal for personal privacy, which was unusual even in his day?

I am reminded of a dream that one of Stern's patient's brought to therapy. The patient was a gifted "executive artist" i.e., an artistic director, orchestra conductor, or movie director, who professed an admiration for Stern that predated their clinical encounter by some time. Eschewing a detailed account of the patient's personal history, Stern recalled that in this dream

> The patient finds himself in a room the one wall of which is lined with books like a study. The patient reaches and finally searches and crawls through an opening in these shelves to find the physician who is crouched naked behind the books. (Stern, 1959b, p. 8)

Stern noted that the patient's own father was a doctor with a book lined study, and that in the process of elucidating the dream, the patient alluded to his own desire to get beyond his own tendency to idealize Stern and get to know him "in the flesh, so to speak." From

Stern's perspective, this dream had obvious transference implications, and betokened a latent homosexual trend; one that was never addressed explicitly, given the brevity of the treatment, and the fact that the patient's acute interpersonal difficulties, which brought him to therapy in the first place, cleared up soon afterwards. Well, yes, perhaps so. But surviving members of Stern's family concur that whenever Stern was upset or irritable, he quickly retreated to *his* book lined study for long intervals of time. It obviously never dawned on Stern that in addition to everything else, perhaps, his patient's unconscious produced an astute assessment of his *analyst's* psychic defenses; that behind the veneer of calm erudition was a man who was profoundly vulnerable, and who feared being exposed to the intense scrutiny of others.

A complicated man

In the course of his career, Stern made some very strong statements about psychoanalysis, psychiatry, and religion. But at several critical junctures, he equivocated or glossed over difficult subjects, particularly in matters of faith. Take the subject of the Church hierarchy, for example. In his very first letter to Dorothy Day, he begged for spiritual guidance because he was besieged by doubts that arose in response to the Vatican's sphinx like silence on the bombing of Hiroshima. But as we already noted, he also feared or condemned these thoughts and feelings, and sought to blame his misgivings on his own sinful inclinations and his wayward attraction to anthroposophy. Then, somewhat later, as Day disclosed some of her own disappointments with high ranking clergymen, Stern frankly advised her to *ignore* the hierarchy's attitude toward her; to trust that she had made a deep contribution to the Church's real mission, by reviving the prophetic spirit of justice and concern for the poor that so many Catholics had lost sight of. Similarly, in 1957, in another letter to Day, he criticized the heavy handed control which the hierarchy exerted over a recent conference of lay Catholic thinkers and activists in Rome, implying that they were prescribing to lay people how they ought to think about their relationship to the Church (and one another).

Finally, despite three decades of strong support for Day and *The Catholic Worker*, in an unpublished interview with Deane Mowrer at

Tivoli Farm, New York, on July 6th, 1968, Stern remarked that Day's anarchist tendencies gave him pause. In his own words:

> Christian anarchism is a contradiction in terms. Christianity is hierarchy and not anarchy. The hierarchic idea is not only transcendental [...] it is also an idea which goes into nature, into society, and so on. (Mowrer, 1968, p. 8, DD-CWC, Series W-9, Box 2, Milwaukee: Marquette University)

Reviewing these various comments in sequence, the cumulative impression one gets is that Stern's feelings toward the Roman Catholic hierarchy fluctuated pretty wildly at times, and that he himself was seldom aware of the full nature and extent of his ambivalence on this score, which was never fully articulated or resolved.

Another sore spot, in retrospect, was his attitude toward heaven and the afterlife. In 1965, as *The Flight from Woman* was going to press, Stern asked Noel Walsh if he actually believed in the resurrection and the afterlife. When Walsh replied that he did, Stern expressed a strong feeling of envy. Walsh, a "cradle Catholic" had imbibed these beliefs with his mother's milk, Stern said, while he himself had to struggle constantly with this issue. This statement suggested to Walsh that he had harbored serious doubts about his faith all along! And yet, there is no hint of this behind-the-scenes struggle in any of his public pronouncements; indeed, quite the contrary. The first documentary evidence we have of his longstanding doubts on this score show up belatedly in his last letter to Dorothy Day, which sadly, is as plaintive as the first one was. In this letter, dated February 24th, Stern confided to Day that he was wrestling with doubts about the Divinity of Christ, and wondered whether the immense suffering he had endured in recent years was actually punishment for the fact that he had converted to Catholicism, and abandoned his ancestral faith. Finally, despite his article on the resurrection five years earlier, he admitted to harboring grave doubts about the afterlife, and indicated that the priest who was ministering to him in his final days was of no help. He begged her, once more, to pray for his soul. And no doubt, of course, she did, with her customary kindness and fervor. But given the tone and content of his last letter to Day, one can only wonder what sorts of thoughts crossed Stern's mind as he prepared to meet his Maker. One can only hope that in the intervening period, he tamed his inner demons, and approached this final threshold with clarity and conviction, regardless of what awaited him on the "other side."

And so we are left ponder the question: why have Stern and his work been so thoroughly forgotten? Unfortunately, there is no single, simple answer to this question. During his lifetime, Stern was studiously shunned by Canadian Jewry. The reasons for this sad but predictable state of affairs will be explored at greater length in Chapter Eight. Similarly, perhaps, with Canada's psychoanalytic community, Jewish and Gentile, who did not shun Stern so much as simply ignore him, since he was openly religious, and never took the crucial step of getting credentialed as an analyst by the International Psychoanalytical Association. Among Québec's Francophones, where Stern had many friends and supporters, his steadfast loyalty to the Church (despite his inner conflicts) probably doomed him to irrelevance as the belated secularization that was the Quiet Revolution took hold in the sixties. Amongst feminists, his pointed attack on de Beauvoir's feminism provoked scorn and indignation, despite generous acknowledgements from outliers like Susan Bordo and Katherine Rudolph. And last but not least, there was the tragedy and scandal of his son's suicide, which was lamented in verse by Daryl Hine, and was particularly damning for Canada's Anglophone intelligentsia, and the more liberal and progressive members of the mental health professions. Why?

A scathing dismissal

When Stern passed away in 1975, Daryl Hine was a nationally renowned poet, with half a dozen collections already in print. Hine produced the first (self-published) edition of *In and Out: A Confessional Poem* in that same year. The second edition appeared more than a decade later with Alfred Knopf (Hine, 1989), this time with glowing endorsements from Northrop Frye and James Merrill. Frye was an internationally renowned literary critic, who described *In and Out* as "a meditation upon the major conflicts of opposites in life and literature: spirit and nature, Christian and pagan, the sacred and the profane" and as "a deeply moving yet very funny poem." Merrill, a Pullitzer prize winning poet described it as "Witty and wise and tender" and as "Daryl Hines' masterpiece."

I do not contest the book's literary merit. It is flawlessly constructed and disarmingly funny in places. Moreover, the book's title—*In and Out*—has a double meaning, referring obliquely to Hine's brief immersion in and subsequent departure from the Church, and to his transformation from a vaguely ascetic teenager in the closet to an openly gay young man. But despite its frequent avowals of truthfulness, and many telling and accurate details about their home, their history and habits, Hines' portrayal of Karl and Liselotte does not ring true. Liselotte was never as skilled musically as her fictional counterpart, and never simply the creature or "confection" of her husband, the dutiful "martyr to marriage and motherhood" that Hine depicted in the character of Charlotte. In fact, in many ways, this description is profoundly inaccurate. Despite multiple miscarriages and hospitalizations, all through her adult life Liselotte was an independent artisan whose services were in steady demand, and whose work Stern himself keenly admired. She not only practiced her craft, but trained others in it as well. Moreover, she was not submissive. She made no secret of her likes and dislikes, even when it ruffled Stern's composure. And she was also prone to bouts of mania and depression—a fact that Hine, who seemed to notice everything, claimed to have learned only *after* Antony's suicide (Hine, 1989, p. 265). In truth, however, it would have been impossible for Hine to remain completely ignorant of this fact for so long if he knew Liselotte and Antony as intimately as he claimed. On this point, he protests too much. Either he knew about these issues sooner than he admitted, or he did not know the Stern family as well as he claimed.

In addition, Hine's suggestion that Liselotte gave her tacit approval to Hines' affair with Antony by turning a blind eye (Hine, 1989, p. 264) strains credulity. Judging from Liselotte's diary (in the Karl Stern Archive at Duquesne University), she was probably oblivious to their intimacies because she was too depressed, or alternatively, too preoccupied with her Farmatorium plans. If there was an element of complicity between her and Hine, it was in their indulgent attitude toward Antony's mocking and derisive comments about the Catholic Church, which Hine described vividly, and which clearly bothered Stern considerably. Indeed, Katherine recalls an episode when Antony and Daryl performed a satirical sketch of priests performing Mass, prompting Karl to storm out of the house, slamming the door behind him. This sort of thing happened more than once, apparently.

And what of Hine's treatment of Karl Stern? By his own admission, even before he met him, Daryl Hine was not a fan of *The Pillar of Fire*, which he re-titled *The Pillar of Salt*, and dismissed on account of its "petrified stance and unsalty opinions"; a clever play on words, to be sure. Hine described Stern's ideas dismissively as a "dubious doctrine, a mixture of Buber and Maritain topped with a dollop of Freud," an obvious oversimplification (Hine, 1989, p. 260). Reflecting on the Sterns' taste in furniture, Hine remarked that "everything bore at the Star's an invisible label, like in those museums, proclaiming its age, in reaction perhaps to the modern world that they found themselves in but not of." The cumulative impression Hine conveyed is that the Sterns were a prosperous but backward looking couple. Like Lot's wife, they were fixated on the past, and by implication, secretly disobedient to God's commands. Rather than being courageous enough to trust Divine Providence and embrace the present, as the title of Stern's book suggested, they lived in a museum—all because they preferred rustic and antique furniture to the kind of modern kitsch that was so fashionable in that era.

So, while he was certainly aloof and pedantic at times, Stern was not simply the humorless, petty tyrant that Hine satirized in the person of "Immanuel Star." His irritability in Daryl Hine's presence may have been strongly influenced by his anxieties about Liselotte's mental status, which was quite precarious when Antony started at McGill. And given the intensely homophobic climate of Canadian culture in the 1950s, Stern's anger and anxiety would only have increased if he suspected the true nature of the relationship between Antony and his Daryl. That being so, it seems likely that Stern's interference in their affair, including the pressure he exerted to send Antony into analysis, was motivated (at least in part) by an anxious desire to spare his son the indignity and the suffering that invariably occur when one is labeled "deviant" for one's entire adult life. This needs to be said, because since Antony's death, attitudes toward sex, gender and psychotherapy have changed dramatically. Sending a teenager for "treatment" in such circumstances seems unthinkable to most people today. But in fairness, given the temper of the times, Stern's motives for acting as he did would have been readily intelligible to all but a tiny handful of his contemporaries, even the most progressive.

Sadly, Hine's characterization of Stern's role in the family's tragedy made no allowance for any of these mitigating circumstances. Indeed, his final verdict on the whole tragedy was that Antony's analysis backfired, and that Karl was solely responsible for his son's death because he was ultra-conservative and homophobic; a self-centered bully masquerading as a real Christian. But even though Hine wrote with conviction, at the end of the day, we cannot really be certain that Antony *was* gay, though he was an extremely tormented soul. Antony may have been experimenting with gay sex, as many curious teenagers do, or he may have been bi-sexual. We will never know for sure. He took that secret to his grave.

Nevertheless, for the sake of argument, let us assume for the moment that Antony Stern actually was gay. What then? Andrew Solomon has written very persuasively on gay shame as a factor in suicide (Solomon, 2001, p. 202). Having studied the subject carefully, Solomon acknowledges that people who suffer from severe mental disorders with a strong genetic component, as Antony did, are also at extremely high risk for suicide, regardless of gender identity issues or the lack thereof (Solomon, 2001, p. 48). So even if Antony was gay, as Hine insisted, he may very well have committed suicide for other reasons, anyway.

In short, the circumstances surrounding Antony's eventual suicide where almost as grim as Daryl Hine made them out to be. But they were also messier and more complicated than his narrative suggests, leaving many questions unanswered. One thing *is* fairly certain, however. Stern probably should have followed Lehmann's advice and put Antony on a trial dose of Lithium. Had he taken this step, Antony might have stood a fighting chance. Lithium does not actually cure anything, and has cumulative side effects that are quite detrimental to one's health. But it alleviates the symptoms of manic-depressive (or bipolar) disorder dramatically in forty to sixty percent of cases (depending on which study you cite). When it does work, lithium dramatically lowers the risk of suicide and other forms of self-harm, and is clearly the lesser of two evils. But lithium was relatively new and untested at the time, so this too was only clear in hindsight, and Stern had good reasons to be wary of lithium.

In addition to the instances of exaggeration and omission just mentioned, there are a few times when Hine actually *fabricated* features of his story in *In and Out*. For example, Hine claimed that:

> Having qualified as a psychiatrist,
> Hyacinth's (Antony's) illness eluded
> the notice of colleagues and patients
> and family, even his father. (Hine, 1989, p. 267)

This statement is patently untrue, and demonstrates how freely Hine invented to humiliate Stern. Similarly, Hine's claim that Charlotte, Liselotte's fictional counterpart, deliberately hurled herself down the stairs out of guilt over her son's suicide, only to "die in madhouse" four years later, is completely false. Liselotte had *already* suffered a broken hip when the news of Antony's death first reached her from her daughter Katherine, and she died of kidney failure in a Montreal Hospital in 1971—not in a madhouse, as Hine evidently preferred to imagine.

Is this merely poetic license? I suppose that depends on your point of view. Changing things up in this fashion made Hine's version of events more compelling for readers, but it begs the question: besides the search for a good story, what other motives prompted this retelling of events, in which the father is utterly oblivious or indifferent to his son's continued suffering, and his mother's guilt and self-loathing prompted self-destructive acts? Despite the book's literary merits, this is a perfectly legitimate question, because at various points in *In and Out* Hine's description of the Sterns adopted the language of psychoanalysis. So long as he maintained this pseudo-clinical posture, probing for unconscious motives, Hine had no right to exempt his own motives for tinkering with the truth from similar scrutiny. Perhaps having Liselotte's fictional counterpart harm herself was intended to reinforce the reader's image of Karl as a tyrannical husband, who left his wife no real avenues for self-expression. And perhaps it was the poet's gratuitous way of punishing Liselotte in effigy—or more precisely, in phantasy—for not acting and he felt she *ought to* have acted at the time he and Antony were forcibly separated. Again, we'll never know for sure. But in retrospect, one cannot help wondering whether Hine's dedication of his volume to Liselotte concealed a more ambivalent and complicated attitude; one that sought to inflict posthumous punishment, while venerating her publicly as a martyr to patriarchy—a clever rhetorical strategy, given the temper of the times.

That said, in fairness to Hine, he was not inventing everything. Antony Stern's youngest child, Eva Marie Stern, is an art therapist who practices in Toronto. After reading a preliminary draft of this book, she wrote to me saying:

> I don't believe my father's suicide was due to any one factor, any one torment. But [...] [I do] [...] believe that my father (Antony) was intractably hurt by his own father. (Karl)

To illustrate her view of her grandfather, Eva Marie Stern cites James Fitzgerald's account of his family's tragedy in *What Disturbs our Blood* (Fitzgerald, 2012). She describes Karl Stern as:

> [...] an equally brilliant and a baleful force. Much like Fitzgerald's father and grandfather, pursuing his humanistic vision and his ideals took precedence over caring for his family. Unlike the immunologist and allergist Fitzgeralds, though, one could expect Stern to try to understand his impact on the people close to him—his wife, his kids [...]. And as [...] James would say, it's what's not openly said that most disturbs our blood. (Letter to the on author, March 28th, 2013)

Agreed. And no doubt, Hine did capture some features of that "baleful force" quite accurately. But Hine did not pause to ask why the sensitive adolescent who was horrified at the carnage of World War I, and the lively, engaged father that James Shaw captured frolicking on the floor with three laughing children in 1951 turned into the dour, demanding father Stern evidently became by the end of that same decade. Nor did he reflect on the impact that Liselotte's multiple miscarriages and hospitalizations had on Karl's marriage, and how depression, insomnia, and severe job-related stress and slowly failing health had already impinged on him by the time he met up with Stern at age fifty-one. Finally, Hine did not wonder whether the man who defended his faith so boorishly at the dinner table, at least in his re-telling, was beset by private doubts, and may have been doubly sensitive to his son's frequent mockery of his faith on that account. Instead, he merely implied that whatever went wrong in the family before, during and after Hine's ill-fated relationship with young Antony Stern was exclusively his father's fault.

In fairness to Hine, I suppose a middle-aged man seeking a long overdue catharsis and some well-deserved recognition for his literary skill may be forgiven for skewering a much older man who caused him so much pain and unhappiness in his youth. But must *we* be so one-sided? Historians and biographers must consider specific relationships and events in the arc of a person's entire life trajectory. If we factor in all the things that Hine deliberately factored out of his narrative, we are left with a different, more nuanced picture of Stern's personality. Stern emerges not merely as an authoritarian and self-absorbed father, or as a miserable buffoon, but as a vulnerable, tragic figure.

Meanwhile, the fact that an artist of Hine's stature laid the responsibility for Antony's death entirely his father's shoulders, minimizing or disregarding other salient factors, contributed enormously to Stern's posthumous neglect, especially in Canada. That being so, one wonders whether (or to what extent) Hine's scathing indictment also deterred potential readers from familiarizing themselves with Stern's body of work. After all, Hine claimed that he actually read *The Pillar of Fire*, which he dismissed as trite and confused. But Hine's appraisal flies in the face of exuberant praise Stern received from Hugh McLellan, C. S. Lewis, Graham Greene, Reinhold Niehbur, Thomas Merton, and many, many other gifted writers. Granted, Hine was extremely gifted. But is it prudent or fair to privilege his glib impressions of Stern's first book over all of theirs? And if not, shouldn't we at least give Stern the benefit of the doubt, and do him the courtesy of reading his *other* books before writing him off completely, as Hine evidently wanted us to do?

How to become a forgotten intellectual

In retrospect, of course, Hine's memoir was merely one of several factors that made Canadians apt to forget Stern and his work. But a multitude of (overlapping) cultural and historical forces have also conspired to bury him in obscurity. One domain in which Stern's influence ought to be felt is, of course, psychiatry. After all, though he was an accomplished musician in his spare time, he was a psychiatrist by vocation. But sadly, the year Stern died, the psychiatric profession made a sharp turn *away* from psychoanalytic modes of thought and practice. Adopting Gerald Klerman's slogan "Return to Kraepelin!" psychiatrists of that era embraced an increasingly blinkered and reductionist version of psychiatry, and were doubtless encouraged in that direction by the (so called) "Freud wars." Most commentators suggest that the "Freud wars" commenced in 1979, with the publication of Frank Sulloway's book *Freud, Biologist of the Mind*. Sulloway is an accomplished historian of science, but also a complete stranger to the literary side of Freud, who argued (contra Stern) that the "real" Sigmund Freud was a biologist manqué, and that many of his underlying biological postulates are demonstrably untrue, and even hopelessly dated when Freud adopted them.

Sulloway's critique of Freud was followed by an avalanche of books and articles by the likes of Elizabeth Thornton (1983), Jeffrey Masson

(1984), Adolph Gruenbaum (1984) Frederick Crewes (1986), Mikkel Borch-Jacobson (1988), and Peter Swales (1989), among others. And contrary to expectation, perhaps, many of Freud's most vehement critics in the eighties and nineties were not psychiatrists, but an unlikely assortment of Sanskrit scholars, English professors, linguists and historians, and philosophers of science—some, like Borch-Jacobsen, with strong deconstructionist leanings. Though there was no conscious collusion among them, as far as I am aware, these anti-Freudian scholars in the humanities were the natural allies of neo-Kraepelinian psychiatrists who were intent on discrediting and demolishing psychodynamic psychiatry (Burston, 2012).

The neo-Kraepelinian movement placed extravagant hopes in the powers of brain imaging and psychotropic medication to unravel the baffling mysteries of mental disorder. Meanwhile, a new "antidepressant" called fluoxetine (Prozac) was introduced in 1988, and the other selective serotonin reuptake inhibitors (SSRIs) that followed in its wake provoked a giddy optimism about the future of psychopharmacology that swept psychiatry (and the culture at large) and persisted into the early twenty-first century (Kramer, 1993). It was not till recently that the harmful side-effects of the SSRIs and the newer ("a-typical") anti-psychotics were exposed, along with big Pharma's dangerous and self-serving policy of suppressing and distorting data in clinical trials (Angell, 2011a; Angell, 2011b; Kirsch, 2010; Olfman & Robbins, 2012). And now, contrary to expectation, genetic researchers are scratching their heads, wondering aloud whether they will *ever* find a clear-cut etiology for any of the severe mental disorders that Kraepelin and his followers attributed to heredity (Craddock, 2010; Crow, 2010; Lake, 2010; Post, 2010). Nevertheless, the smug triumphalism of neo-Kraepelinian psychiatry has prevailed from Stern's death until very recently, rendering him an irrelevant has-been, a footnote to an embarrassing episode in the history of psychiatry in the eyes of most psychiatrists.

Another area where Stern might be expected to show up more often nowadays is in psychoanalysis and the humanities. However, there is not a single reference to Stern in Alan Parkin's *History of Psychoanalysis in Canada* (Parkin, 1987) or George Awad's more recent recounting of that same history (Awad, 2002). Meanwhile, Francophone authors who acknowledge Stern's existence are sometimes quite disparaging (e.g., Desgroseilliers, 2001). Even in the academy, where he might have stood a chance, owing to his many essays on literature, Stern's reputation has suffered, because his probing reflections on Goethe, Dostoyevsky, Tolstoy, Ibsen, Thomas Mann, Eugene O'Neill, and others breathe an air of old fashioned humanism that is completely out of fashion in the academy nowadays. In a field now dominated by anti-humanist rhetoric, only someone whose career is already on an even keel (and therefore indifferent to collective disapproval) would risk wrangling with an intriguing oddity like Stern.

Another arena where Stern might have had a more enduring impact was in the field of feminist studies. Taken on their own merits, Stern's critique of the hyper-masculine character of modernity, of Freud's androcentric theories about women and the libido, and his corollary emphasis on women's ways of knowing and engaging with others in the world—empathy and intuition—still strike some feminists as sensible, if not prescient in some respects. After all, many feminists since Stern's day have stressed the intensely (and intrinsically) relational and embodied character of "women's ways of knowing" (e.g., Gilligan, 1993; Belenky, Clinchy, Goldberger, & Tarule, 1997). But in the age of queer theory, Stern's firm belief in innate gender differences dooms him from the start for the vast majority of academic readers.

Nevertheless, and despite these impediments, the time has come for a searching and sympathetic appraisal of Stern's contributions to psychiatry and psychoanalysis. In the following chapter, I will attempt a preliminary assessment of his main contributions and legacy to the mental health professions today. With that task behind us, we can finally turn our attention to the more delicate and potentially controversial issues surrounding Stern's conversion and his efforts to combat anti-Semitism in the Church.

CHAPTER SEVEN

Freud, faith, and phenomenology

Freud's revenge and Stern's challenge

The relationship between psychoanalysis and Christianity is a complex and contentious one. After all, though born Jewish, Freud was a materialist and an atheist, so when Stern published *The Third Revolution* in 1954, most Catholics regarded Freud as a menace. Even among the Catholic intelligentsia, resistance to psychoanalysis was strong, and with good reason. In his last book, *Moses and Monotheism* (1939a), Freud contended that it was not Jesus, but Paul (Saul) of Tarsus who founded the Christian religion, and invented the concept of Original Sin (Freud, 1938). In so doing, said Freud, St. Paul and his followers borrowed extensively from the mystery cults of pagan antiquity, eventually substituting a mother-and-son oriented religion for the older, father-centered religion of the Jews, thus putting a new and decidedly Oedipal twist on the older, Jewish faith. While more inclusive and congenial to non-Jews, said Freud, Christianity marked a decisive shift *away from* Judaism, which had placed a complete ban on magic and superstition. Freud's contention that Catholicism represents a concession to paganism prompted him to conclude that Christian anti-Semitism arose from lingering pagan sympathies and inclinations, and an unconscious hostility towards the Jews for inventing monotheism in the first place (Burston, 2014b). Freud was hardly alone in this. In *The Pillar of Fire*, Stern recalled a conversation with a biochemist that worked at the German Institute for Psychiatric Research around 1933. This young man was a neo-pagan, but unlike most of his Nazi colleagues, had no reservations about dining with Stern on occasion. Since seating in the cafeteria was segregated along racial lines, Stern was quite curious about this fellow, who told him:

> I used to be terribly anti-Semitic, you know, until I began to study the writings of Dr. Hauer. Then I found out that what we hate in Jews is not the Jews. It is Christ and the Christian religion. This religion is something so utterly alien to the very spirit of the European peoples that they revolt with their entire being against it. But although they feel revulsion they are not aware of its true origin. Hence that irrational hatred of Jews, because people vaguely feel that it is actually a Jewish way of feeling, thinking, acting, a Jewish norm of living that has been stuffed down their throats for the past two thousand years. Once you have found out that it is actually Christianity that is the painful foreign body in your flesh, something curious happens. You stop hating Jews. You regard them with the same kind of sympathy or antipathy that you might regard any other foreign nation. (Stern, 1951, p. 133)

Stern then wondered what features of the Judaeo-Christian tradition were contrary to the European spirit. Echoing Nietzsche, his Aryan colleague replied that it imbued people with an unbearable sense of guilt. Then citing Tacitus' book *Germania*, he argued that Indo-Germanic people had a much higher idea of "the destiny of man," and even faulted Hitler for deflecting constructive anti-Christian sentiments into vulgar Jew baiting.

Of course, the striking similarity between Freud's theory of anti-Semitism and the beliefs of Stern's biochemist do not alter the fact that Freud saw neo-paganism as a regressive cultural force, and not as a (highly desirable) return to some authentically Aryan form of spirituality (Burston, 2014b). But more importantly, for our purposes, the fact that Freud explained the triumph of Christianity as a partial *regression* to paganism illustrated his belief in the superiority of the Jewish faith. So though it attempted to deprive Jews of their greatest prophet,

Moses—treating Moses as an Egyptian, after all—*Moses and Monotheism* (1939a) was also rejoinder to the demeaning anti-Semitic stereotypes that were prevalent at the turn of century, and which had tormented Freud since early childhood.

Though obviously open to dispute, the claim that Judaism is a more rational religion than Christianity was widely shared by Jews of that era; especially those who, like Freud, had been influenced by the Enlightenment (Gilman, 1992; Elon, 2002). But the immediate and inescapable upshot to this line of thinking is that conversion from Judaism to Christianity *must* be a regressive step, a move backwards (or "downwards") towards mother-worship, Oedipal entanglements and magical thinking. No surprise then that Freud and his followers regarded Jews who converted to Christianity as deeply neurotic, and that many still do.

So, Stern faced an uphill battle in attempting to "baptize" Freud. And he knew it, too. In an introduction to a book by another Catholic psychoanalyst, Stern noted that:

> A man like Dr. Gorres […] is in danger of finding himself in a no man's land between hostile camps; to psychoanalysts he may be suspect as a Catholic, and to Catholics he may become suspect as a psychoanalyst […]. [Yet] at no time since the 13th century has there been a greater need to integrate to assimilate the seemingly alien into the corpus of Christian philosophy […]. The present book, like any other attempt at synthesis, is a product of necessity, and at the same time, a manifestation of moral courage. (Stern, 1975, pp. 262–263)

Stern's appraisal of Gorres' work—a product of necessity, and an act of courage—could be applied with equal justice to Stern's own publications. Stern knew that his conversion to Catholicism would discredit him in the eyes of many psychoanalysts, and that most Catholics feared he was siding with the enemy. Nevertheless, a strong sense of mission compelled him to bring Freud to Catholic audiences. And while dismissing Freud's theory about the origins of Christianity, Stern acknowledged that Freud's description of organized religion as a "collective obsessional neurosis" was a very astute description of the distortions that Christianity underwent over the centuries. As to Freud's contention—in *The Future of An Illusion* (1927c)—that science and religion are adversaries, and that science is destined to prevail in the fullness of time, Stern dismissed that idea as a legacy of Freud's Enlightenment positivism, arguing that faith and reason are ultimately compatible. To make this point clearer, he compared new scientific discoveries to pieces of a puzzle that somehow fit into a bigger picture. In his own words

> No fragments of a jig-saw puzzle mean anything unless you are convinced that they are a part of a whole which will finally turn out to be a picture. Every good scientist has a cosmology. He may be dimly aware of it and carry it with him as an ill defined shadowy image, or it may be elaborate like that of the great Christian thinkers of the middle ages, or that of the evolutionists of the nineteenth century. There is no scientist who does not try to fit his findings, which are by their very nature fragmentary, into the jigsaw puzzle of some universal idea. (Stern, 1951, pp. 250–251)

So, by Stern's account, "Every good scientist has a cosmology" and tries to fit their findings "into the jigsaw puzzle of some universal idea." The tacit implication of this remark is that much scientific research is motivated by a search for cosmological coherence—the hope or belief that the universe comprises an integrated and intelligible totality or system. Is this actually the case? Yes and no. On the face of it, the claim that *every* scientist tries to fit his (or her) findings into a broader cosmological framework is simply untrue, and there is no shortage of counterexamples one could furnish along these lines. But then as Thomas Kuhn observed, all scientific findings (including many born of serendipity) are integrated (at one point or another) into a more comprehensive *paradigm* that is shared by other practitioners of the same discipline. And it is also the case that many *great* scientists really do search for cosmological coherence. Thus, for example, Albert Einstein once remarked to Niels Bohr that "God does not play dice with the universe." And on another occasion, he was moved to say that "Science without religion is lame; religion without science is blind."

Furthermore, as Freud's friend Oscar Pfister observed, religion and science are both animated by the conviction that "the Truth shall make you free" (Pfister, 1928). The problem is that while science and religion converge impressively on this point, they diverge sharply on what constitutes "the truth," and on the most appropriate criteria and methods for obtaining it. As a result, the fact that Stern received an archbishop's imprimatur for *The Third Revolution* must have seemed like an archaic gesture to the majority of his peers in psychiatry, if not an attempt to revive the dubious practice of submitting scientific books to religious authorities for approval.

In fairness to Stern, there was something slyly contrarian about his simultaneous efforts to make Freud kosher for Catholics, and to disconcert his psychoanalytic readers with his frank religiosity. In this roundabout way, Stern was attempting to move *both* sides to reconsider their rigid, rejectionist stances and find a reasonable middle ground. But one doesn't have to be a scientist to discern that the existence of a list of "approved" books implies the existence of another list of books that are banned, and therefore, of a censorship that is inimical to the process of free inquiry and discussion. Why would any scientist even want to ingratiate himself to religious authority like that?

Psychoanalysis and existential-phenomenology

Another reason Stern faced an uphill battle was that leading representatives of existentialism and phenomenology, intellectual movements which were more acceptable to Christian audiences, also regarded Freud quite warily. Consider the appendix VIII of Husserl's *The Crisis of the European Sciences and Transcendental Phenomenology* (Husserl, 1970). It is called "On the problem of the unconscious." This lengthy fragment fairly bristles with reproaches towards the new "depth psychology." Husserl's appraisal of Freud was shared by Karl Jaspers, who dismissed *Moses and Monotheism* (1939a) as being "clueless and impudent" (Jaspers, 1952).

Not all phenomenological thinkers were as dismissive as Husserl and Jaspers, however. The philosopher Max Scheler—a pupil of Husserl's and a friend of Jaspers'—was the first phenomenologist to engage Freud's theory of repression sympathetically in "The idols of self knowledge" a paper that first appeared in 1913, the same year as Jaspers' *General Psychopathology* (see Scheler, 1973). Another book of Scheler's, called *Ressentiment*—which Stern valued highly—appeared two years later, in 1915, and sought to integrate some Freudian theses into an explicitly Catholic frame of reference (Scheler, 2000; Burston, 2009b). Now, a century after Scheler, the literature on the psychoanalysis and phenomenology has become quite substantial. But oddly enough, this literature contains no sustained commentary or reflection on Karl Stern's contribution. Nevertheless, the fact remains that Stern's evolving dialogue with Freud was interwoven with illuminating discussions of Husserl, Scheler, Jaspers, Buber, Marcel, and Maurice Merleau-Ponty, among others. How did Stern bridge the gap between their respective contributions and Freud's theories of mind? In his introduction to Gorres' book, Stern noted that:

> Psychoanalysis has had a strange evolution. There is a line leading directly from Goethe's philosophy of nature, a romantic philosophy of nature, through Carus, Schopenhauer, Nietzsche and the great Russian novelists—to Freud. No matter how divergent those contributory streams may have been they have one thing in common—the fact that they go against the current of nineteenth century materialism and positivism. They represent the "other" nineteenth century [...]. (Stern, 1975, p. 262)
>
> Freud himself was not consciously aware of any of this. A typical child of the nineteenth century, trained in the laboratories of Vienna and the neurological wards of Paris, he professed the current scientific positivism of his time, a philosophy that is quite heterogeneous to the true meaning of his own genius. It is for all these reasons that we now have the duty to place Freudian findings (not Freud's philosophy) where they belong, namely, in a Christian anthropology—to "baptize" psychoanalysis. (Stern, 1975, p. 263)

So, what is "the true meaning of Freud's genius?" Stern claimed that Freudian thought represents a fusion of two distinct—and antagonistic—currents of European thought; the Cartesian, reductionistic mindset of the natural and experimental sciences, and a romantic, Goethean philosophy of nature, whose belated representatives presumably included Carus, Schopenhauer, Nietzsche, and Bergson. It is the latter, not the former source of Freud's ideas that evinces a close kinship with existential-phenomenology, and accounts for Freud's deepest insights, said Stern. Moreover:

> No matter what Freud writes about, be it anxiety or hostility, paranoia or mourning—the primary tool of insight is *knowledge by connaturality*. The fact that these observations are then expressed as "mechanisms" and presented *more geomtrico*, as it were, is due to the need for clinical shorthand and to the need to establish "laws," i.e. to establish a predictability, as in the natural sciences,

of certain pathological phenomena as regular outcomes of certain inner constellations. It is, however, interesting that Freud adduces, to confirm his theories, the works of Shakespeare and Sophocles, Goethe and Dostoyevsky—much more frequently than the academic psychology of his time. (Stern, 1975, p. 31)

The concept of "knowledge by connaturality" dates back to St. Thomas Aquinas and before that, said Stern, to Dionysus the Aeriopagite. But to make this argument more intelligible to contemporary audiences, Stern invoked Karl Jaspers' distinction between a *verstenhende* psychology, which seeks to *understand* human experience and behavior empathically, in human terms, and a psychology based on *erklaren* or explanation, which seeks to *explain* experience and behavior in causal, naturalistic or reductionistic terms. The former is based on empathy, and yields an immediate, intuitive understanding of another's person's state of mind. The latter, which Stern called "knowledge by disassembly," is based on the exact or experimental sciences, and yields theories and empirical generalizations that help us to predict and control behavior, whether we understand it humanly or not (Jaspers, 1913).

To illustrate the difference between causal explanation and comprehension, Stern asked us to imagine a psychiatric institution where two researchers are studying the incidence of psychoses following childbirth—a fairly common psychiatric syndrome associated with post-partum depression. One investigator is a psychoanalyst, the other, an endocrinologist. Each investigator wants to know *why* some mothers become psychotic, but bases their research on fundamentally different premises. Thus, for example:

> When the psychoanalytical observer finds that the patient suffers from a psychosis following childbirth because she herself had not been wanted by her mother, he *comprehends* ("takes into") in the sense of having intellectual sympathy (feel with). In finding that the patient was deficient in a certain ion in the blood, the other observer *explains* ("lays outside," the movement opposite to comprehending), and no act of intellectual sympathy is involved. (Stern, 1965a, p. 46)

Stern was relying on etymology to make his point, but it is a valid one. Both in English and in German, the phrase "to comprehend" implies an act of (mentally) enclosing, enfolding, encompassing or internalizing an external object or entity. And "to explain," by contrast, implies a movement to externalize, to expel. Put differently, if we comprehend a depressed mother's rejection of her infant as the result of her being rejected by her own mother many years previously, we understand her behavior *humanly*, and not as an anomaly or chemical imbalance that is presumably taking place in her blood or brain. In fact, in many cases, we only search for chemical imbalances in cases like these *because* we are ignorant of her developmental history, and therefore *fail* to comprehend her humanly. As a result, her behavior strikes us as profoundly mysterious, if not meaningless, in the circumstances.

Unfortunately, said Stern, Freud's need to cloak his intuitive-empathic insights in the language of the natural sciences abetted a tendency to self-deception among the Freudian faithful. In *The Third Revolution*, he wrote:

> The fact that psychoanalytic insight is primarily empathic insight, as contrasted with scientific knowledge, is concealed and complicated by several features, particularly by the fact that Freud himself from the beginning presented his discoveries within a framework of terms which were borrowed from the natural sciences. There are several reasons for this. The originator of psychoanalysis was a child of the nineteenth century. He had been educated in the laboratory and the neurological ward [...]. Therefore it was most logical for him and his early followers to use the language of the natural sciences. As we have seen, there are certain aspects of physics (particularly thermodynamics) and biology (particularly ontogenesis) which lend themselves splendidly to conveying basic psychoanalytic concepts by way of approximate analogy. When we speak of an "amount of libidinal energy" which is "split off" or "channeled into" something or "sublimated" or "displaced," we use the language of physicists of chemists to make concepts out of something essentially preconceptual. The preconceptual, archaic world of imagery, which forms the key to the world of neurosis, reminds us of Edgar Allan Poe's "unthought-like thoughts that are the thoughts of thought." Technical terminology for such things at best partakes of the nature of a parable. As Karl Jaspers has pointed out, we fool ourselves if we think that the terminology of psychoanalysis really proves that it is something of the same order as physics or chemistry. Actually, there is no such thing as

an "amount of libidinal energy" which would fit into a system of references comparable to that of the sciences. Love and hate, joy and mourning cannot be quantified. (Stern, 1954, pp. 154–155)

It is hard to overstate the importance of this passage. Unlike dogmatic Freudians of that era, Stern clearly understood that the topographical, hydraulic, energetic and embryological metaphors that suffuse Freud's metapsychology were useful heuristic schemata, but nothing more. Thus, in the clinical setting, or in case formulation, it is quite legitimate to speak of a libidinal "cathexis," or "counter-cathexis," or about sublimating sexual energy into non-sexual interests or activities, and so on. But at the end of the day, all such talk is simply conjuring with unknown quantities of a purely hypothetical energy. The same holds true of the id, ego, and superego. These theoretical constructs enable us to describe how we deceive ourselves about our own experience and intentions, or how we harness or deflect our fears and desires in the process of adaptation to reality. But we're deluding ourselves if we think that they actually exist in the same fashion as atoms, molecules, magnetism, electricity, and so on.

So in effect, if not so many words, Stern was warning psychoanalysts not to reify their heuristic schemata. But while Stern's clarity on this score was commendable, he sometimes conveyed the misleading impression that Freud *himself* invited or expected that his readers to read him in this non-dogmatic, if not metaphorical fashion. Whether Stern gave this impression to readers intentionally or unintentionally is not clear. But either way, this was simply not the case. And even if it were, many of Freud's followers were determined to turn his sophisticated heuristics into articles of faith for a new secular religion—which is why Jaspers looked down on them (Jaspers, 1952). Clearly, Stern was immune to that sort of thing. Indeed, he lamented the widespread transformation of psychoanalytic *method*, which is appropriate and illuminating in the clinical setting, into an all-encompassing *mentality* that colonizes domains of human experience and endeavor where the psychoanalytic method is inappropriate or misplaced. Once it strays beyond or outside its domain of competence, the many metaphors that inform psychoanalytic discourse can do considerable mischief. Stern gives two examples. He says:

> If I go to a symphony concert, the fact that the composer's creative impulse may have been fueled by a period of sexual frustration

> adds nothing to my understanding of the music. It is possible that a great teacher of youth is a man who in this way sublimates his latent homosexuality. To confirm or disprove this interpretation is a scientific problem. I may find this piece of information useful when the teacher comes to consult me for some problem for which he needs psychiatric help. But we all know that the phenomenon of a "great teacher" or "leader of youth" possesses an autonomous facticity that has nothing to do with psychological genetics—as little as the fact that the professor needs a certain amount of calories to be able to teach. And yet almost all psychoanalytic writings on philosophy and theology, and particularly those by Freud himself—which had such an impact on the popular imagination and on the nihilistic climate of our time—succumb to the fallacy of such psychologism. (Stern, 1975, p. 32)

So, according to Stern music and teaching are two domains that possess an "autonomous facticity." Flat-footed or heavy-handed psychoanalytic interpretations tend to conceal more than they reveal in these areas, giving *the illusion of insight*, rather than the real thing. Another domain of human experience that possesses an autonomous facticity, said Stern, is ethics. Though he deemed Freud's theory of the id, ego, and superego to be indispensable for clinical work, Stern freely acknowledged that the misuse of Freudian theory contributes to ethical relativism. But Stern was somewhat equivocal on this score, too. On some occasions, he flatly reproached Freud for promoting scientism or psychologism, as he did in the preceding quote. On others, he appeared to absolve Freud from any responsibility for this sorry state of affairs. For example, he writes:

> Life in Europe in the nineteenth century had many aspects of complacency and hypocrisy. And those who looked into the motives "behind" faiths and philosophies were often moved by a need for purity and truthfulness. They were the great purgers, and their ruthlessness was the ruthlessness of the prophets. They shook us up, and due to them, self-deception has become much more difficult than before. Nietzsche was right: one must not exploit one's suffering to exert power over others. Marx was right: woe unto those who use religion as opium for the people. Freud was right: faith devoid of the primacy of love is a compulsive-obsessive neurosis. In other

words: Nietzsche or Marx or Freud were heirs of an aristocratic humanism to whom the reductive method was a means of exhortation and an expression of ascetic courage [...] Whereas thinkers like Nietzsche and Marx and Freud were still working in the tradition of [...] aristocratic humanism, the procedure has in our time become incredibly vulgarized. (Stern, 1965a, pp. 65–66)

In short, in his more charitable moods, Stern obviously wished to group Freud with the other "masters of suspicion," as Paul Ricoeur called them, and to blame the corrosive impact of scientism on Freud's followers, or on post-Freudian positivists whose pursuit of methodological purity prompted them to reject psychoanalysis completely. But while it is wrong to tax Freud (or any other thinker) with all the crude distortions and oversimplifications that his apologists and interpreters engage in subsequently, one can also err in the opposite direction, and exonerate a misunderstood thinker completely out of a misplaced sense of loyalty. This was probably the case with Stern, who should have let Freud shoulder more of the blame for the widespread tendency to "colonize" the ethical sphere with reductive explanations. Remember, in *Group Psychology and the Analysis of the Ego* (Freud, 1921c), Freud claimed said that political demands for equality are nothing more than unconscious derivatives of sibling rivalry, based on collective envy. Freud's disparaging gloss on modern social movements probably owes much to Nietzsche, and is obviously in keeping with what Stern calls their "aristocratic humanism" (Burston, 2009b). But there was nothing particularly prophetic about it. If anything, this was a smug, condescending dismissal of people who cherish or champion democratic values—one calculated to diminish their credibility, and put their moral courage into question.

Two ways of knowing

But while Stern skirted these issues, intentionally or not, he did address the apparent incompatibilities between the scientific and religious modes of apprehending the truth. In *The Flight From Woman*, Stern took a cue from Henri Bergson, and argued that there two fundamental ways of grasping reality—the poetic mode of knowledge, and the scientific one. While quite different, Stern insisted, they are both necessary and integral to the full and harmonious development of the human person. Citing Jean Piaget, Stern noted that children are not capable of fully rational abstract thought (formal operations) till the age of twelve or later, as a rule. Meanwhile, there are other modes of knowing and engaging the world that precede discursive rationality. Piaget argued for three stages in the development of human intelligence—the sensori-motor stage, concrete operations, and formal operations, or reason proper. According to Piaget, before formal operations commence, human beings are not fully rational, but are proto-rational, and Stern insisted that before the emergence of formal operations—or the capacity to reason abstractly, like an adult—the child knows the world in other, more concrete and immediate ways.

If Stern is right, children inhabit a different experiential universe than adults, and engage the world in a more immediate, participatory way, through what the anthropologist Lévy-Bruhl called "participation mystique," Stern argued that this primordial way of engaging the world is never superseded or vanquished by abstract thought completely. On the contrary, Stern insists that this way of knowing and relating to the world (through what Maurice Merleau-Ponty called "the flesh" (1964)) persists all through the human life cycle, even when it recedes to the background of consciousness. Even when that happens, says Stern, it is not a question of one way of knowing *replacing* another, as Freud or Piaget imagined. It is a question of maintaining a harmonious balance between them.

This early, non-discursive, participatory way of engaging the external world, said Stern, is intimately tied up with the infant's relationship to its mother. In his own words:

> The function of the mother is not exhausted with sheltering, protection and dependence. By the very act of birth she puts us into the world; you might almost say that the first encounter with her involves being pushed away by her. At birth the umbilical cord is severed, and if the mother's love for the child is healthy, a gentle process of severing continues, not only physically but mentally [...].
>
> Today we know that this early drama, more than anything else, is decisive for the formation of character. [...] Man's earliest love story takes place before the advent of reason; yet it is more profoundly experienced than anything he experiences later [...]. Our experiences with father and with siblings enter into that

pattern, of course, but the drama of "mother–child" leaves traces at the rock-bottom of the human condition. (Stern, 1965a, p. 19)

Following on the observations of the anatomist Portmann and psychiatrist John Bowlby, Stern pointed out that at the moment of birth, the human infant is more helpless and dependent on its mother's care than the newborns of any other species on the planet. And this of course is not controversial. Somewhat more controversial, perhaps, are the inferences Stern draws from this about the psychology of the newborn. According to Stern, the act of severing the umbilical cord—the physical connection between mother and child—does not sever the *psychic connection* between mother and child, which remains strong throughout infancy. Indeed, in optimal circumstances:

> There exists a deeply knowing relationship between the child and the mother—a mode of knowledge much stronger than the tie to the father, which only arises somewhat later. (Stern, 1965a, p. 32)

According to Stern, in optimal circumstances, the relationship between mother and child remains so close that the boundaries between them are actually quite diffuse. They form a somewhat undifferentiated mother–infant matrix, from which the child only extricates itself slowly. While this long process of individuation takes place, there exists "a psychic flow between mother and child" that gives them an immediate and intuitive knowledge of one another.

Now the question is, how well does Stern's stance square with contemporary research on infancy and brain development? Despite the somewhat archaic language Stern employed, it actually anticipates many recent research findings, albeit without addressing the role of hemispheric dominance in these processes of unconscious and nonverbal communication. For example, in Chapter Twelve of *Affect Regulation and the Repair of the Self*, psychiatrist Allan Schore noted that:

> [...] the mother of the securely attached infant psychobiologically attunes her right hemisphere to the output of the infant's right hemisphere in order to receive and resonate with fluctuations in her child's internal state. This bond of unconscious emotional communication [...] facilitates the experience-dependent

maturation of the infant's right brain. Neuroscientists are now writing that:

"Spontaneous communication employs species-specific expressive displays in the sender that, given attention, activate emotional pre-attunements and are directly perceived by the receiver [...]. The 'meaning' of the display is known directly by the receiver [...]. This spontaneous emotional communication constitutes a *conversation between limbic systems* [...]. It is a biologically-based communication system that involves individual organisms *directly* with one another: the individuals in spontaneous communication constitute literally a biological unit (Buck, 1994, p. 266, my italics)." (Schore, 2003, p. 70)

After surveying the growing literature on infancy and right hemispheric functions, Schore concludes that:

Most neuropsychological studies of "the minor hemisphere" have focused solely on motor behaviors, visuospatial functions, and cognition, but only recently have neuroscientists delved into the fundamental activity of the right brain in the recognition of facially-expressed nonverbal affective expressions (Kim et al., 1999; Muller et al., 1999; Nakamura et al., 2000; Narumoto et al., 2000). This research demonstrates that the right hemisphere is specialized for both the receptive processing (Blair et al., 1999) and expressive communication (Borod, Haywood, & Koff, 1997) of facial information during spontaneous social interactions, such as in "natural conversation" or within "interpersonal family communication" (Blonder et al., 1993). This hemisphere is also dominant for evaluating the trustworthiness of faces (Winston et al., 2002). (Schore, 2003, p. 71)

So, where does this leave Stern? If the research of Schore et al., is any indication, Stern was obviously on to something pivotal. The fact that this intuitive, unconscious and preverbal way of knowing and engaging the world develops in earliest infancy and persists into adulthood may also explain why he called this knowledge through union or communion with others, and why so many of the metaphors he used to describe it involve oral metaphors of swallowing or being swallowed, incorporating or being incorporated. For example, he wrote:

> All knowledge by *union*; all knowledge by incorporation (incorporating or being incorporated); and all knowledge through love has its natural fundament in our primary bond with the mother. The skeptic warns the believer not to "swallow" things, not to be "taken in." And from his point of view he is right. Faith, the most sublime form of non-scientific knowledge, is (if we consider its natural history, independent of all questions of grace) a form of swallowing or being taken in. This is also true about Wisdom. *Sapientia* is derived from *sapere*, to taste, and *Sophia* is the She-soul of Eastern Christendom. (Stern, 1965a, p. 54)

Leaning on Merleau-Ponty again, Stern then argued that faith is based in a non-discursive way of knowing the world that has its own logic, its own validity, even if positivism and rationalism are hostile to it. In fact, in Stern's opinion, faith is the most *mature* form that this intuitive or poetic form of knowledge can take.

But Schore's research, which vindicates Stern on many levels, also provides a potent corrective on one important issue. Stern was inclined to equate the poetic and scientific modes of knowing the world with feminine and masculine, respectively. This essentialist perspective prompted Stern to conclude that the ascendancy of rationalism and positivism and the concurrent decline of "womanly values"—i.e., receptivity, empathy, and intuition—in the population at large are the result of the hyper-masculinization of modern society; a trend that, in his estimation, poses a serious threat to our collective mental health. While feminist theory supports Stern's contention that Cartesian rationalism was grounded in severe "gynophobia" (Bordo, 1986), and that modern society is becoming "hyper-masculine" (Burstyn, 1999), recent research on hemispheric dominance simply does not support Stern's contention that the poetic and scientific modes of knowledge are gendered in the ways that Stern imagined (McGilchrist, 2009). Even though there *are* measurable differences between the brains of men and women (Miller & Halpern, 2013), very few neuroscientists nowadays imagine that they are of sufficient magnitude to warrant such broad generalizations. According to psychiatrists Allan Schore and Iain McGilchrist, the (supposedly feminine) traits of empathy, altruism, and intuitive, holistic (though mostly unconscious) processing of social and emotional cues occurs chiefly in the right hemisphere, while the abstract, analytical, and discursive intellect develops and "resides" (for the most part) in the brain's left hemisphere (Schore, 2003; McGilchrist, 2009). This means, in effect, that the fundamental duality of human existence need not be addressed through what Stern called "the metaphysics of the sexes"—that the poetic and scientific modes of knowledge are simply generic human attributes, rather than intrinsically gendered epistemologies.

Nevertheless, if we reject Stern's gender essentialism, and situate his poetic mode of knowledge in the right hemisphere and the scientific mode of knowledge in the left hemisphere, then *The Flight From Woman* foreshadows many of Iain McGilchrist's central theses in his monumental book, *The Master and His Emissary*. Indeed, the convergences between these thinkers are so deep and extensive, it is a wonder no one has pointed them out before.

Like Stern, Iain McGilchrist is profoundly influenced by existential phenomenology, and above all, by Max Scheler and Maurice Merleau-Ponty. And it is in light of these shared philosophical commitments that both men construed Descartes' philosophy as the embodiment of a new brand of rationalism that, on close inspection, is actually extremely *irrational*. Moreover, both Stern and McGilchrist see Cartesianism as a reductive, mechanistic mentality which favors abstract thought over embodied experience, leading to a dramatic decline in what some elderly feminists still refer to as "women's ways of knowing," namely empathy and intuition (Serlin & Criswell, 2000).

Again, like Stern and Scheler, McGilchrist insists that ethical values possess an "autonomous facticity," and are not merely the result of cultural conventions. Moreover, both see the societal process they describe taking place in the last 500 years or so as leading to a dramatic increase in knowledge, and a corresponding decline in wisdom. And both hope somehow to halt, reverse or at least slow down the seemingly inexorable march of this historical trend that has hijacked and diminished our humanity.

Moreover, there are striking parallels in the way Stern and McGilchrist take up Freud. Both men categorically reject Freud's attempt to reduce religious faith to the level of a symptom, and yet both attempt to derive the constitutive dualism that they believe underlies human existence from their readings of Freud. For example, McGilchrist writes that the unconscious, while not identical with, is more strongly associated with the right hemisphere. Conversely, says McGilchrist:

> [...] conscious processing tends to go on in the left hemisphere. This dichotomy can be seen at play even in the realm, such as

> emotion, with an admittedly strong right-hemispheric bias; the right hemisphere processes unconscious emotional material, whereas the left hemisphere is involved in the conscious processing of emotional stimuli. Certainly the right hemisphere experiences material that the left-hemisphere cannot be aware of; and according to Allan Schore, Freud's preconscious lies in the right orbitofrontal cortex. Freud wrote of non-verbal, imagistic thinking that it 'is therefore, only a very incomplete form of becoming conscious. In some way, too, it stands nearer to unconscious processes than it does to thinking in words, and it is unquestionably older than the latter both ontogenetically and phylogenetically [...]. (McGilchrist, 2009, p. 188)

Describing the pre-conscious as a form of "non-verbal, imagistic thinking" that is older than the discursive intellect puts one in mind of "Edgar Allan Poe's 'unthought-like thoughts that are the thoughts of thought'" (Stern, 1954, p. 155). The crucial difference between Freud on the one hand, and Stern and McGilchrist, on the other, is that in Freud's estimation, primary process thought is invariably an obstacle or impediment to reason, because it steadfastly resists adaptation to reality (Freud, 1923b). So, for example, when Freud wrote "Where the id is, there shall ego be" in *Civilization and Its Discontents* (1930a), he was siding with the materialist and rationalist mentality that seeks to *replace* one way of knowing (or being) with another (as much as possible), and which therefor belittles faith, treating religion and reason as adversaries. According to Stern and McGilchrist, by contrast, the poetic mode of knowledge precedes the abstract, discursive intellect (both ontogenetically and phylogenetically), but also *exceeds* it in depth and acuity, at least in most domains of human experience. Therefore, the goal of human development lies in a harmonious balance between these two disparate ways of knowing or "being in the world," not in the hegemony of reason. The "poetic mode of knowledge" is also the source of what Stern refers to repeatedly as "the metaphysical sense," the loss or attenuation of which reflects the malaise of modernity. In a similar vein, McGilchrist traces the roots of religious convictions to right-hemispheric attitudes, as follows:

> Believing is not to be reduced to thinking that such and such is the case. It is not a weaker form of thinking laced with doubt. Sometimes we speak like this: "I believe the train leaves at 6:13"

where "I believe" means simply that I think (but am not certain) that.' Since the left hemisphere is concerned with what is certain, with the knowledge of facts, its version of belief is that it is just the absence of certainty [...].

But belief in terms of the right-hemisphere is different [...]. For it, belief is a matter of care [...]. Thus, if I say that "I believe in you", it does not mean that I think such and such is the case. It means that I stand in a certain sort of relation [...] towards you, one that entails me in certain ways of behaving [...] toward you, and entails on you the responsibility of acting and being in certain ways as well. It is an acting *as if* certain things were true [...] that in the nature of things cannot be certain [...].

This helps illuminate belief in God. This is not reducible to a question of a factual answer to the question "Does God exist?" [...] It is having an attitude, holding a disposition toward the world, whereby that world, as it comes into being for me is one in which God belongs [...]. An answer to the question whether God exists could only come from my acting as if God is, and in this way being true to God, and experiencing God (or not, as the case may be) as true to me [...]. This [...] is not a [...] "cop out", an admission that really one does not believe what one pretends to believe. Quite the opposite; as Hans Vaihinger understood, all knowledge, particularly scientific knowledge, is no more than acting *as if* certain models were, for the time being, true. (McGilchrist, 2009, pp. 170–171)

Like McGilchrist, Stern was apt to link faith in God and "the metaphysical sense" with a caring disposition. Referencing Freud's theory of human development, Stern observed that:

Libido has the dual meaning of desire and the fulfillment of desire. It is a global term for all forms of human loving. However, the transformations of love are expressed no longer in the semantics of quantifiable energy but in those of stages of growth. The libido of the newborn infant can be seen as a kind of gastrula, undifferentiated but with a high capacity to receive. It is a capacity to be loved rather than to love which, however, contains potentialities of active, outgoing, giving love and the capacity to endure frustrations. The decisive point about all this is the fact that the dim world of the undifferentiated polymorph instinctual drives and the most mature forms of human love are unified by a mysterious bond of *becoming*. I say "mysterious" because neither the semantics of quantifiable energy nor the semantics of embryology are sufficient to "explain" the adult personality [...].

That is why all metaphysical questions, when treated with purely psychological tools, fill us with such as sense of embarrassment. It is as though somebody were to take a portrait by Rembrandt or Leonardo, with its areas of light and darkness, and replace it with an anatomical chart, because the latter is so much clearer and leaves nothing unrevealed. In other words, the philosophical idea of man—which is not a matter of technical knowledge—implies a *chiaroscuro*, an irreducible sense of the unrevealable that heightens the sense of truth. This is the reason why on the transcendental plane all psychological exploration appears so strangely flat and pedestrian. (Stern, 1975, p. 33)

Stern's contrast between a Rembrandt or Leonardo and an anatomical chart converges powerfully with McGilchrist's description of the differences between two ways of apprehending human reality beautifully. One is true to experience, mindful of the implicit and unknown, and attentive to the subtleties and nuances of the person-in-context; the other is somehow *about* the body and yet utterly disembodied, a product of monumental abstraction, referring to everyone and to no one all at once. Does the latter necessarily invalidate or supersede the former? Can these two ways of grasping human reality co-exist in a kind of fruitful tension, or is the increasing dominance of left-hemispheric values, attitudes and ways of grasping reality inevitable? That is the question that both Stern and McGilchrist pose in their critiques of the modern (and postmodern) world. The answer, of course, remains to be seen.

CHAPTER EIGHT

A Hebrew Catholic

What is conversion?

The literature on religious conversion is vast, affording a multitude of perspectives from which to view Stern's transformation from a Jew wavering on margins of orthodoxy, Zionism and Marxism into a committed "Hebrew Catholic." In the following chapter, we explore several ways in which this lengthy, awkward and often tormenting process shaped Stern's sense of personal identity, and his attitudes towards Judaism, anti-Semitism, Zionism, and the Catholic Church.

However, before doing so, we need to be clear what we actually mean by the term "conversion." After all, most authors argue that the term conversion encompasses both the "inner" (or spiritual) and "outer" (or public) dimensions of religious identity formation (e.g., Neuhaus, 1988). But Jewish history demonstrates that, in many instances, the word "conversion" merely refers to the *public* embrace or avowal of a new religious identity, and does not address the *inner* experience or motives that may propel someone to embrace a new faith. After all, at the end of the day, a public gesture of this kind may not be backed up by deep conviction, especially when it is motivated by fear, a desire for acceptance, or a longing for upward social mobility.

Historically speaking, Jewish conversions in response to threats of death or exile were commonplace in Germany, Spain, Portugal, North Africa, Eastern Europe, and elsewhere. Conversions like these often resulted in a (highly conflicted) form of dual religious identity, in which the believer's public and private "selves" were at variance with one another. A dual identity of this kind often entailed an elaborate pretense, a performance sustained for the sake of survival. Conversions like these were commonplace in pre-modern times, but not in Stern's own milieu. Indeed, he scarcely mentions them—a significant omission, from the Jewish perspective.

After the Enlightenment, another pattern of conversion among Jews emerged, in which converts were given positive incentives to assimilate and perhaps thrive in an environment that was still actively hostile to Judaism—a decision made easier if the convert lacked religious convictions to begin with. One of Freud's favorite satirists, Heinrich Heine, furnishes a splendid example of conversions like these, which were commonplace in Europe in the nineteenth and early twentieth century. But the relevance to Stern's case is only indirect, because unlike Heine, Stern possessed of what one critic aptly termed "a raging hunger to believe." Nevertheless, the collective sense of disappointment and betrayal that greeted such expedient identity shifts do help explain the response Stern received from the Jewish community over his decision to convert.

Since the word "conversion" is ambiguous and open-ended with respect to questions of motive and belief, *especially* where Jews are concerned, let us consider the word *epiphany* as a way to describe the "inner" dimensions of Stern's experience. According to the Oxford Etymological Dictionary, the word *epiphany* originally referred to the appearance of a divinity, or a manifestation of a supernatural being. In other words, it denotes a rare, involuntary experience, involving feelings of reverence, awe or the uncanny; a transformed state of consciousness, rather than a public ritual solemnizing a new social role or affiliation. Stern describes at least three experiences of that sort: once, while listening to Cardinal Faulhaber's Advent sermon of 1933, another while living in the Silk family's boarding house in Oppidans Road in 1937, and again, in 1941, in conversation with Maritain about his lingering misgivings about becoming Catholic and his longing to experience the Shekinah—the Hebrew term for the Divine Presence. Experiences of this kind are transformative, but also rare and brief. Besides, the word *epiphany* is now used to denote almost any sudden and singular experience of insight—Arthur Koestler's "Aha!" experience—regardless of whether it encompasses or even touches on the sacred or not.

Another term sometimes applied to people like Stern is "religious awakening," a phrase that may also describe whole societies or cultures when matters of faith suddenly acquire renewed relevance and urgency. For purposes of this discussion, however, a religious awakening is simply a process that occurs within the individual. And whereas conversion refers to the public embrace of a new faith or identity (with or without conviction), a religious awakening refers to an "inner" process that may or may not be shared openly with others, but is often long and fraught with "inner" complications of various kinds.

For example, for some people, a religious awakening effects a dramatic alteration of their theological frame of reference, and leads to the assumption of a new name and a new identity, a new religion, or the creation of a new, hybrid faith that fuses elements of pre-existing religious. Then again, for many people, a religious awakening returns them to the faith that they (or their parents) abandoned, or to new modes of piety within their original faith. For a smaller number, a religious awakening *radicalizes* their religious outlook, and in the process, turns them away from—and to some extent, against—the denomination they were born into, rendering them heterodox figures or religious reformers. The two pre-eminent examples of this sort of religious awakening in the nineteenth century were Kierkegaard, who turned against the Danish Lutheran Church, and Tolstoy, who turned against Russian Orthodoxy (Stern was intimately familiar with Kierkegaard and Tolstoy, whom he discussed at length in *The Flight from Woman*).

So when all is said and done, a religious awakening may or may not result in conversion, draw one closer to one's ancestral faith, or propel someone into a leadership role, all depending on circumstances. But from a phenomenological standpoint, a religious awakening *does* entail the experience of being addressed and in some sense claimed by God, and a profound conviction of being in possession of existential truths that eluded one beforehand, as well as a newfound sense of purpose going forward. In the case of Karl Stern, his religious awakening was a prolonged affair, accompanied by deep inner conflicts and punctuated by several epiphanies that unfolded over more than a decade, which culminated in his conversion to Catholicism in 1943.

Conversion to Christianity: flight or fulfillment?

The question then arises: Did Stern's conversion to Christianity represent the fulfillment of Stern's spiritual development as a Jew, as Stern believed? Or did it really constitute *a turning away* from Judaism, as Franz Rosenzwieg and—for different reasons—Sigmund Freud would have us believe? Perhaps it is a matter of perspective. Why? Well, Judaism and Christianity share some devotional attitudes and structures of piety which register strongly in our liturgy and prayers. For example, when Jews and Christians address the Almighty in prayer, we both tend to speak of God as our Creator, our Judge, and as our Redeemer. Considered as the Creator of the universe, the God of the Bible typically evokes a sense of admiration and gratitude and above all, a sense of awe and humility, because according to tradition, all living creatures owe their existence to God. The beauty and the mystery of the world are all His handiwork, which we can never hope to match, or to fathom fully.

Considered as a Judge, the God of the Bible evokes more mixed feelings—feelings of guilt and fear, but also of hope that if we strive to be just and merciful, to emulate God in our conduct with our fellow creatures, we will be loved and honored, at least by Him. Why? Because the God of the Bible is a great equalizer. On the Day of Judgment, we are told that God is completely indifferent to our worldly status or accomplishments. It doesn't matter whether we are kings or Presidents, on the one hand, or just "ordinary folks," because we are all made in God's image, and God's omniscience permits Him to see into the inner recesses of our hearts, to discern our true motives, and to ignore any misunderstandings and misconceptions that others harbor about us after we pass on.

Our feelings toward God as cosmic Judge are closely aligned to our beliefs about God as our Redeemer, or liberator. According to the Bible, God liberates us from idolatry and belief in false gods who cannot save us, and if we are currently enslaved or brought low by the malice or indifference of others, faith in God sustains us spiritually so that we can endure, and keep our hope and our dignity intact, despite all, until we are finally free.

Why do Jews and Christians share these core beliefs? Quite simply, because they were already rooted in the religious environment Jesus grew up in. Nevertheless, many Christians mistakenly believe that

Jesus first taught or inspired this kind of faith, while his friends and followers were sadly lacking in these attitudes and sensibilities, being robotically enslaved to "the law." That being so, it is important to remind readers that the habits of the heart which Jews and Christians share today were simply Jewish in the first instance (Crossan, 1994; O'Hare, 1997).

With that said, when Jews address God as their Creator, Judge or Redeemer, they are always talking about one and the same person. Not so for their Christian counterparts. In Christianity, as in Judaism, God the Father is always the Creator. But according to the New Testament God's Son is the Redeemer, not God the Father. Depending on the believer's denomination, the judging function of God may be allocated to the Son or the Father, and is sometimes shared by both. To complicate matters further, when Jews say that Moses or King Saul were infused with the Holy Spirit—*Ruach Elohim*, in Hebrew—we are not referring to a person of the Trinity, but to a state of spiritual exaltation that confers extraordinary insight or courage on ordinary mortals.

Furthermore, note that the religious education of the average Jew imbues him or her with sense of sacred history that is punctuated by pivotal events—the Creation, the Flood, the Exodus, Sinai, the Temple, Exile and return, and so on. Most Christians share this sense of sacred history, but only up to a point. For the average Christian, pivotal events in the Hebrew Bible merely *prepare the way* for Jesus' ministry, and the passages that are most pertinent to the Christian's faith are the (alleged) predictions or premonitions of Jesus' birth, the events surrounding Jesus' birth, his ministry, his trial, his crucifixion and resurrection, and so on. For the average Christian, everything pivots around this particular story, which is as timeless, fresh and relevant today as it was two millennia ago.

By contrast with Christians, who are apt to forget or to minimize the importance of people and events that occurred before and after Jesus' birth, ministry, and crucifixion, Jews are commanded to remember them vividly. This injunction is summed up in a single Hebrew word—*zachor*. This injunction is repeated often during the Passover Seder as an antidote to the ever-present threats of identity-diffusion, assimilation and conversion. Of course, no one, not even professional historians, can actually remember or reconstruct the entire panorama of Jewish history, spread out as it is all over more than three millennia. But by the same token, no one—not Abraham, Moses, Samuel, Elijah, or David—is as *central* to Jewish identity as Jesus is to the Christian narrative.

So unlike the average Jew, who identifies with the patriarchs, Moses and the prophets, the rabbis of old, and so on, the average Christian's sense of identity hinges overwhelmingly on the life and example of a single man. And a recurrent theme in Stern's conversion narrative is his gradual realization that Jesus' crucifixion was, in Hegel's words, *the hinge of history*. Absent this belief, said Stern, human history—and the Holocaust in particular—are senseless and unintelligible. Indeed, Stern asserted that whenever any human being is suffering, Jesus Christ is present, and suffering alongside of them.

In light of these disparate perspectives, the Christian believer almost always assumes that Stern's conversion to Catholicism represents the apex or culmination of his spiritual development as a Jew, just as Jesus' ministry represents the true fulfillment of the divine Logos in history. From the Jewish perspective, however, the unique status attributed to Jesus' crucifixion by Christians is unwarranted, since the Roman authorities crucified more than 10,000 Jews in the century of Jesus' birth. From the Jewish perspective, Jesus was merely one of many martyrs from that era, and a somewhat obscure one at that. So his death was tragic, but by no means *unique*. In time, however, Stern became fully persuaded that this tragic event was not merely *a* crucifixion, but *the* crucifixion, In so doing, Stern took a decisive step *away from* Judaism, because in adopting this philosophy of history, and this particular brand of theodicy, he embraced beliefs and attitudes that, from a Jewish perspective, are not the expression or culmination of developments that are integral to Judaism itself. Though he wasn't referring to Stern's case specifically, no one grasped this point more clearly than Rabbi Arthur Hertzberg, who wrote that ever since *Nostra Aetate*:

> [...] the Church condemns undue pressure for conversion and [...] respects those who are committed to the first Biblical revelation. What is between the lines of these Catholic documents—and what has appeared again and again at discussion tables between the leaders of the two faiths—has been a profound desire (I would even say need) of Catholics to have Jews to agree that Jesus is part of their religious history and that Jewish theology must take account of him no less seriously than Catholic theology takes account of the Patriarchs and the revelation to Moses on Sinai. Every time I, for

one, (and I have, of course, not been alone) have said at such tables that Jesus is no more important to Judaism than Muhammad is to Christians faces have fallen.

In my view, Christianity at its deepest level continues to grapple with the problem of the rejection of the New Dispensation by Jews [...]. Even liberal Catholics regard the renewed dialogue with Jews as an opportunity to [...] make some sense of what to Christians appears incomprehensible; that the people which best knew Jesus ignored him when he appeared and continue to do so. In this expectation, Catholics in dialogue with Jews will continue to be disappointed, and this despite the attempt to "solve" this problem through "two covenant theology" that was proposed by Franz Rosenzweig. (Hertzberg, 1994, p. 200)

Why Christianity?

This brings us to a slightly different question. Why did Stern convert to Catholicism, and what were the factors that ultimately led him to embrace Christianity, rather than Orthodox Judaism, for example? Having chronicled Stern's life in some detail, I am obviously in no position to deny that he suffered from severe neurotic difficulties, or that they played some part in his decision to convert. But it is also abundantly clear now that Freud's anathema on conversion was motivated by neurotic needs of his own, and that any effort to reduce Stern's spiritual struggles to the mere by-product of neurotic trends or infantile needs completely trivializes or ignores his *conscious* experiences of doubt and transcendence (Hewitt, 2014).

By contrast with Freud, whose attitude toward Christianity reflects the deep injuries of anti-Semitism, Erik Erikson provided us with a more useful way of understanding Stern's conversion. Without negating Freud's discoveries, Erikson appreciated how lop-sided and incomplete Freud's theory of human development was, and by way of compensation, placed as much emphasis on the vagaries of adolescent and adult development as he did on infancy and childhood. It was from this *epigenetic* perspective that Erikson described how highly sensitive, creative, and original thinkers—Luther, Darwin, James, Freud, and Gandhi, among others—underwent an unusually deep and protracted identity crisis that often lasted well into their thirties (Erikson, 1958; Erikson, 1964; Erikson, 1968).

The word "crisis" is a bit off the mark here, because the sense of urgency that haunts people like these is not sudden or acute, but chronic and persistent, rooted in a potentially paralyzing state of identity confusion, which in turn obligates the sufferer to engage in a process of careful self-scrutiny over extended periods of time. But unlike Freud, who focused on psychopathology, Erikson sought to elucidate the sources of health and resilience—what he called *ego-strength*—in "crises" of this kind (Erikson, 1964). As they wrestle with doubt and self-doubt, teetering dangerously close to madness, these creative souls gradually achieved a new kind of internal equilibrium, and the courage they needed to fulfill their cultural mission—what Ellenberger called "creative illness" (Erikson, 1958; Ellenberger, 1970; Burston, 2007).

Another reason Erikson's approach makes more sense here is that it is genuinely impartial in its appraisals of Judaism and Christianity. Despite his militant atheism, Freud took the superior rationality of the Jewish faith for granted, just as many Christians believe they have privileged access to the truth, and that Jews and Muslims have merely been granted fragmentary or distorted premonitions of the truth, rather than the plenitude of Divine grace.

In the final analysis, however, psychoanalysis is really not authorized or equipped to adjudicate rival claims like these. On the contrary, it must bracket and set aside all beliefs in cultural or spiritual superiority, or else direct attention to their social-psychological roots and ramifications. Erikson's theory of identity formation is admirably impartial, and can be fruitfully applied to any identity shift—religious, political or scientific—that is kindled in adolescence and propels the believer into an irrevocable commitment that defines their adult lives.

A third reason to apply Erikson's epigenetic perspective in Stern's case is that, like Stern, Erikson sought the developmental roots of the sense of the sacred in the infant's experience of its mother. Remember, Freud traced the sense of the numinous back to the child's (highly ambivalent) relationship to the father, and ignored or effectively ruled out the maternal imago as a source of feelings of reverence, awe and dread (Burston, 1989). Erikson, by contrast, believed that our first intimations of a "hallowed presence" are evoked in the intimate (preverbal) communion between mother and child, and are closely connected with "basic trust" and the foundational virtue of hope. According to Erikson, these experiences are a necessary and integral part of human development—not a neurotic distortion or aberration of some kind (Erikson, 1966).

With that said, however, we still owe Stern the courtesy of bracketing *all* theories of unconscious motivation and summarizing the reasons that *he* gave for his conversion in *The Pillar of Fire*, as well as relevant observations he made about his family and educational milieu. As Stern recalled, his father and mother were both quite estranged from Judaism, and celebrated Christmas with their neighbors. His grandfather, the leader of the local synagogue, dressed up as Father Christmas every year, and evidently relished that role. Karl's first religious instruction was actually from Catholic nuns, who clearly impressed him with their piety. Stern himself stressed the importance of "praeter-verbal" religious instruction—teaching by example, or the embodied way in which a religious teacher lives his or her faith. The fact that nuns furnished little Karl with the first example of deep religious devotion may explain his unqualified admiration for the untutored piety of devoted spinsters like Kati Huber and Babette Klabel. One thing seems certain—for the first five years of his life (at least), the boundaries between Judaism and Christianity must have been extremely fluid.

The next phase of Stern's religious instruction was Jewish, yes, but entrusted to a now nameless Cantor who was remembered as "hateful." He was followed by a series of indifferent tutors who left no impression whatsoever. Admittedly, Cantor Mohrmann, who followed in their anonymous footsteps, was quite musical, and knew his Hebrew—or so little Karl imagined. But Mohrmann was also a compulsive gambler, whose behavior outside of synagogue was slightly shady.

This summary covers the first nine years of Stern's childhood. What of the five that followed? When Ludwig arrived, Karl was sent to Ebenburg, where his religious instruction was anything but inspired. In Munich, with the Kohen family, Stern finally encountered Jews who prayed with passion and conviction. But his own Bar Mitzvah was a profound disappointment, and his first efforts to emulate the orthodox and embrace their world-view, one year later, alarmed and offended his parents. Even his grandfather mocked his sudden upsurge of religiosity, rather than offering encouragement or understanding.

Obviously, none of these things actually *explains* Stern's conversion to Christianity. After all, many Jews who grew up in similar circumstances would have simply become Zionists or "secular Jews" instead. Stern's recollections merely demonstrate that there was a lack of coherence and parental concern for his religious education. Indeed, he was treated to a kind of casual, take-it-or-leave-it approach that was often confusing and frustrating for him. He never said this in quite so many words, of course. But this fact registers indirectly in his disdain for middle-class Jewish liberals. Thus, he wrote:

> There has never been a Sinclair Lewis to describe the peculiar void, the lack of purpose, the absence of anything which would give roots or blossoms to this environment—the colorless "goodness," the efficiency without inner goal, the peculiar anemia deprived of the red blood of the Jewish tradition, and transfused with the saline solution of political liberalism. (Stern, 1951, p. 54)

Meanwhile, as Stern grew older, he found that the people who derived the greatest solace and inspiration from their religious beliefs were often quite old fashioned and out of step with modernity. They performed devoted acts of service for others, and were not ambitious in a worldly way. They prayed daily, believed in miracles and the afterlife, and waited patiently for the coming (or the return) of the Messiah. Only seldom were non-believers—like Franz Burger or Bruno Schultz—accorded the same respect in *The Pillar of Fire* as Liselotte's nanny, Katie Huber, or the Hirschs' housemaid, Babette Klebl, or Rabbi Ehrentreu and Dr. Frankel in Munich. These pious souls had the passion, the conviction and the certainty that Stern craved. They became his role models, his "ego ideal"—the kind of person he longed to become.

But if these were the people that Karl trusted and admired instinctively, what finally tipped the scales in favor of Catholicism? Was it because he encountered more Christians who lived life in this deeply committed fashion than he did in the Jewish community? Perhaps, but that is not the whole story. Another factor that scholars have studiously neglected thus far was Stern's passion for sacred music—Beethoven's *Missa Solemnis*, Bach's *St. Matthew's Passion*, and so on. But this topic furnishes the subject matter for most of Chapters Three and Nineteen in *The Pillar of Fire*, and really needs no further elaboration here.

Another cultural factor that drew Stern into the Christian orbit was Christian theology, which is at once much more speculative, more systematic and, as Edith Stein correctly observed (Stein, 1986, p. 82), more otherworldly than Jewish theology is. In addition to providing Stern with an abundance of role models and soul stirring music, Christianity's finely honed "metaphysical sense" afforded him a better medium for sublimating his inner contradictions. After all, by any common sense criteria, Stern *was* a bundle of contradictions; a fact that contributed to his love of singularity, his fondness for soulful and unconventional people, no matter what their faith or walk in life. This trait of Stern's is evidenced throughout *The Pillar of Fire*, especially in his portrait of Franz Volhard (p. 76), and later indirectly, in his reflections on Rudi Herz, who:

> [...] changed from a business clerk into a strict ascetic who sat in the evenings stooped over huge volumes of Talmud [...]. He quit the career that his parents had chosen and became a farmer. He was one of the first leaders of the farming schools for the Mizrahi, the Zionist movement of orthodox Jews [...] whose central theme is a movement back to the land and to handicraft and to life in co-operatives. Incidentally, he had a genuine inner relationship to art, particularly the Primitives and Renaissance painting. He always had reproductions of medieval altar pictures and Giotto on his walls. All this belonged to him in a way that I cannot define—a Jewish orthodox farmer with a Madonna of the early Rhenish school.
>
> Today, when I think of the invisible Church, I see [...] Rudi Herz with his ascetic features and his skull cap, and behind him reproductions of Giotto and Michaelangelo. (Stern, 1951, pp. 54–55)

Rather than scolding or dismissing people as colorful and Quixotic as this, we should acknowledge that the energy and imagination they expend in attempting to reconcile sensibilities and world-views this disparate often reflect considerable ego-strength. If harnessed creatively, their inner contradictions become fertile and dynamic, a source of creative tension. And if not, they promote paralysis and neurotic disability. Stern's extraordinary creativity and profound mental suffering are equally unintelligible unless we take these factors into account.

With all that said, however, there are several neurotic trends that probably contributed to Stern's decision to convert to Catholicism. In so saying, I have no wish to trivialize his decision or to diminish his new-found faith, nor to suggest that neurotic needs or motives were the dominant, much less the *only* factors in his decision. But conversions that require so much soul-searching beforehand are seldom, if ever, undertaken without attempting to express or overcome unresolved neurotic difficulties. Anyone who thinks otherwise is either extremely naïve or unduly defensive. In an unpublished paper entitled, "Brief memorandum on the psychological problems associated with the priesthood and religious life," Stern himself wrote that

> Neurosis in itself has often been the soil for great spiritual development, and if one excluded neurotic personalities as such from the priesthood one would exclude some of the giants of the Christian tradition such as Saint Augustine. (KSA, Series 3, Box 11, Folder 16, p. 6)

Stern's remarks are quite prescient, in some ways, anticipating more recent discussions of Augustine (Parsons, 2013). Besides, as Gregory Baum points out:

> In the last chapters of [...] [*The Third Revolution*] Stern emphasizes the neuroses of the saints. He argues that divine grace does not make them healthy, but uses their brokenness and allows their symptoms to sustain the marvelous and elevated things they do. For Stern, the saints are divinely bizarre. (Baum, letter to the author, March 29th, 2013)

Of course, Stern was not a saint, nor was he bizarre, despite his contradictions. But the fact that he saw no necessary conflict between deep religiosity and neurosis means that no one should be unduly defensive on this score—or at least, not on *his* behalf.

In any case, among the various neurotic motives that colored Stern's burning desire to convert, adolescent rebellion and resentment figure prominently. In Chapter Four of *The Pillar of Fire*, Stern observed that:

> For some unknown reason, the relationship between generations, particularly between father and son, seems much more problematic in Germany than in Anglo-Saxon countries. Generalizations like this are usually questionable but there is something quite characteristic. If only one could put one's finger on it. (Stern, 1951, p. 50)

These observations are hardly original, and were written with reference to the *Wandervogel*, rather than himself or his family of origin. And in fairness, Adolf Stern was not the typical authoritarian father German teenagers of that era rebelled against. On the contrary, Adolf routinely deferred to his own father—Stern's grandfather—as the chief dispenser of discipline around the house. Altogether, it seems that Adolf Stern played a relatively minor role in his son's emotional life. As a result, Stern may have never experienced the kind of tortured Oedipal ambivalence toward his own father that Freud declared is virtually universal (Burston, 1989).

But the relationship between Stern and his father was disturbed nonetheless. By his own admission, at an early age, Karl Stern found his father embarrassing, and if *The Pillar of Fire* is any indication, Adolf Stern was simply unable to anchor Karl in his ancestral tradition, or to assist him in meeting the challenges of the future. Having to look elsewhere for such things, and suffering ridicule from his elders when he began groping for a new identity, Stern eventually rebelled against their values and life style. Adopting Christianity rather than Judaism as his spiritual path may have gratified some deeply repressed resentment toward his entire family. These unconscious currents probably co-existed with his conscious (and completely genuine) love and affection for them—expressed, for example, in his fantasy of their presence at his baptism. The lingering consequences of this unconscious conflict might account for his religious doubts toward the end of his life, and his disturbed relationship with his own sons, Antony and Michael. Put another way, the problem was not that Adolf Stern was authoritarian. The problem was that he wasn't *authoritative* enough to inspire loyalty and confidence, and a desire to follow his example. So when it came to raising his own sons, Karl overcompensated in the opposite direction—with equally unfortunate results for "the relationship between the generations," which were profoundly disturbed as a consequence.

Another, less obvious neurotic trend that colored Stern's decision to convert was survivor guilt. He wrote frequently—in his published work, and in agonized letters to Dorothy Day and John Öesterreicher—about his "traitor complex." At the level of consciousness, his misgivings were simply based on a realistic appraisal of the situation of Jews in Hitler's Europe, and Stern's fear of alienating his friends and family. Unconsciously, however, his "traitor complex" was probably linked to guilt feelings about his unresolved (and belatedly consummated) adolescent rebellion against his father and family of origin.

Another component of his "traitor complex" was the vivid realization that, from 1933–1935, he was one of a tiny handful of Jews who were still gainfully employed in German universities, thanks to Spielmeyer's sponsorship and his Rockefeller grant. This fact alone confers a certain historic status on him. While this was an extremely privileged position, no doubt, it could not have been a *comfortable* one. Quite the contrary, we find Stern asking himself—both in Chapter Nineteen of *The Pillar of Fire*, and elsewhere—why *he* was spared while others were trapped, gassed, burned or buried in mass graves. This kind of talk is typical of traumatized survivors. Clearly, the effort to make sense of his extraordinary good luck made him wonder about the *meaning* of his situation, and indeed, the meaning of history, because the idea that his survival was a mere fluke was simply intolerable to him. Consequently, Stern *consciously* rejected the idea that the universe is meaningless, or that his fate was a random occurrence in favor of a Christian view of history. Whether, or to what extent, his adoption of a new theological frame of reference assuaged his underlying sense of survivor guilt is uncertain, but this factor cannot be ruled out completely.

Another thing that probably contributed to Stern's eventual conversion was his intense need for what psychoanalysts call an "idealized object," or a "good object"—a person, entity or institution that symbolizes purity and goodness, and remains constant, reliable, and will not disappoint us at the end of the day—or less figuratively, for believers, at the end of our lives, or history itself. After all the trauma and uncertainty he had undergone prior to his conversion, Stern needed to have an idealized object, and that "object" was the "invisible" Catholic Church. The idealizing trend was evident when he wrote the following, for example:

> Christianity never demands of you to deny anything positive you have ever loved. You can find it all again in Christ, but you find more. He does not want you to be nostalgic for the past, because the past is in Him. He asks you not to look back at the burning city lest you will turn into a pillar of salt. (Stern, 1951, p. 231)

Of course, Stern knew very well that many Catholics were anti-Semites, ardent nationalists, or even fascists, for that matter. But from his perspective, these blemishes pertained only to the "visible Church." Presumably, the "invisible Church" remained intact, with deep, pristine springs of piety that were hidden from view feeding the streams that insured its continued existence.

Sadly, Stern's tendency to idealize the "invisible Church" was expressed in his idealization of some of its more visible members. Consider his enthusiastic response to Cardinal Faulhaber's sermon of December 17th, 1933, which Eric Vogelin quotes in *Hitler and the Germans* (Vogelin, 1999). This sermon, which elicited an epiphany, said Stern, actually provoked a very worried response among most members of the Jewish community. Guenther Lewy writes:

> Cardinal Faulhaber's Advent sermons in 1933, in particular, are remembered for their eloquent vindication of the sacred character of the scriptures of the Old Testament. But Faulhaber went out of his way to make clear that he was not concerned with defending his Jewish contemporaries. "We must distinguish," he told the faithful, "between the people of Israel before the death of Christ, who were vehicles of divine revelation, and the Jews after the death of Christ, who have become restless wanderers over the earth. But even the Jewish people of ancient times could not justly claim credit for the wisdom of the Old Testament. So unique were these laws that one was bound to say: 'People of Israel, this did not grow in your own garden of your own planting. This condemnation of usurious land-grabbing, this war against the oppression of the farmer by debt, this prohibition of usury, is not the product of your spirit.'" (Cited in Vogelin, 1999, p. 190)

Contrast Faulhauber's remarks in 1933 with Pope John Paul II's address in the Great Synagogue of Rome in 1986. John Paul II acknowledged the special kinship between the Jewish and the Christian faith, and described Jews as "our elder brothers" (Dionne, 1986). In so doing, John Paul II completely contradicted Faulhauber's hostile (and preposterous) claim that the Jews "can not justly claim credit for the wisdom of the Old Testament." The point here is that, judging from Stern's recollection of Faulhauber's sermon, he responded to it *as if* he had been listening to John Paul II. Remember, he wrote of Faulhauber's sermon that:

> It had a profound and irrevocable influence on me [...]. I felt like a child who had known its own house from inside and from the garden, and who is now, for the first time, shown it from far away as part of the landscape. (Stern, 1951, p. 158)

The fact that Stern was so charmed by Faulhaber's sermon demonstrates that the idealizing trend I am referring to either permitted or necessitated a tendency toward distortion, and that on some level, Stern was already ripe for conversion. Meanwhile, the metaphor Stern chose, of suddenly being afforded a (metaphorical) view of his own house, his own tradition, from afar, already appeared in Faulhaber's sermon, albeit with a view to demonstrating that the prophetic pursuit of justice and mercy has nothing to do with the Jewish people—an assertion that is transparently anti-Semitic and quite contrary to what Stern himself actually believed. Worse still, Cardinal Faulhaber described contemporary Jews as "restless wanderers," ignoring the fact that their migrations throughout Europe were almost always *involuntary*, prompted by vicious persecution, rather than by some collective character flaw. Faulhaber's characterization of Jews as "wanderers" was not an isolated case, of course. This was a widely sanctioned way of blaming victims for their own suffering, and absolving those who were actually responsible.

That being so, it is instructive to note that none of Cardinal Faulhaber's animus toward the Jewish people was evident in Stern's recollections of this historic speech. And in fairness to Stern, perhaps, Faulhauber's high-brow, low intensity anti-Semitism was a far cry from the low-brow, high-intensity anti-Semitism of the Nazis. Only the latter constituted an immediate threat to the safety of the Jewish community. But looking back, Faulhauber's denigrating assessment of Jewish spirituality furnished the perfect pretext for collective passivity and indifference toward the fate of Jews, as Hitler moved steadily toward "the Final Solution." As is often the case in anti-Semitic milieus, high-brow, low-intensity anti-Semites provide a measure of cover and legitimacy for the more violent, low-brow variety; a collusive relationship that is no less potent or dangerous for being unconscious (Burston, 2014b). Because of his need to idealize the Church and its representatives, Stern was oblivious to this historical dynamic. The fact that he did not find Faulhaber's sermon alarming indicates that by December of 1933 Stern *already* viewed his ancestral faith from a considerable distance. In Freudian terminology, his ambivalent attachment to Judaism had been divested of much of its libidinal energy and significance, which were being re-directed into new, subterranean channels of piety.

Contexts of conversion

So far, Stern's religious awakening and subsequent conversion have been subject to searching analyses by David Neuhaus (Neuhaus, 1988), Sherry Simon (1999), and Robert McFarland (McFarland, 2007). Neuhaus and McFarland attempt to understand Stern's conversion by comparing his experiences with those of other prominent converts from Judaism; Simon, by contrasting Stern's attitude towards Judaism and Christianity with that of another prominent Montrealer, Stern's contemporary, the poet A. M. Klein. We will address these analyses in chronological order, and attempt to synthesize what we've learned from each of them as we press toward our conclusion.

Fr David Neuhaus, SJ, himself a convert from Judaism, is the Patriarchal Vicar of Hebrew speaking Catholics in Israel. In an illuminating article entitled "Jewish Conversion to the Catholic Church," Neuhaus draws on ideas gleaned from William James and Robert Lifton, comparing Stern's experience with that of two other well-known converts, Edith Stein (1891–1942) and Eugenio (Israel) Zolli (1881–1956). Stein was a student of Husserl and Scheler (Bello, 2000) who converted to Catholicism in 1922 (Stein, 1933), perished in Auschwitz twenty years later, and was canonized by Pope John Paul II in 1998. Zolli was the chief Rabbi of Rome who was sheltered during World War II by Pope Pius XXII, and converted to Catholicism in 1945 (Zolli, 1954). Unlike Stern, Stein and Zolli were born into observant Jewish families. But like Stern, they left detailed accounts of their conversions, prompting Neuhaus to search for overarching patterns and similarities in their experiences (Neuhaus, 1988).

Based on their first person accounts, Neuhaus argues that most converts from Judaism undergo a discernable three-stage process. The first is characterized by "a personal sense of sinfulness or unfulfilment," a realization that "sin is everywhere and can only be redeemed by a radical change of life." The second stage is characterized by a "persistent pursuit of the numinous" or a sense of transcendence, and the third is characterized by a sense of "happiness, fulfillment and higher control" (Neuhaus, 1988, pp. 42–43).

Neuhaus notes that for Jews who contemplate conversion, the transition from stage two to stage three is usually complicated by a sense of guilt engendered by:

> [...] the hold the community left behind continues to have on the convert [...]. Aspects of this can be seen in many conversions—the English aristocrat who becomes a Communist, the Protestant who becomes a Catholic, or the Italian middle class teenager who joins the Red Brigade—yet one would be hard pressed to find equal depth to the feeling of betrayal inherent in the Jew joining the Roman Catholic Church. Not only does he leave a community living in reduced circumstances, priding itself on a survival ethos [...] but he joins a Church seen as built up on deep anti-Judaism, associated with virulent anti-Semitism, which has often taken the role of the persecutor, culminating in its supposed acquiescence to Nazi barbarism. (Neuhaus, 1988, pp. 44–45)

Of course, this was precisely Stern's dilemma, the one that propelled him to seek counsel from Maritain (among others). But once the decision to become Catholic has actually been made, says Neuhaus, the (formerly Jewish) convert can adopt one of several paths to defining their relationship to their previous community. He (or she) can completely repudiate the Jewish faith, distancing himself from the Jewish community physically, socially, and emotionally. Alternatively, the convert may actively repudiate and even demonize his former faith, and perhaps devote his life to converting his former community to the one true faith. And for converts who are unashamed of their Jewish origins, and unafraid to acknowledge them, a third solution to alleviate their lingering sense of guilt is for them to address, expose and eliminate anti-Semitism among their fellow Catholics, and to minimize their sense of alienation from their former communities by supporting Zionism or studying Judaism and/or the Judaeo-Christian heritage.

Finally, says Neuhaus, there is a fourth strategy, the one adopted by Stern, Stein, and Zolli, which involves the development of a sophisticated theological rationale to explain the Jewish role in history, and the reasons for the Jews' continued suffering and persecution. These theological musings represent a compromise between frank condemnation and a vigorous affirmation of their former faith's validity. Moreover, he notes, they usually:

> [...] concentrate upon an end eschatology, where redemption is taken for granted, usually seen as a time when the Jews will be

re-united as the Chosen People within the Church. (Neuhaus, 1988, p. 46)

In the process, notes Neuhaus, Stern, Stein, and Zolli all present Christianity as a religion of love and peace, extolling the piety of the simple Christian believer, thereby negating "the essence of the past community's historiography, of deep anti-Semitic content to past Christian history (p. 49)." Moreover, says Neuhaus:

> The price of cleansing the convert's new community is one of systematizing and rationalizing the Holocaust and anti-Semitic pogroms of the past, attempting to find their meaning in the overall eschatological process. Unable to remain silent about this peak of un-Christian behavior to their past community, the Holocaust is placed within the system of cause and effect which will bring about their ultimate redemption. (Neuhaus, 1988, p. 49)

Despite the frank realism of this appraisal, Neuhaus also claimed that it is "baseless" to suggest that Stein, Zolli or Stern changed their religion from ulterior motives, or that their experiences were anything but genuine revelations that led them to "a higher truth." And yet, he freely concedes that:

> [...] the construction of this framework of rationalization, addressed to both the former and present communities, is essential to the continued commitment of the convert [...] In this way converts re-write history, a common phenomenon among those who have undergone conversion. With history rewritten and the present redefined, the future can be approached with a new certainty, where answers are provided to the insoluble conflicts of the past. (Neuhaus, 1988, p. 51)

Father Neuhaus' description of the stages that precede or accompany conversion to Catholicism do ring true. Most of the evidence he presents for a deepening consciousness of sin (phase one) comes from Stein and Zolli's narratives, but there is plenty of evidence of this in Stern as well. For example, in *The Pillar of Fire*, Stern said that:

> [...] psychoanalysis has reaffirmed what the Church has taught all the time; namely, that potentially there is inside every man a den of

> murderers and thieves. Why these potentialities become manifest in your neighbor and remain latent in you, this is not for you to judge. The veil which separates the potential evil in you from the manifest evil in the man you are going to read about in tomorrow's headlines in thinner and more mysterious than you think—this is the catharsis which emanates from the great Russian writers of the nineteenth century, and from psychoanalysis [...]. But it is only an elaboration of an old truth. (Stern, 1951, p. 226)

Stern is right, of course. This idea is not new. But neither is it uniquely Christian. The Hebrew Bible (and Rabbinic commentaries) reflect at length on the *yetzer ha'ra*, or the evil inclination, which is deemed to be present in everyone. What renders the budding convert's situation different from that of the average Jew is that they are suddenly confronted by an overwhelming sense of the potential for evil inherent in everyone, everywhere, and do not believe that their community of origin provides an adequate answer to this problem (for one reason or another).

While phases one and two in Neuhaus' stage theory are descriptively accurate, there is a problem with his third (post-conversion) stage, which is characterized by a sense of happiness and fulfillment. In public, as we know, Stern always seemed quite secure in his newfound faith. But with the passage of time, the onset of illness, family discord and his eldest son's suicide, Stern was sometimes beset by agonizing doubts. To Noel Walsh, he confided his fear that his son's suicide and his final stroke and paralysis were Divine punishment for abandoning Judaism—his "traitor complex" returned to haunt him. To Dorothy Day, in his last letters, he confided doubts about salvation and the afterlife. Did Stein and Zolli experience similar doubts? I do not know. But if Stern's life is any indication, the third stage Neuhaus described is not *always* the end of the story.

Similarly, problems arise in connection with the varieties of Catholic identity formation that Neuhaus describes among Jewish converts. On the whole, his descriptions are quite useful for understanding the attitudes Jewish converts adopt toward their community of origin. Nevertheless, they beg some urgent questions. For example, even if we grant that Stein, Zolli, and Stern did not convert for ulterior motives, it does not necessarily follow that their (admittedly very difficult) decisions led them to "a higher truth." In so saying, of course, Neuhaus privileges the Catholic perspective over the Jewish one. While he is amply entitled to do so, such claims have no scientific standing—even to psychoanalysts who treat religious experience with respect, rather than the kind of hostile deconstruction that Freud accorded to religious belief.

On a different note, for the sake of discussion, let us suppose that in converting to Catholicism, Stein, Zolli, and Stern really did embrace a "higher truth." Nevertheless, according to Neuhaus, their path represents merely *one* route to Catholic identity formation. The other three modes of identity formation Neuhaus describes prompt one to wonder whether a convert who distances himself completely from his ancestral faith, denying or hiding his former religious affiliation, has also embraced a "higher" truth, or whether his motives are actually more complicated. Similarly, what do we make of converts who openly repudiate or demonize their former community, or work tirelessly to convert them to Catholicism? Finally, what of those who are unashamed of their ancestry, and seek to minimize the sense of distance and estrangement between the two faiths? Are all three types also free of "ulterior motives"? And if so, how do we reconcile that claim with the fact that their attitudes toward Judaism are so disparate?

Then again, let us assume once more that Neuhaus is right, and that Stein, Zolli, and Stern were all in possession of a higher truth after their conversions. Even so, there is something disconcerting about Neuhaus' observation that converts like these rewrite history to insure their continued commitment to their newfound faith, and that this process entails a tendency to minimize their Church's past misdeeds towards the Jews. Why? Because it suggests that successful converts *must* abandon historical truth to remain in possession of a religious or metaphysical truth; an extremely problematic position, from both a logical and psychological point of view. To put the issue more crudely, how can a tendency to self-deception, minimization or denial ever be pressed in the service of the truth? The answer to these questions are far from evident, and call for a more detailed exploration of the issues than Neuhaus provided at this juncture.

In fairness to Neuhaus, of course, converts to *any* religion must rewrite their personal histories to justify their decisions, whether these decisions are rooted in an adolescent identity crisis or the fact that, for one reason or another, their community of origin simply fails to meet their spiritual needs. But rewriting one's personal history is one thing. Rewriting social, collective or world history so that it accords with a theological preconception is not just a private or devotional act but a political statement, or at the very least, an interpretive stance which has political roots and ramifications. Must the two go hand in hand? Remember, six decades have elapsed since Vatican II, and many Catholic scholars have finally acknowledged that the theological anti-Judaism of medieval Christendom contributed mightily to the cultural climate in which nineteenth century racist anti-Semitism flourished, and conversely, that the theological anti-Judaism of many devout Catholics in Hitler's Germany (and throughout Europe) was colored by crudely racist beliefs and convictions (Carroll, 2001; Connelly, 2012). Perhaps it is a reflection of their cognitive style, or of their moment in history, or of the inherent difficulties facing Jewish converts to Catholicism. But the fact remains that Stein, Zolli, and Stern all glossed over or denied these inconvenient truths in the process of elaborating their theological rationales for the Holocaust. In light of all we know now, is this is a benign or desirable state of affairs, or one we should encourage or accept, going forward?

Sherry Simon is a professor of French at Concordia University who writes very perceptively about the complexities of language politics and translation issues in her native Montreal (e.g., Simon, 2002). Instead of contrasting Stern's experience with that of older, European contemporaries like Stein and Zolli, Simon situates Stern in the context of Québec's cultural politics during the forties and fifties. In "A. M. Klein et Karl Stern: Le scandale de la conversion," she compares Stern's attitude and choices with those of Melech Davidson, a Holocaust survivor and long-lost uncle of the protagonist of *The Second Scroll*, a novel by Stern's younger contemporary, Canadian poet, Abraham Moses Klein (1909–1972).

Though born in Ratno, Ukraine—Melech Davidson's ostensible birthplace—A. M. Klein was brought to Montreal at three, and grew up in the bustling, diverse and predominantly Yiddish-speaking Jewish community. While they lived in the same city, in reasonably close proximity to each other, Simon notes that Klein and Stern never met because they moved in different social circles, and were worlds apart, psychologically speaking. And yet, by a curious coincidence, Klein's celebrated novel—one of the finest in Canadian literature—was published in 1951, the same year as *The Pillar of Fire*. In one section of the novel, Klein explores the psychological life of the narrator's uncle, who longed to fuse his Jewish and Christian sensibilities in an inclusive, universalistic identity, much as Stern did—or tried to do—after his conversion. Whereas Stern was drawn into the Christian orbit through sacred music, Klein's character, like Stern's friend Rudi Herz, was enchanted by Christian art and architecture, and felt that the ban on "graven images" (or visual representations of the divine) left Judaism somewhat impoverished by comparison with Christianity. Nevertheless, despite strong temptation, Melech Davidson does not convert, but remains loyal to his ancestral faith.

Stylistically speaking, *The Second Scroll* was inspired by James Joyce's *Ulysses*. But it is a masterpiece in its own right, and probably the first English language novel to address the psychological complexities besetting Jews in the aftermath of the Holocaust. Not surprisingly, Klein's novel was greeted by Montreal's Jewish community, and by Jews everywhere, with pride and pleasure, as a kind of cautionary tale. By contrast, as Simon points out, Stern's book was experienced as an insult and a provocation, because Stern compared the exclusivity of the Jewish people with Nazi racism. In Chapter Seventeen of *The Pillar of Fire*, Stern put the matter bluntly, as follows:

> Let there be no mistake. Jewish religion [...] is based on the axiom that Revelation is a national affair [...]. Do not be misled by the fact that in their personal ethics they are anything but exclusive and racist. Do not be misled by certain noble Talmudic principles such as "the just of all nations have share in the world to come" [...]. Do not be misled by the fine cosmopolitan sentiments of reformed Judaism, which are often prompted by noble hearts but at the same time by much vague thinking and a lukewarm dilution of the most profound and earthshaking elements of the Judaic treasure. No, there is no getting away from it [...]. I only had to look at our liturgy to see that this was so. Jewish religion was racial exclusiveness. Mind you, it was racial exclusiveness in its noblest, most elevated form [...] but it was racism just the same. (Stern, 1951, p. 159)

A few pages later, in Chapter Eighteen, Stern quoted a Lutheran writer, Ricarda Huch, who once remarked that:

> [...] for Jews to become converted to Christ means an extraordinary sacrifice. Not only, says she, must the individual die with Him in order to live; it is the whole people who must die with him. By some mysterious twist of fate, the Jews are the only people which

> cannot remain a people and be Christian at the same time. (Stern, 1951, p. 169)

Elaborating further on this theme, Stern suggests that Huch's reflections on Jewish identity reveal:

> [...] why Jewish shortcomings, Jewish vices, Jewish impurities are hated more than those of other people. Because the physical existence of the Jewish people is, from the point of view of the metaphysics of history, an incongruity. The Jews are here, they are living, whereas the ultimate meaning of their existence as a people is that it should transcend itself. (Stern, 1951, p. 170)

Stern then went on to add that the collective self-transcendence he was urging on the Jews had nothing to do with the liberal idea of assimilation. Absent real piety, conversion means nothing. Indeed:

> A religious Jew who chose to be burned at the stake by the Inquisitor was obviously closer to God than a modern Jew who is baptized to solve the problem of anti-Semitism for his children. (Stern, 1951, p. 171)

So, Stern spoke with respect of orthodox Jews, despite the fact that, as a rule, they were far more reclusive and mistrustful of their pious Christian counterparts than their more modern kin. Nevertheless, Stern's philosophy of history prompted him to regard *all* Jews as "incongruities," who can't fulfill their historic mission until they willingly embrace Jesus as the Messiah and simply cease to exist as a nation. This way of framing the issue suggests that at the end of the day, there is nothing that is distinctively *Jewish* about Jewish culture or civilization that is inherently worth saving.

Simon does not mention this, but the flip side of Stern's argument, which probably startled Christian readers, appeared in a paper composed in Rome in 1965, entitled "Some religious aspects of anti-Semitism," which was published a decade later, in *Love and Success* (Stern, 1975). Here Stern suggested that in the great drama of salvation, Jews will not relinquish their claims to nationhood until Christian anti-Semitism has completely ceased, and Christians fully embrace the mystery of the Incarnation, which—among other things,—means fully accepting the Jewishness of Jesus. Here, Stern observed that:

> The Christian child who in the course of his religious education, is early imbued with a love of Jesus, frequently hears the very word "Jews" for the first time in the context of the crucifixion. The fact that the mother of Jesus was a Jewess, that all his early friends and followers were Jews, that he himself in the flesh was a Jew is kept from the child's conscious with what seems at time almost bad intention. (Stern, 1975, p. 259)

Stern then went on to observe:

> Many years ago Jacques Maritain remarked to this writer that, just as to Jews the divinity of our Lord is a seemingly insurmountable obstacle, Christians have a similar difficulty with his humanity. At first sight this seems like a specious comparison. After all, acceptance of the divinity of the person who lived in the flesh, in history, seems the very proof of faith. Yet this is not so. The psychology of the "cradle" Christian is such that the Christ of the icon is often not a truly incarnated being.

According to Stern, then, Christians' inability to acknowledge Jesus' basic Jewishness results in anti-Semitism and an impoverished grasp of their own faith. And as long as that remains the case, Stern said, it is not reasonable to expect Jews to relinquish their stubborn particularity. Were Catholic audiences as offended by Stern's later remarks on anti-Semitism as Jews were by *The Pillar of Fire*? That is doubtful, because these remarks never reached the same vast audiences. But one thing is certain. These caveats—which exonerate Jews until Christians cease to act hatefully, and live up to their own religious precepts—appeared long after *The Pillar of Fire*. Because of their belated appearance, they had absolutely no effect on Jewish audiences. And why would they, after so long an interval? Despite the compliments paid to orthodox Jews in *The Pillar of Fire*, Stern was profoundly insulting to Jews of all denominations when wrote:

> *Do not be misled* by the fact that in their personal ethics they [Jews] are anything but exclusive and racist. *Do not be misled* by certain

> noble Talmudic principles such as "the just of all nations have share in the world to come" [...]. *Do not be misled* by the fine cosmopolitan sentiments of reformed Judaism [...]. (Stern, 1951, p. 159, emphasis added)

It is not clear precisely whom these admonitions were directed towards. But the phrase "Do not be misled [...]" repeated three times, consecutively, implies to all Stern's readers that Jews who abhor racism and embrace the more universalistic dimension of their religious tradition are either insincere, prone to self-deception, or worse yet, harbor a hidden agenda, hoping to put one over on gullible Gentiles. Even now, more than sixty years later, it is *extremely* difficult to reconcile this harsh appraisal with Stern's frequent avowals of love and concern for his community of origin.

Further below, in the very same paragraph, Stern made another comment that is not merely insulting, but positively incendiary. He wrote:

> There is no getting away from it [...]. I only had to look at our liturgy to see that this was so. Jewish religion was racial exclusiveness. Mind you, it was racial exclusiveness in its noblest, most elevated form [...] but it was racism just the same. (Stern, 1951, p. 159)

By time you read these words, Stern manages to convey the impression that Judaism is inherently or intrinsically racist, while Catholics are only racist in a contingent manner, as a result of faulty education and some unfortunate historical accidents. To qualify this judgment by calling Judaism racism "in its noblest, most elevated form" does nothing to soften the blow. On the contrary, it immediately invites the counter-accusation that Catholicism (or Christianity in general) is inherently anti-Semitic. After all, the textual evidence in favor of this charge is at least as robust, as some Catholic scholars freely concede nowadays (e.g., Ruether, 1997).

Now, when Jews and Christians trade accusations like these in an actual face to face discussions, only two outcomes are possible. The best-case scenario is an unpleasant (and ultimately sterile) stand-off that is apt to stifle or severely reduce prospects for further dialogue. The other, even less desirable outcome is that an exchange like this will push participants to the brink of a slippery slope, from the bottom of which there is no possibility of return, and little (if any) prospect for building lasting trust and friendship.

So if Stern imagined that *The Pillar of Fire* would one day contribute to a constructive dialogue with Jews on matters of faith or identity, he was utterly mistaken. Statements like his still provoke consternation and dismay among Jewish audiences, reinforcing the worst fears of Holocaust survivors and their families—namely, that Christians seek to de-legitimate Judaism, and in certain circumstances, will collaborate with fascists who are bent on their ultimate annihilation; the former, by conversion, the latter, by genocide. And besides, ever since Constantine, Jews have suffered far more grievously at the hands of Christians than vice versa, rendering Christian claims to moral superiority suspect *a priori*. (Freud was right about that, after all). So wouldn't it be more prudent and productive for Jewish/Christian dialogue to set aside invidious comparisons like these—to simply agree that many (but not all) Christians are anti-Semites, and that many (but not all) Jews are indeed racist, and to acknowledge our joint responsibility to address these issues in a vigorous, proactive fashion in the context of our children's religious education?

So, despite his many gifts to posterity, Stern's brand of Catholic apologetics is a splendid example of how *not* to conduct interfaith dialogue (at least from the Christian side). And as Sherry Simon reminds us, when *The Pillar of Fire* first appeared, Rabbi Bernard Heller expressed the horror and indignation most Jews felt toward Stern in *Letter to An Apostate* (Heller, 1952). By contrast with Heller, A. M. Klein, whom Simon discusses so insightfully, adopted a very different strategy. He said virtually nothing to or about Stern, preferring to carry on as if Stern did not exist—an eloquent statement in itself. But if Klein's silence was eloquent, even more interesting, and certainly more revealing, was Stern's reception among French Canadians. To get this matter into perspective, Simon notes that most French Canadians were kindly disposed to conversion narratives, but that Stern's critique of Judaism in *The Pillar of Fire* mirrored his critique of French Canadian culture, which combined fervent religiosity with strong nationalistic sentiments. Stern objected to nationalism in any form, and felt that any admixture of nationalism and religion opened the door to prejudice, hatred and divisiveness. Moreover, and more importantly, it was a serious impediment to the conversion of the Jews. In his own words:

> To the outsider, on the plane of a low natural order, the Church itself is just another hostile camp. Indeed, to some the Church is

> an Irish institution (in the United States), a French institution (in Canada) and so forth. In the true mystical body there is no trace of an ethnic structure. However, my Jewish friends do not perceive that. Can you blame them? Their next-door Irish neighbors, or the priest around the corner, may be extreme nationalists. (Stern, 1951, p. 236)

Nevertheless, writing in the pages of *Le Devoir*, Montreal's leading French-language newspaper, Gilles Marcotte gave *The Pillar of Fire* a very favorable reception, and even acknowledged the prevalence of nationalist and anti-Semitic sentiments among Francophones. At the same time, Marcotte endorsed Stern's charge that Judaism is inherently racist and exclusionary, and that true Christianity, which still thrives in many corners of Québec, presumably, preserves the essence of Judaism *minus* all these odious features. Furthermore, notes Simon, Marcotte's review was predicated on the idea that all Jews—both in the newly founded state of Israel, and those remaining in the Diaspora as well—are really proto-Christians or prospective converts, whether they know it yet or not. No Christian who took these statements to heart could possibly have supported Zionism, except as a prelude or pathway to conversion.

Now, let us turn our attention to Robert McFarland's illuminating essay, "Elective divinities: Exile and religious conversion in Alfred Döblin's *Schicksalreise* (Destiny's Journey) Karl Jakob Hirsch's *Heimkehr zu Gott* (Return to God) and Karl Stern's *Pillar of Fire*." Robert McFarland is an Associate Professor of German Studies at Brigham Young University. Unlike David Neuhaus, who compared Stern's evolving Catholic identity to two older European converts—one who perished in the Holocaust, one who narrowly survived—McFarland situates Stern among the community of exiled intellectuals who fled Germany before World War II, most of whom settled in the United States. Most of these exiles were politically engaged artists or writers of one sort or another. Most of them were indifferent (or openly hostile) to religious ideas and sentiments. The lives and careers of some of these exiles have been studied closely, but Döblin, Hirsch and Stern were neglected, notes McFarland, because they were deliberately excluded by this group—and by religious Jews, as well.

McFarland's goal is to demonstrate how his three subjects used their conversion narratives to infuse their own brands of spirituality into the political, literary and aesthetic debates that enveloped and engaged them prior to their conversions, and to "minimize the potential ethical problems" that arose from their conversions in the midst of the Holocaust. McFarland notes that Döblin and Stern's narratives belong in a genre of modern apologetics that begins with Cardinal John Henry Newman, who sought "to create a voice of dissent against the secularizing tendencies of European culture," to restore religion to the public sphere, as a critical and potentially world-changing praxis. That being so, Döblin, Hirsch and Stern found secular ideologies like Marxism and Zionism to be extremely problematic, and so sought to create "heretical" narratives:

> [...] that criticize the dogmatic secularism and politicization of the exile community and to restore a spiritual heterodoxy to the literature of exile. (McFarland, 2007, p. 40)

Though it is rooted in experiences he had before he fled Germany, Stern's critique of Zionism is noteworthy in this context. He freely conceded that the young *halutzim* he befriended in his teenage years were wholesome, principled, unselfish, and brave. Yet we also find Stern scolding young Zionists who, by his own admission, were motivated by a strong sense of justice and charity, and capable of extreme self-sacrifice because they "[...] did not realize that they themselves were living on the immense treasure of orthodoxy."

Moreover, while they embraced noble values, said Stern,

> [...] orthodox Jewry has preserved Judaism unadulterated in its purest and richest form over thousands of years. Pure Ethics is an artifact isolated by a purely rationalist, modern process from the huge organism of tradition. (Stern, 1951, p. 151)

Actually, on reflection, there are two separate reproaches here. The first was directed towards Zionists for their secularism; an attitude that, before World War II, was perfectly aligned with orthodox Jewish opinion on this matter. After all, the kibbutz movement drew inspiration from socialists like Moses Hess (1812–1875) and David Aharon

Gordon (1856–1922). While a few Mizrahi kibbutzim had a religious orientation, most religious Jews opposed them completely (Burston, 2014b). The other, more encompassing complaint here is directed against modernity and rationalism as such; a reproach for severing ethics from "the huge organism of tradition." The point is that the former, more targeted complaint was necessitated by the latter, more encompassing mistrust of modernity, and by Stern's deep religious traditionalism.

Having noted Stern's misgivings about Zionism, McFarland points out that *The Pillar of Fire* follows a rhetorical strategy very similar to those of Döblin and Hirsch. For example, he says, all three authors begin their narratives by drawing a somewhat idyllic picture of their early childhood experiences of Judaism. In his words: "The spirituality of childhood is portrayed as a lost paradise, a place of childlike wonder at the outward expressions of a family's faith" (McFarland, 2007, p. 46). Unfortunately, McFarland goes astray here. I cannot speak for Döblin and Hirsch, but Stern's descriptions of "the spirituality of childhood"— or *his* childhood, anyway—are punctuated by long interludes of dull estrangement, brief episodes of acute disappointment and a growing sense of confusion.

Next, says McFarland, Döblin, Hirsch, and Stern describe their gradual absorption into the prevailing German cultural milieu, with its characteristic philosophical, artistic and literary dimensions, which draws them away from their Jewish roots. In Stern's case, this entailed an intensive immersion in "canonical" readings from the German cultural pantheon—Lessing, Goethe, Schiller, and other well-known poets, playwrights, and philosophers. This stage, says McFarland, was followed by their introductions to modernism (in various artistic and intellectual forms), which engendered reactions against the perceived soullessness of modernity, leading, in all three cases, to experiments with orthodox Judaism, which began on a hopeful note, but left the future converts unconvinced and unsatisfied. This phase was followed by a fresh crisis followed by an ardent embrace of Christianity, which Hirsch and Stern in particular construed as the consummation or fulfillment—and emphatically not as the negation—of their spiritual development as Jews.

In some ways, McFarland's rendering of the (self-described) stages in identity formation among converts like Stern is less problematic than Neuhaus' typology because it traces the outlines of overarching themes in the converts' own narratives. It also alerts readers to the supercessionist overtones of Hirsch and Stern's discourses, which serve a proselytizing function that, in McFarland's estimation "[...] is counter-productive in any kind of interfaith discussion." Truer words were never spoken. Gregory Baum, Professor Emeritus at the Université Québec a Montréal, a former Professor of Theology (University of Toronto) and before that, an Augustinian priest who served as a special advisor to the Ecumenical Secretariat at the Second Vatican Council, points out that:

> Dialogue is a conversation based on trust and mutual acceptance, in which the partners feel free to reveal their own problems and unresolved questions. Dialogue is unguarded conversation. Dialogue is an exchange that transforms both partners, leading them to a better self-understanding [...]. It would be utterly deceitful to lure a partner into dialogue, attempting to create a community of trust [...] and then abuse this confidence in an effort to persuade the partner to change his or her religion. It may happen, of course, that in such a trusting dialogue a partner decides to move to another religious tradition. But interreligious dialogue would be a form of manipulation if its aim were to make Christians of the participants. (Baum, 2000, p. 3)

Stern, Vatican II, and beyond

Baum's sentiments are grounded in historical experience, and in a deep respect for the suffering and dignity of the Jewish people. After all, in the immediate aftermath of the Holocaust, many Jewish leaders including Martin Buber, Abraham Joshua Heschel, and Emile Fackenheim (among others) called on the Church to stop the centuries-long effort to convert the Jews, and to halt what French historian (and Holocaust survivor) Jules Isaac called "the teaching of contempt"—i.e., the tendency to vilify Jews in Catholic liturgy and religious instruction. Indeed, on June 13th, 1960, Jules Isaac had a private audience with Pope John XXIII in which he urged the Pope change the language of the Mass. After all, before 1962, the Tridentine Mass contained the following language, recited annually on Good Friday:

> Let us pray also for the faithless Jews: that our God and Lord may remove the veil from their hearts; that they also may acknowledge Our Lord Jesus Christ.

> Let us pray. Almighty and Eternal God, Who dost not exclude from Thy mercy even from the faithless Jews: hear our prayers, which we offer for the blindness of that people; that acknowledging the light of Thy Truth, which is Christ, they may be delivered from their darkness. Through the same Lord Jesus Christ, Who livest and reignest with God the Father in the unity of the Holy Ghost, God, through all endless ages. Amen.

After 1962, thanks to John XXIII, the pertinent passage read as follows:

> For the conversion of the Jews. Let us pray also for the Jews that the Lord our God may take the veil from their hearts and that they also may acknowledge our Lord Jesus Christ.
>
> Let us pray: Almighty and everlasting God, You do not refuse Your mercy even to the Jews; hear the prayers which we offer for the blindness of that people so that they may acknowledge the light of Your truth, which is Christ, and be delivered from their darkness.

Lingering references to Jewish blindness, darkness, etc., all metaphors for spiritual ignorance or inadequacy, were hardly cause for celebration, of course. But they represented progress of a sort. Then in 1970, Pope Paul VI took a much more radical step, and abbreviated the prayer even further, as follows:

> Let us pray for the Jewish people, the first to hear the word of God, that they may continue to grow in the love of his name and in faithfulness to his covenant. Almighty and eternal God, long ago you gave your promise to Abraham and his posterity. Listen to your Church as we pray that the people you first made your own may arrive at the fullness of redemption.

On reflection, the hope that Jews will "arrive at the fullness of redemption" was probably worded in a deliberately ambiguous way. Depending on one's attitudes or inclinations, this phrase could be interpreted by old-fashioned Catholics as a wish for the eventual conversion of the entire Jewish people, and by more liberal souls as a hope that salvation can still be achieved within the framework of the Jews' (pre-existing) covenant. Nevertheless, this calculated ambiguity was a welcome change, precisely because it *could* be interpreted more charitably, and was therefore a huge and purposeful step away from the Church's historic mission to convert the Jews, and the negative stereotypes of Jews that colored the Catholic religious imagination in the preceding centuries.

Jews everywhere greeted Paul VI's Mass with gratitude and relief. But sadly, it was revoked, because it provoked a good deal of dissent within the Church itself. One ultra-conservative group did not merely greet Vatican II with dismay, but with outright hostility, flatly rejecting the Second Vatican Council's declarations on human dignity, religious liberty and ecumenism, arguing that these new principles undermined the sanctity and unity of the Church (Venarri, 2013). This group was called the Society of Saint Pius X (or SSPX), and was founded in 1970 by Archbishop Marcel-François Lefebvre (1905–1991).

Archbishop Lefebvre began his ecclesiastical career as a Holy Ghost Father in 1932, and spent many years in Africa before his election as Superior General of the Order from 1962 to 1968. When he resigned that post, he said, it was because the Holy Ghost Fathers would not accept his spiritual guidance any longer. In addition to being a theological conservative, Archbishop Lefebvre was an outspoken supporter of Marshal Philippe Pétain and the Vichy regime in France (1940–1944). Lefebvre was also known for his outspoken support of the Franco and Salazar regimes in Spain and Portugal. In short, he was nothing like Stern or Maritain (Lefebvre's support for authoritarian regimes with abysmal human rights records, and for Jean-Marie Le Pen are all well documented).

Meanwhile, in 1976, despite warnings from Paul VI, Archbishop Lefebvre ordained a group of Tridentine priests to perform the old Latin Mass, and was suspended from performing *any* of the sacraments under Canon Law. Shortly after his election, in 1978, Pope John Paul II had a private audience with Lefebvre in the hopes of healing the breach, but no resolution was reached. Roughly ten years later, in 1987, Lefebvre announced his intention to consecrate a bishop to carry on his work after his death. In May of 1988, he signed an agreement with Cardinal Ratzinger (later Pope Benedict XVI) to insure that the new bishop would be legitimate in the eyes of the Vatican—an agreement he soon reneged on. On June 30th, 1988, Lefebvre ordained not one, but four bishops to minister to traditionalist congregations, prompting Cardinal Joseph Ratzinger, who led the Roman Congregation for the Doctrine of the Faith, to excommunicate all of the Lefebvrist bishops and priests, on the grounds that Archbishop Lefebvre lacked the authority to ordain them without the Vatican's consent. That same year, 1988, Paul Touvier (1915–1996), the first Frenchman convicted of crimes against humanity for vile misdeeds as an officer in the Millice in World War II, was found sheltering in an SSPX Priory in Nice; a source of considerable embarrassment to the Catholic Church.

Then on August 6th, 2000, the Roman Congregation for the Doctrine of the Faith, led by Cardinal Ratzinger, issued a new proclamation entitled *"Dominus Iesus."* As Gregory Baum observed, this new proclamation deviated significantly from the spirit of the Second Vatican Council in two important respects. First, Baum noted that while the Council:

> [...] stresses the universality of Christ's redemptive work, it also acknowledges, for the first time in the Church's history, that the Jewish people remains a covenanted community, the recipient of the divine promises, and a worshipping assembly in which God's word is heard and God's grace received. Not only in *Nostra Aetate* does the Council acknowledge God's abiding covenant with the Jews; it also states in *Lumen Gentium* (no. 16) that "the people to whom the covenants and the promises were given [...] remain, on account of their fathers, most dear to God because God does not repent of his gifts" [...]. The Catholic Church no longer tries to convert Jews to the Christian faith since they are already in a covenant relationship with God. This acknowledgement does call for a certain rethinking of Christology, even if a theology acceptable to all Christians has not been found yet. Because Cardinal Ratzinger makes no mention of this conciliar teaching, relevant though it is to his topic, his theology remains defective. (Baum, 2000, p. 3)

Second, Baum lamented Ratzinger's contention:

> [...] that dialogue with the world religions is compatible with the intention of making converts [...]. The proposal that dialogue and convert making can go together is unethical. (Baum, 2000, p. 3)

Needless to say, *"Dominus Iesus"* had a chilling effect on Catholic-Jewish dialogue, prompting some Jewish leaders to say that it was irrevocably damaged, if not actually dead. Nevertheless, after a decent interval, fences were mended, and things sputtered along again until March 15th (Ash Wednesday), 2004, when Mel Gibson, the Hollywood actor and director, released *The Passion of the Christ*. This film was wildly popular with Christian audiences, despite the fact that it violated many of the Catholic Church's own guidelines for the performance of Passion plays, and that Mr. Gibson openly rejected the second Vatican Council (Burston & Denova, 2005). Because of the Jewish community's negative response, the Vatican did not publicly endorse it, but rumors that John Paul II had previewed the film, and privately approved of it, were widespread. These suspicions were only intensified by John Paul II's decision to beatify Sister Anne Catherine Emmerich (1774–1824) on October 3rd, 2004. Emmerich is a favorite of Tridentine Catholics (including Mel Gibson), and well known for her anti-Semitic rants. These developments left many Jewish leaders scratching their heads, wondering why the Vatican was silently condoning Gibson's film and beatifying a well-known anti-Semite, eroding the trust developed since Vatican II, despite repeated assurances that they were doing no such thing.

When John Paul II passed away, in 2005, Joseph Ratzinger ascended the Papal throne, and on February 5th, 2008 *L'Osserartore Romano* published the current version of the prayer, with full Vatican approval. It reads:

> Let us pray for the Jews. May the Lord our God enlighten their hearts so that they may acknowledge Jesus Christ, the savior of all men. Almighty and everlasting God, you who want all men to be saved and to reach the awareness of the truth, graciously grant that, with the fullness of peoples entering into your Church, all Israel may be saved.

Obviously, there is no equivocation, no room for interpretation here. Benedict XVI, formerly Cardinal Ratzinger, re-introduced the call to convert Jews *en masse* without explanation or apology. These liturgical changes, which called to mind the Roman Missal of 1962, were interpreted by Vatican watchers as a concession to conservative Catholics who were alienated by the doctrinal and liturgical changes introduced by the Second Vatican Council more than four decades previously (Thavis, 2008). Then on January 21st, 2009, Benedict XVI formally revoked the excommunication of the Society of Saint Pius X and the four Lefebvrist bishops, prompting the Rabbinate in Israel to sever relations (briefly) with the Holy See. Why did they take this drastic step? As it turned out, one of the four, Bishop Richard Williamson, made public remarks that were patently anti-Semitic, and was guilty of Holocaust denial. Embarrassed by this stunning reversal, which it should have anticipated, the Vatican insisted that Bishop Williamson publicly retract his views on the Holocaust, and when he failed to do so, his re-entry into the Church was revoked. Nevertheless, the other three Lefebvrist bishops were accepted back, though they never dropped their opposition to the Vatican II reforms. Indeed, the Society of Pope Pius X had not altered their theological position since 1988, when the stigma of heresy was first imposed. Weary of controversy, and the many scandals that plagued his papacy, Joseph Ratzinger stepped down as Pope on February 11th, 2013. And shortly after his resignation, on October 16th, 2013, the SSPX showed its true colors again by offering to perform a public funeral for an unrepentant Nazi war-criminal, Erich Priebke—an offer that was later rescinded, due to adverse publicity.

So, reviewing these events in sequence, the cumulative impression one gets is that the Church today will not tolerate overt expressions of anti-Semitism or Holocaust denial. Nor does it plan to proselytize Jews openly and publicly anytime soon. But neither will it relinquish its communal prayers for the conversion of Jews, for fear of alienating the more conservative elements it is attempting to bring back into the fold, including some with strong fascist sympathies. How would Stern have greeted these developments? Obviously, he would have found the politics of the Lefebvrist faction deeply reprehensible. But he was no fan of Vatican II, either. Why? As Gregory Baum pointed out:

> Stern's lack of interest in the Church's new understanding Jews and Judaism is puzzling, to say the least. Attempting to explain this, I think, one has to look at several creative Catholic thinkers, spiritual leaders in the pre-conciliar Church, who became doctrinal conservatives and showed little sympathy for the rich unfolding of post-conciliar theology. Among them was Jacques Maritain in his last book, the German author (Joseph Pieper) who wrote the book on hope that impressed the young Stern, and Dietrich von Hildebrand, a Catholic philosopher, a refugee from Hitler's Germany living in New York, and several other prominent thinkers.
>
> These thinkers, including Stern, made a clear distinction between the supernatural life in the Church carried by God's

grace and the natural life in the world outside the Church based simply on human willing. The virtues of Catholics were supernatural, while the virtues of non-Catholics were simply natural, thus excluding them from salvation. These authors acknowledged occasional exceptions to this division, the Holy Spirit blowing where It will, but as a rule they were unable to recognize brothers and sisters in the world. They were in fact worried about the salvation of their non-Catholic friends and family members. (personal communication, December 2nd, 2014)

Stern, of course, faced this dilemma when his stepmother passed away. And indeed, any Catholic who took *"Dominus Jesus"* to heart would be in precisely the same position. What accounts for Stern's affinities with more conservative elements in the Church today? Baum points out that:

Karl Stern greatly admired Dorothy Day [...]. She was otherworldly in a worldly way, expressing a higher love capable of changing the lives of those who suffered [...]. This radicalism attracted Karl Stern. He was not a reformer: he did not believe that society could be improved. He was a radical of sorts. He longed for alternative practices of love that gave witness to the Gospel, even though these practices had no chance of being applied universally.

In his letters Karl expressed the curious idea that Protestant Christians wanted to reform the world, while Catholics longed for the manifestation of holiness. He mentions that Quakers and Protestants started the movement to abolish slavery, while the Catholic ethos was expressed by Peter Claver, who loved the slaves and joined them in their desperate conditions of their lives. Stern believed that the Church's mission was to give witness to the otherness of God, to the infinite distance between God and the dominant culture. According to him, the Gospel does not fit into the world [...].

Disappointed by the reformist orientation of the Vatican Council, Stern expressed the idea that [...] Catholicism now no longer stands against the world, but like Protestants at their best, Catholics now advocate in the name of co-operation with all people who love justice to reconstruct the social order.

In his letters Stern presents himself as theologically conservative and as socially radical, at odds with a world dominated by

> the rich and powerful. […] Yet he is not entirely consistent since he criticizes a congress on the laity in Rome because it had been controlled by the hierarchy and because bolder lay Catholics were not represented. He praises Dom Hélder Câmara for his radical social practices without acknowledging his liberation theology, which he, Karl, criticizes in other contexts. (Baum, 2011, pp. 4–5)

On the whole, Baum's characterization rings true, although the remark that Stern "was not entirely consistent" is a remarkable understatement. After all, as we've seen in the preceding pages, Stern was an accomplished scientist who mistrusted rationalism and believed in miracles; a Christian who remained a Jew—at least in his own mind; a Freudian who was also a Jungian (with reservations); a man who admired medieval ascetics and their contemporary counterparts, yet admonished modern philosophers, beginning with Descartes, who despised, disparaged or disavowed the flesh for being latter day Manicheans (and so on).

The same could be said of the otherworldliness that Stern harbored alongside the activist, social-justice orientation he celebrated in Dorothy Day and Dom Hèlder Câmara. Perhaps the best way to describe Stern's inconsistencies along these lines is to say that the tension between an otherworldly interpretation of the Gospels, one that placed Christianity outside or *against* the world, and a progressive, social justice orientation that demands positive engagement in the world—and presages liberation theology in many ways—were always present in Stern. When it came to social issues (other than interreligious dialogue), Stern generally led with his activist, social justice agenda, and only retreated to the more otherworldly sensibility indigenous to Catholic piety as a kind of default position. Judging from his biography, certain events or states of affairs (e.g., his waning sense of efficacy as a public intellectual, his failing health) might have elicited a preponderance of one attitude over the other, but without ever eliminating either attitude completely.

The fact that Stern was like this should come as no surprise. Indeed, it might help explain his conversion. Because whatever else it may be, Judaism is not an *otherworldly* faith. Yes, as some scholars insist, otherworldly elements and attitudes occasionally surface in the history of Judaism, particularly in Jewish mysticism, but they seldom take hold for long. By contrast, the tension between otherworldliness and social activism seems to be an integral feature of the Catholic soul, or less figuratively, of the whole Catholic intellectual tradition. If one of these dimensions or polarities were suddenly eliminated from the picture, Catholicism would morph into something entirely different. It would not be Catholicism anymore. Moreover, to complicate matters further, if you study Church history, it dawns on you that there are strong correlations but no straightforward equivalence between otherworldliness and traditionalism, on the one hand, and social activism, ecumenism and "liberalism" on the other. Strains of all these outlooks or sensibilities can be found in the same culture, the same religious order, and indeed, in the same individual. So if Judaism did not satisfy Stern, it may be partly because it gave him far less scope to harness and express his internal contradictions creatively.

CHAPTER NINE

Judaism and Catholicism in Stern and Lacan

Given the enormous influence that Jacques Lacan (1901–1981) has exerted on psychoanalysis since the sixties, no appraisal of Stern's legacy would be complete without exploring their similarities and differences, particularly on religious issues and their attitudes toward Freud. But despite the fact that they were contemporaries, Lacan and Stern are seldom compared to one another, or even mentioned in the same breath. Why? Perhaps because neither one actually mentions the other in their published work, and because many of Lacan's admirers are not conversant with or even interested in his views on religion. Indeed, for most Lacanians, the Catholic roots and ramifications of Lacan's ideas are still *terra incognita*.

This is a puzzling state of affairs, because evidence of Lacan's Catholic sensibilities abound. Though he formally renounced Catholicism at age sixteen, opting for atheism, fifteen years later, in 1932, Lacan dedicated his doctoral dissertation to his younger brother, a Benedictine monk, in the following words "*Au R. P. Marc-François Lacan, bénédictin de la Congrégation de France, mon frère en religion,*" i.e., to "my brother in religion," not just "my brother." Moreover, his writings are filled with references to St Paul, Augustine and Aquinas, among others, and in later life, Lacan saw to it that all of his children were baptized

(Roudinesco, 1999). In 1954, when the International Psychoanalytical Association revoked his status as a training analyst, Lacan complained bitterly that he had been "excommunicated," and quoted the New Testament and some celebrated Catholic authors in his ongoing polemics with the Freudian faithful. And in 1964, when he formed L'École freudienne de Paris, Lacan joined forces with three Jesuit Fathers, namely, Louis Beirnaert, Michel de Certeau and Francois Roustang. Other key figures in the school, though not priests, were also devout Catholics (Parker, 2011).

Then, ten years later, in *The Triumph of Religion*, Lacan declared that Catholicism is the "one true religion" (Lacan, 2013, p. 66)—implying that others are false, or at least defective by comparison. He even argued that Catholicism would triumph over psychoanalysis and science because it supplied an abundance of meaning—though having devoted most of his career to disparaging or dismissing questions of meaning (from a structuralist and arguably poststructuralist perspective), what Lacan actually meant by meaning in this context remains obscure, and a matter for considerable conjecture (Dunlap, 2014).

Finally, it is instructive to note that on November 16th, 2011, three decades after his passing, Lacan's daughter, Judith Miller sued historian Elizabeth Roudinesco, who recalled that Lacan had asked for a proper Catholic burial, despite his atheist pretensions. Miller alleged that Roudinesco's remark, in her recent book, *Lacan: In Spite of Everything* (Roudinesco, 2014), implied that his immediate family had disrespected his last wishes, and sought to suppress or delete this passage. The court ruled in Miller's favor, but their verdict was overturned on appeal, when the presiding judge discerned that this was not really a conflict between Roudinesco and Miller, but "between Lacan and himself."

Assuming the court ruled correctly, on the whole, Lacan's attitude toward Catholicism need not be framed in terms of an "internal conflict," conscious or otherwise. Judging from the available evidence, it seems more likely that Lacan was not conflicted at all, but simply wanted to have it both ways—to be a loyal Catholic, in some sense, and to be an atheist, simultaneously. What else are we to make of this bizarre history?

In any case, as Ian Parker observes "[…] the Lacanian break with the IPA was to some extent a break that gave voice to a Catholic current inside French psychoanalysis" (Parker, 2011, p. 156). And as a result, there are some striking similarities between Lacan and Stern. In talks to Catholic audiences, both of them took pains to differentiate the tasks of the analytic vocation from those of the priesthood, and the analytic process from the Catholic rite of confession (Stern, 1954; Lacan, 2013). Both rejected the view of organized religion and mysticism espoused by mainstream psychiatry and psychoanalysis, and positivist or biologically reductionist readings of Freud, albeit for different reasons (Stern, 1948a; Stern, 1948b; Lacan, 1953).

That said, Stern was a Christian humanist and existentialist in the spirit of Jacques Maritain and Gabriel Marcel, and read Freud in that spirit (Stern, 1954). By contrast, Lacan was an anti-humanist, who sometimes described Freud as one as well (Lacan, 2013, p. 29). Moreover, and by his own admission, Lacan reveled in ambiguity and willful obscurity, while Stern cultivated a lucid and straightforward prose style. Finally, despite the galloping de-Christianization of Europe after 1968, Lacan declared that Catholicism would eventually triumph over all contending social forces, converting the entire world (Lacan, 2013). Writing after Québec's Quiet Revolution in the late sixties, Stern had obviously lost the robust optimism that had infused *The Pillar of Fire* two decades previously, speculating gloomily on the coming age of the machine, a kind of spiritual Dark Ages (Stern, 1975, pp. 238–257).

In terms of their overall perspectives on human development, Lacan followed Freud in stressing the primacy of the father imago (Lacan, 2013, pp. 22–23), insisting, unlike Freud, that the subject is constituted through language, and that any vestiges of pre-linguistic subjectivity are thoroughly repressed or abandoned in the process of language acquisition (Lacan, 1953). By contrast, Stern stressed the primacy of the maternal imago, and the persistence of pre-linguistic and paralinguistic communication between mother and child that forms the basis for an intuitive/empathic mode of engagement with the world that he called "the poetic mode of knowledge." Indeed, *The Flight From Woman* is a plea for the restoration of the poetic mode of knowledge, and an argument for the intrinsic compatibility of faith and reason—something Lacan never attempted, to the best of my knowledge (Stern, 1965).

Lacan and Stern differed sharply on other aspects of human development as well. For example, in *The Pillar of Fire* (1951) and *The Third Revolution* (1954), Stern described Freud's psychosexual stages an "embryology of love," which explain how a passive infant dependent on a mother's love becomes an adult capable of active commitment and concern for others (Stern, 1951; Stern, 1954). And on a similar note, in an unpublished document entitled "Brief memorandum on the psychological problems associated with the priesthood and the religious life," Stern observed that an oral-passive orientation may lead to maternal fixation, and as a result, interfere with the priest's capacity to fulfill to his vocation. But conversely, he added:

> On a non-neurotic, "sublimated" level, "oral-passivity" makes for the highest forms of spirituality. Indeed, the very idea of spiritual childhood implies that the character structure, which is disastrous when manifested at a regressive level, under the impact of Grace, predisposes a person to a truly evangelical life. (KSA, Series 3, Box 11, Folder 16, p. 1)

Unlike Stern, however, Lacan argued that Freud's whole theory of character and object relations is misbegotten—a moralistic intrusion on the real business of psychoanalysis. In *Discourse to Catholics*, Lacan deplored:

> [...] the famous Freudian definition of sexuality, from which people wanted to deduce a supposed "object relation" said to be oral, anal or genital. This notion of object relations harbors within itself a profound ambiguity, if not a pure and simple confusion, for it gives a natural correlate a characteristic of value that is camouflaged behind reference to a developmental norm.
> It is with such confusions that (Christ's) malediction regarding those who "bind heavy burdens, hard to bear, and lay them on men's shoulders" (Matthew 23: 4) will strike those who authorize in man the presupposition of some personal shortcoming at the core of dissatisfaction. (Lacan, 2013, p. 42)

Another striking feature of Stern's Catholicism was his emphasis on the activist dimension of the priestly vocation. In the "Brief memorandum on the psychological problems associated with the priesthood and the religious life," for example, Stern observed that in pre-modern times a priest could practice his vocation:

> [...] quite unaware of the larger issues of the society of his time, the ideas of the French Revolution, etc. Contrary to this, the priest

of our time cannot help being involved in the larger issues of the society in which he lives. The Gospel often demands to "take a stand" on these issues. This creates a problem. On the one hand, such a "stand" may lead away from a Christocentric and sacramental concept of the sacerdotal. We encounter this pitfall so often in contemporary Protestantism where humanitarian and social causes usurp entirely the place of Christian spirituality. On the other hand, in Catholicism there exists concepts of sacerdotal life which deny the living Christ in the burning issues of society around us. (KSA, Box 11, FF 16, pp. 2–3)

By contrast with Stern, Lacan never tasked priests with taking a stand against injustice, or even acknowledged serious gaps between theory and practice among the faithful. But he frequently invoked scripture to chastise other analysts. So, for example, in his seminar of December 1st, 1954, Lacan delivered a blistering broadside against orthodox Freudians, saying that:

[...] even when one does show willingness to follow Freud, mouthing *the death instinct*, one doesn't understand it any more than the Dominicans, so prettily ridiculed by Pascal in *Les Provinciales*, had a clue about the principle of sufficient grace. (Lacan, 2006, p. 162)

To put these remarks in context, Lacan was suggesting here that Freud wrote *Beyond the Pleasure Principle* (1920g) to recapture his original ground and disabuse readers of earlier ideas like character structure and object relations, which are not relevant to the phenomenon he was *really* trying to elucidate. Is that actually the case? No, probably not. But the tacit implication of these remarks is that psychoanalytic theory is analogous to religious doctrine, and that, unlike Lacan, the leaders of the IPA merely deluded themselves in thinking that they followed Freud, though they did not grasp his deeper meaning.

This also tallies with Jeffrey Mehlman's interpretation of Lacan's use of the myth of Acteon at the end of "La chose freudienne." On the one hand, notes Mehlman:

[...] the myth is a parable of psychoanalysis properly construed: The analyst, upon confronting the truth of castration (Diana in her nudity) is called upon to play Acteon, bearing witness to the

> violation of the integrity of his ego by his "own" unconscious drives (allegorically, the hounds). On the other hand, the myth is a somewhat paranoid allegory of the historical tragedy of psychoanalysis—the work of Freud-Acteon, having encountered truth, is torn to shreds by his inferior followers. Now those followers are referred to as a "diaspora" of "emigrants." Lacan's villains, in this case, are less Americans than Jews. Freud—Acteon, on the other hand, is said to be inspired by a "properly Christian concern for the soul's movements." In … this reading of the myth, moreover, the role of Diana in her bath falls to none other than the Statue of Liberty. All of which—the castigation of ego-psychology as a Jewish cultural formation, the outlandish identification of Freud with Christianity—join to revive a Christian typological reading of the myth—Acteon/Freud the hounds/the Jews […]. (In: Roudinesco, 1999, p. xiv)

Mehlman's gloss on Lacan's reworking of the myth of Acteon rings true, prompting the suspicion that Lacan's historical imagination was deeply infused with imagery and attitudes native to the clerical/Catholic anti-Semitism that enveloped France during the Dreyfus era (Brown, 2010). And this is not an isolated case. In his essay "Kant with Sade," published in 1963, Lacan quotes Alfred Dreyfus' older contemporary, the Catholic historian Ernest Renan (1823–1892) as follows:

> "Let us be thankful," [Renan] writes, "that Jesus encountered no law against insulting a whole class of citizens. For the Pharisees would have been inviolable." Renan continues:
> His exquisite mockery and magic provocations always hit home. The Nessus tunic of ridicule that the Jew, the son of the Pharisees, had been dragging in tatters behind him for eighteen centuries was woven by Jesus with divine skill. A masterpiece of high-level mockery, his scathing remarks have become burned into the flesh of the hypocrite and of the falsely devout. Incomparable remarks, worthy of a Son of God! […]. (Cited in Lacan, 1963, pp. 665–666)

This passage warrants close scrutiny. Renan began by describing the Pharisees as "a […] class of citizens," suggesting that they were merely a portion of the Jewish population in Jesus' lifetime. But then Renan shifts his ground, arguing that *all* Jews are descended from Pharisees, implying that *all* Jews today are hypocritical and "falsely devout." This rhetorical device, of seeming balanced or judicious at first, then escalating rapidly into full blown calumny, is quite commonplace in anti-Semitic literature. And the suggestion that Jesus himself "wove the tattered Nessus tunic of ridicule" that Jews have born for eighteen centuries, i.e., that Jesus himself was the source of Christian anti-Semitism, is complete and utter nonsense, as any competent scholar nowadays will attest.

A charitable interpretation of Lacan's use of Renan might be that Lacan believed that scathing ridicule is actually an art form associated with moral, intellectual or spiritual superiority, as he argued in connection with Pascal and the Dominicans, for example. This is probably true, as far as it goes, and if we read Lacan this way, we might argue that he simply did not notice Renan's anti-Semitism. But this face-saving maneuver begs the obvious question—*why didn't Lacan notice Renan's anti-Semitism?* Perhaps Lacan thought of the guardians of Freudian orthodoxy who "excommunicated" him as "Pharisees," and imagined himself as the true (if somewhat belated) apostle of Freud; a kind of secular version of St Paul, who truly understood the teaching of Freud/ Jesus, unlike his Jewish followers, who supposedly "tore him to shreds" (see also Hackett, 1982).

Mehlman finds Lacan's suggestion that Freud possessed a "properly Christian concern for the soul's movements" to be "outlandish." True enough, but it was much more than outlandish. After all, in *Moses and Monotheism* (1939a), Freud claimed that Christianity gained converts rapidly because it made deep concessions to paganism and to mother-worship, constituting a cultural and historical regression to a lower developmental level than Judaism (Burston, 2014b). Of course, Freud's statements along these lines are as odious to Christian readers as Lacan's anti-Semitic tropes are to Jewish ones. But that is just the point, isn't it? From early childhood onwards, Freud was enveloped in a predominantly Catholic culture awash in anti-Semitic attitudes and stereotypes. Among other things, perhaps, Freud's appraisal of Christianity as a massive cultural regression was a spirited retort to precisely the kind of prejudiced polemics Lacan was pedaling. Indeed, if nothing else, Lacan's weird fantasies demonstrate that he utterly failed to grasp the cultural-historical context in which Freud lived and theorized, and more importantly, to reflect critically on his own cultural biases. After all, Lacan's depiction of Jesus as being unsullied by Jewish attitudes and habits of the heart reflects a commonplace defect in Catholic education that Stern, the convert from Judaism, put his finger on very astutely. In many cases, Stern noted:

> [...] Christian faith is full only if there exists a living awareness of the historical Jesus, of that almost anonymous "heretical" rabbi—obscure and utterly peripheral in the secular history of the Roman Empire of his time. This latter image comes "naturally" to every Jew, and I could quote innumerable examples. But for the Christian, in order to "see" this fully, something like a conversion is necessary. (Stern, 1975, p. 260)

Stern's phrase, "something like a conversion," is interesting. It appears to imply that the ability to comprehend Jesus as a flesh and blood human being—and a Jewish one, at that—is somehow *trained out of* the average Christian, who by the time he reaches adulthood, "naturally" thinks of Jesus in purely a-historical, disembodied terms. But in fact, as Padric O'Hare points out, there is nothing really "natural" about this way of thinking (O'Hare, 1997). If you have not already been reared to think this way, there is something profoundly counter-intuitive about it.

That being said, we applaud Ian Parker, who notes that:

> Despite the generous defences of Lacan against the charge of anti-Semitism, for example in terms of the argument that he was nasty about everyone and did not single out the Jews in particular for contempt, there are some unpleasant eruptions of spite against the IPA that are then condensed into complaints about Judaism [...] Lacan's "Proposition of 9 October, 1967", for example, includes the appalling factually incorrect claim that 'the IPA of Mittel Europa has demonstrated its preadaptation [...] in not losing a single member in the said [concentration camps] [...]. (Parker, 2011, p. 165)

In truth, of course, many IPA members perished in the camps. Commenting on the "Proposition of 9 October, 1967," Parker notes, one long time analysand of Lacan's acknowledged that:

> Lacan's argument in the first version of the 1967 proposition—that "the religion of the Jews must be questioned in our hearts"—was a

call for searching inquiry "came to be understood as an unbearable hostility toward Judaism." (Parker, 2011, p. 1965)

In Lacan's defense, some argue that it was his rupture with the IPA that provoked these bad tempered tirades. After all, Lacan seldom invoked the New Testament or well-known Christian authors unless he wanted to rebuke the Freudian faithful for their intellectual poverty, or for betraying their master's legacy. But if Lacan had not already harbored "an unbearable hostility toward Judaism"—the product, perhaps, of his Jesuit education—his anger would have found others targets, other forms of expression. Fortunately, unlike Freud, a resident of Vienna, a hotbed of anti-Semitism, Stern grew up in a rural environment where Jews and Christians lived amicably side and by side. Open expressions of anti-Semitism in his home town were quite rare until the late 1920s. And unlike Lacan, Stern never actually joined the International Psychoanalytical Association. And as a result, Stern was never demoted or "excommunicated."

But let us be frank. Even if he endured a similar fate, Stern had too much respect for his ancestral faith to carry on like Lacan. And while there are certainly many supercessionist motifs in *The Pillar of Fire*, Stern never harbored "an unbearable hostility toward Judaism," and admonished Catholics that unless or until they recognized the Jewishness of Jesus and relinquished the hatred in their hearts, most Jews would never dream of converting.

Clearly, the reception of Freud's ideas in Catholic circles is subject to extremely diverse cultural-historical influences and agendas. Stern's commitment to Catholicism prompted him "baptize Freud," and in the process to modify the Freudian theory of human development in *The Flight from Woman* (1965). By contrast, Lacan's Catholicism was seldom evident in the substantive changes he made to Freud's theories. Instead, as Parker points out, it shows up in meta-theoretical and organizational features of the movements he spawned, including:

> [...] the composition of the apparatus of the school formed after the break with the IPA, in its appeal to particular conceptual lines of work, in the imagery deployed to convey its meaning, in the formal structures elaborated to transmit it, and then by way of the frames retroactively mobilized by some of its supporters.

> These five aspects—personnel, reference, semiotics, form and devotion—constitute the background against which we might grasp the logic of Lacan's own comments about rival traditions, comments which cannot simply be dismissed as accidental or spiteful side-effects of the split in the IPA. (Parker, 2011, pp. 153–154)

Of course, there is a profound irony in this situation. Lacanians often pride themselves on being uniquely qualified (and motivated) to resist and repudiate the normalizing "technologies" that other schools of psychoanalysis presumably employ to promote their patients' adaptation to contemporary capitalism. But if Parker is correct, then Lacan was adapting psychoanalysis to a specifically French Catholic culture with strong anti-Semitic overtones, and doing so in a semi-deliberate fashion. Indeed, the anti-Semitic sensibility he channeled was more in keeping with the monarchism of Paul Maurras and Vichy France than with the Catholic piety of his philo-Semitic contemporaries, Jacques Maritain and Dorothy Day. In other words, when subjected to careful scrutiny, this dimension of Lacan seems more *pre-capitalist* than anti-capitalist in outlook and derivation. So how do we square the abundant and incontrovertible evidence of Lacan's hidden agenda—which is *extremely* conservative, theologically speaking—with the radical rhetoric of so many of his followers?

Someday, perhaps, someone will write a comprehensive history of the reception of Freud in Catholic culture. And when they do, no doubt, they may actually answer this question, Meanwhile, we can summarize their different agendas by saying that while Stern tried to introduce Freud's ideas into the core of Catholic (humanist) culture, and did so explicitly, Lacan sought to smuggle Catholic thought patterns into psychoanalysis, but without really owning up to that fact. Moreover, even if Stern dismissed much of Vatican II theology as "meretricious," many of his own ideas and sentiments vividly prefigured those newer theological shifts in perspective. But surveying Lacan's work, and the recent efforts of some of his theologically minded critics and expositors (e.g., Earle, 1997; Pound, 2007; Kotsko, 2008; Dunlap, 2014), one wonders if the Second Vatican Council ever touched Lacan and his circle in a meaningful way, and if so, where—if anywhere—this registers in his texts, and why this issue has remained dormant for so long.

AFTERWORD

On December 10th, 2015, as this book appeared nearly ready to go to press, the Vatican released a statement to commemorate the fiftieth anniversary of *Nostra Aetate*, one of the most important documents to emerge from the second Vatican Council. This new document is called "The gifts and calling of God are irrevocable." Though not a Papal encyclical, it is of considerable importance because it appears at a time of rapidly escalating anti-Semitism throughout Europe (and elsewhere), and was unveiled by Cardinal Kurt Koch, Father Norbert Hoffmann, and by Rabbi David Rosen and Dr. Edward Kessler, prominent representatives of the Jewish community. The document placed *Nostra Aetate* in historical context, emphasizing that section four, the heart of the document, signaled and helped to catalyze a dramatic shift in the Church's attitude toward the Jewish people, which included ending what Jules Isaac called "the teaching of contempt," and a historic decision to relinquish its mission to convert the Jews.

This robust re-affirmation of *Nostra Aetate* comes at a welcome time, because the Church's second promise, to relinquish the mission to the Jews, is in constant danger of being diluted and in due course, perhaps abandoned by conservative forces who downplay just how dramatic a change in emphasis *Nostra Aetate* actually was. For example, John

Thavis, the award winning Rome bureau chief for the Catholic News Service, notes that as Pope Benedict XVI commenced negotiations with the SSPX about re-joining the fold in January of 2009, his agenda went far beyond re-integrating a splinter group he himself had excommunicated (as Cardinal Ratzinger). Thavis points out that, if the negotiations transpired as planned, they:

> [...] would offer Benedict a chance to recast Vatican II teachings in his "hermeneutic of continuity" mode—not a rollback exactly, but a more conservative trajectory that, in the long run, would be much better than a rollback. He was convinced that ten or twenty years in the future, this course correction would take the Church back to its traditional identity. *Ad extra*, some things would not be completely undone, like dialogue with other churches and other religions. But Benedict's goal was to restore evangelization as the priority in dialogue and curb the church's participation in worldly enterprises that did not explicitly spread the Gospel. *Ad intra*, the pope had much more leeway: restoring a much more traditional liturgy, retooling religious orders as frontline missionary forces [...]. And in this project, the SSPX would be eminently useful. It was classic triangulation: Benedict would play Fellay [the leader of the SSPX] against the liberal wing of the church, thus creating a new "middle" ground over which the pope, as the protector of unity, would reign. This was Benedict's grand design. (Thavis, 2014, pp. 178–179)

Fortunately for posterity, and for Jewish/Catholic relations, Benedict's "grand design" came to naught, largely because of the stubborn and spiteful anti-Semitism of Bishop Richard Williamson, which in addition to embarrassing Pope Benedict profoundly, called the world's attention to the SSPX's lingering fascist sympathies, and prompted a brief (but noteworthy) severing of relations between Rabbinate in Jerusalem and the Vatican. Thankfully, judging from "The gifts and calling of God are irrevocable," and from many public statements he has made since his papacy began, Pope Francis has absolutely no intention of going down this road. Quite the contrary, he has downplayed the call to convert members of other faiths, calling instead for deeper mutual understanding.

What is the relevance of all this to the history of psychoanalysis—if any? Well, for one thing, judging from his warm enthusiasm for Renan, and many statements concerning the IPA, it appears that Jacques Lacan never got the news about ending the centuries long "teaching of contempt" towards Jews, despite his close and life-long ties to the Catholic Church. Indeed, from one point of view, his tirades against the IPA could be construed as an attempt to convert analysts (and aspiring analysts) to a kind of crypto-Catholic movement that promised to rescue Freud/Jesus from his followers, and to repudiate the Pharisaic distortions of his thought. And in view of Fink's recent translations (Fink, 2014), one can only wonder if Lacan saw his Herculean efforts as little more than a prelude to the ultimate triumph of Catholicism over all other ideologies and social forces. Either way, his was not a stable platform for respectful dialogue or peaceful co-existence with members of other faiths, was it?

Will Lacanians find this characterization of Lacan's sense of mission and identity persuasive, even plausible? Probably not. Despite Ian Parker's sagacious reflections on the Catholic underpinnings of Lacanianism, most secular and left-leaning Lacanians will probably continue to argue that Lacan's religious metaphors and flights of fantasy, prompted by his animosity towards the IPA, are regrettable in retrospect, but have nothing to do with the essence of his thought, or indeed with the future of psychoanalysis, Lacanian or otherwise. By contrast, Jewish Lacanians may feel obligated to devote more serious attention to this subject, and unless they have already sided decisively with the conservative wing of the Church, Lacanians who are Catholic (or members of several other Christian denominations) will have a harder time ignoring these issues, since their faith now obligates them not to ignore, but to renounce and to challenge anti-Semitism—not just in Lacan, but among his students and followers, presumably. The long term consequences of serious and sustained reflection and debate among Lacanians on Lacan in relation to *Nostra Aetate*, should it ever come to pass, are impossible to foretell. Only one thing is certain; they will be *extremely* interesting.

And what of Stern? Well, Stern had no following to speak of in psychoanalytic circles, and for a variety of reasons, it is doubtful that most Lacanians, Catholic, Jewish or otherwise, will give him a sympathetic hearing, now or in future. Nevertheless, analysts of all theoretical and religious persuasions should at least take note of Stern's generous and thoughtful response to Freud's critique of Christian anti-Semitism, which Lacan studiously ignored, to the best of my knowledge. They may also take note of Stern's exhortations to Christians everywhere to acknowledge and embrace the Jewishness of Jesus and his followers, to relinquish the hatred in their hearts, to close the gap between theory and practice, and actually live by the central precepts of their faith.

REFERENCES

Abella, I. & Troper, H. (1983). *None is Too Many: Canada and the Jews of Europe 1933–1948*. Toronto: Lester, Orpen and Dennys.
Angell, M. (2011a). The epidemic of mental illness: Why? *The New York Review of Books*, June 23rd.
Angell, M. (2011b). The illusions of psychiatry. *The New York Review of Books*. July.
Awad, G. (2002). Canada, and psychoanalysis. In: *The Freud Encyclopedia: Theory, Therapy and Culture*. Erwin, E. (Ed.). New York: Routledge, pp. 65–66.
Baum, G. (2000). Cardinal Ratzinger's theology. A response to Dominus Jesus. *The Ecumenist, 37, 4, Fall 2000*.
Baum, G. (2011). Karl Stern, a Catholic intellectual troubled by Vatican Council II. *Open House*, 211: 4–5.
Baum, G. (2015). Karl Stern's Letters to Dorothy Day. *The Ecumenist, 52, 4*: 5–7.
Belenky, M., Clinchy, B. M., Goldberger, N. R., & Tarule, J. M. (1997). *Women's Ways of Knowing. The Development of Self, Voice and Mind*. New York: Perseus (Basic Books).
Bello, A. A. (2000). The study of the soul between psychology and philosophy in Edith Stein. *The Eighteenth Annual Symposium of the Simon Silverman Phenomenology Center*. Duquesne University, Pittsburgh PA.

REFERENCES

Berdyaev, N. (1935). *The Fate of Man in the Modern World*. Donald Lowrie (Trans.). Reprinted by Ambassador Books, Toronto, 1961.

Borch-Jacobson, M. (1988). *The Freudian Subject*. Stanford, CA: Stanford University Press.

Bordo, S. (1986). The Cartesian masculinization of thought. *Signs, 11*, 3: 439–456.

Bordo, S. (1987). *Flight to Objectivity: Essays on Cartesianism and Culture*. New York: SUNY Press.

Bordo, S. (Ed.) (1999). *Feminist Interpretations of Descartes*. The Pennsylvania State University Press.

Breggin, P. (1993). Psychiatry's role in the Holocaust. *International Journal of Risk & Safety in Medicine, 4*: 133–148.

Bronner, S. (2000). *A Rumor About the Jews. Antisemitism, Conspiracy and the Protocols of the Elders of Zion*. New York: Oxford University Press.

Buber, M. (1927). *I and Thou*. W. Kaufmann (Trans.). New York: Charles Scribners & Sons, 1970.

Burston, D. (1989). Freud, the father and the philosophy of history. In: *Sigmund Freud: Critical Assessments*. Laurence Spurling (Ed.). London: Routledge, volume 3, pp. 46–55.

Burston, D. (1996). *The Wing of Madness: The Life and Work of R. D. Laing*. Cambridge, MA: Harvard University Press.

Burston, D. (1999). Archetype and interpretation. *The Psychoanalytic Review, 86 (1)*: 35–62.

Burston, D. (2003). Nietzsche, Scheler and social psychology. *Journal of The Society for Existential Analysis, 14 (1)*: 2–13.

Burston, D. (2007). *Ego, Ethics and Evolution: Erik Erikson and the American Psyche*. New York: Jason Aronson.

Burston, D. (2009a). Nazism. *The Encyclopedia of Psychology and Religion*. David Leeming (Ed.). New York: Springer Press, volume 2.

Burston, D. (2009b). Ressentiment and religion. *The Encyclopedia of Psychology and Religion*. David Leeming (Ed.). New York: Springer Press, volume 2.

Burston, D. (2012). Psychoanalysis and psychiatry in the 21st century: Historical perspectives. *The Psychoanalytic Review, 99 (1)*: 63–80.

Burston, D. (2014a). Zionism. In: *The Encyclopedia of Critical Psychology*, T. Teo (Ed.). New York: Springer, pp. 2093–2098.

Burston, D. (2014b). Anti-Semitism. In: *The Encyclopedia of Critical Psychology*, T. Teo (Ed.). New York: Springer, pp. 115–120.

Burston, D. (2014c). Our imperiled age: An unfinished dialogue between Carl Jung and Karl Stern. *International Journal of Jungian Studie*.

Burston, D. & Denova, R. (2005). *Passionate Dialogues: Critical Perspectives on Mel Gibson's "The Passion of the Christ"*. Pittsburgh: Mise Press.

Burstyn, V. (1999). *The Rites of Men: Manhood, Politics and the Culture of Sport.* Toronto: University of Toronto Press.

Carroll, J. (1996). *An American Requiem: God, My Father and the War that Came Between Us.* Boston: Houghton Mifflin.

Carroll, J. (2001). *Constantine's Sword: The Church and the Jews.* Boston: Houghton Mifflin.

Cleghorn, R. (1984). The emergence of psychiatry at McGill. *Canadian Journal of Psychiatry, 29 (7)*: 551–556.

Cleghorn, R. (1990). The McGill experience of Robert A. Cleghorn, MD: Recollections of D. Ewen Cameron." *Canadian Bulletin of Medical History, Volume 7*: 53–76.

Cocks, C. (1991). The Nazis and C. G. Jung. In: A. Maidenbaum & S. Martin (Eds.). *Lingering Shadows: Freudians, Jungians and Anti-Semitism.* Boston: Shambala.

Collins, A. (1988). *In The Sleep Room: The Story of the CIA Brainwashing Experiments in Canada.* Toronto: Lester, Orpyn and Denis.

Connelly, J. (2012). *From Enemy to Brother: the Revolution in Catholic Teaching on the Jews 1933–1965.* Cambridge, MA: Harvard University Press.

Craddock, N. (2010). Molecular genetics and the Kraepelinian dichotomy: One disorder, two disorders, or do we need to start thinking afresh?" *Psychiatric Annals, volume 40 (2)*: 88–91.

Crewes, F. (1986). *Skeptical Engagements.* New York: Oxford University Press.

Crossan, J. D. (1994). *Jesus: A Revolutionary Biography.* San Francisco: Harper Collins.

Crow, T. (2010). The continuum of psychosis—1986–2010. *Psychiatric Annals, 40 (1)*: 115–119.

Day, Dorothy (1952). *The Long Loneliness: The Autobiography of the Legendary Catholic Social Activist.* Reprinted 1997, with an introduction by Robert Coles. New York: Harper Collins.

De Beauvoir, S. (1949). *The Second Sex.* Constance Borde & Sheila Malovany-Chevalier (Trans.). New York: Alfred Knopf, 2010.

Delisle, E. (1993). *The Traitor and the Jew. Anti-Semitism and extremist right-wing nationalism in Québec from 1929–1939.* Montreal: Robert Davies Books.

Delisle, E. (1998). *Myths, Memories and Lies: Québec's Intelligensia and the Fascist Temptation 1939–1960.* Montreal: Robert Davies Books.

Desgroseilliers, R. (2001). L'historie de la psychoanalyse a Albert-Prevost. *Filigrane, Volume 10 (1)*: 6–22.

Dionne, E. J. (1986). Pope speaks in Rome Synagogue in first such visit on record. *New York Times, April 13th.*

Dru, A. (1966). The "Eternal Feminine". Review of *The Flight from Woman*, by Karl Stern. *The Tablet*, December 31th, p. 1476.
Dubner, S. (1998). *Turbulent Souls: A Catholic Son's Return to His Jewish Family*. Reprinted 2004, New York: Harper Collins.
Dudek, L. (1965). Karl Stern's work of profound scholarship. *Montreal Star*, Sept. 18th, p. 6.
Duhaime, J. & Gignac, A., (Eds.) (2003). Juifs et Chrétiens: L'a-venir du dialogue. *Theologiques, 11*, 1–2. Montreal: University of Montreal.
Dunlap, A. (2014). *Lacan and Religion*. Bristol, CT: Acumen Publishers.
Du Plessix Gray, F. (2010). Dispatches from the Other. Review of *The Second Sex. New York Review of Books*. May 30th, pp. 6–7.
Earle, W. J. (1997). Illusions with futures: Jacques Lacan. In: *Religion, Society and Psychoanalysis*. Jacobs, J. L. & Capps, D. (Eds.). Westview, CT: Westview Press.
Ellenberger, H. (1970). *The Discovery of the Unconscious*. New York: Basic Books.
Elon, A. (2002). The Pity of It All: A Portrait of the German-Jewish Epoch, 1743–1933.
Englund, S., Levenson, J., Senior, D., & Connelly, J. (2014). "Who do you say that I am?": Why Jewish Catholic dialogue cannot avoid the question." *Commonweal*, Feb. 27th, pp. 13–26.
Erikson, E. (1958). *Young Man Luther*. New York: W. W. Norton.
Erikson, E. (1964). *Insight & Responsibility*, New York: W. W. Norton.
Erikson, E. (1966). The ontogeny of rituaization. In: R. Lowenstein, L. Newman, M. Schur, & A. Solnit, (Eds.). *Psychoanalysis—A General Psychology: Essays in Honor of Heinz Hartmann*. New York: International Universities Press.
Erikson, E. (1968). *Identity, Youth and Crisis*. New York: W. W. Norton.
Erikson, E. (1969). *Gandhi's Truth: A Study in Militant Non-Violence*, New York: W. W. Norton.
Fay, T. (2002). *A History of Canadian Catholics*. Montreal: McGill-Queen's University Press.
Fisher, J. T. (1989). *The Catholic Counterculture in America: 1933–1962*. Chapel Hill: University of North Carolina Press.
Fitzgerald, J. (2012). *What Disturbs our Blood: A Son's Quest To Redeem the Past*. Toronto: Vintage Canada.
Foschi, R., Giannone, A., & Giuliani, A. (2013). Italian psychology under protection: Agostino Gemelli between Catholicism and Fascism. *History of Psychology, 16(2)*: 130–144.
Freud, S. (1912–1913). *Totem and Taboo. S.E., 13*. London: Hogarth.
Freud, S. (1920g). *Beyond the Pleasure Principle. S.E., 18*. London: Hogarth.

Freud, S. (1921c). *Group Psychology and the Analysis of the Ego*. S.E., 18. London: Hogarth.
Freud, S. (1923b). *The Ego and the Id*. S.E., 19. London: Hogarth.
Freud, S. (1927c). *The Future of An Illusion*. S.E. 21. London: Hogarth.
Freud, S. (1930a). *Civilization and Its Discontents*. S.E. 21. London: Hogarth.
Freud, S. (1939a). *Moses and Monotheism*. S.E., 23. London: Hogarth.
Fromm, E. (1941). *Escape From Freedom*. New York: Avon Books, 1965.
Fromm, E. (1951). A modern search for faith. Review of *The Pillar of Fire*. *New York Herald Tribune Review of Books*, April 15th, p. 12.
Gauvreau, M. (2005). *The Catholic Origins of Québec's Quiet Revolution, 1931–1970*. Montreal: McGill-Queen's University Press.
Gilbert, M. (2006). *Kristallnacht: Prelude to Destruction*. New York: Harper Collins.
Gilligan, C. (1993). *In a Different Voice*. Cambridge: Harvard University Press.
Gilman, S. (1993). *The Case of Sigmund Freud: Medicine and Identity at the Fin de Siecle*. Baltimore: Johns Hopkins University Press.
Goldblatt, D. (1992). Star: Karl Stern (1906–1975). *Seminars in Neurology*, 12 (3): 279–282.
Goldbloom, R. (1999). Prisoners of ritual. *Canadian Medical Association Journal*, 161 (5). Sept 7th.
Gruenbaum, A. (1984). *The Foundations of Psychoanalysis: A Philosophical Critique*. Berkeley: University of California Press.
Guttman, H. (2010). Personal communication with the author.
Hackett, C. D. (1982). Psychoanalysis and theology: Jacques Lacan and Paul. *Journal of Religion and Health*, 21 (3): 184–192.
Healy, D. (2003). *Let Them Eat Prozac*. Toronto: James Lorimer and Company.
Heft, J. (Ed.) (1999). *A Catholic Modernity? Charles Taylor's Marianist Award Lecture*. Oxford: Oxford University Press.
Heller, B. (1952). *Letter to an Apostate*. New York: The Bookman's Press.
Hertzberg, A. (1992). *Jewish Polemics*. New York: Columbia University Press.
Hewitt, M. (2014). Rivalry or difference? Contemporary psychospirituality and the psychoanalytic study of religion. *Religious Studies Review*, 40 (4): 175–185.
Hine, D. (1989). *In and Out: A Confessional Poem*. New York: Alfred Knopf.
Hitler, A. (1925). *Mein Kampf*. Ralph Mannheim (Trans.). New York: Houghton Mifflin, 1999.
Hogenson, G. (1984). *Jung's Struggle with Freud*. Notre Dame: Notre Dame University Press.
Husserl, E. (1962). *Ideas: General Introduction to Pure Phenomenology*. W. R. B. Gibson (Trans.). New York: Collier.

Husserl, E. (1964). *The Idea of Phenomenology*. W. P. Altson & G. Nakhnikian (Trans.). The Hague: Martinus Nijhoff.
Husserl, E. (1970). *The Crisis of the European Sciences and Transcendental Phenomenology*. D. Carr (Trans.). Evanston, IL: Northwestern University Press.
Jaspers, K. (1913). *General Psychopathology*. Hoenig, J. & Hamilton, M. (Trans.). Chicago: University of Chicago Press, 1965.
Jaspers, K. (1952). *Reason and Anti-Reason in Our Time*. G. Stanley (Trans.). New Haven, CT: Yale University Press.
Kane, P. (2014). Invited address for the dedication of the Karl Stern Archive, Simon Silverman Phenomenology Center, Duquesne University, Pittsburgh PA, October 10th.
Kaplan, M. (1998). *Between Dignity and Despair: Jewish Life in Nazi Germany*. New York: Oxford University Press.
Kertzer, D. (2014). Th*e Pope and Mussolini*. New York: Random House.
Kirsch, T. (2000). *The Jungians: A Comparative and Historical Perspective*. London: Routledge.
Kirsch, I. (2010). *The Emperor's New Drugs: Exploding the Antidepressant Myth*. New York: Basic Books.
Koestler, A. (1949). *The God that Failed*. Richard Crossman (Ed.). New York: Harper & Brothers.
Kotsko, A. (2008). *Zizek & Theology*. London: Continuum.
Kraepelin, E. (1901). *Lectures in Clinical Psychiatry*. New York: Hafner, 1968.
Kramer, P. (1993). *Listening to Prozac*. New York: Viking Press.
Kung, H. (1969). Blame everything on the council! *The Critic, 27*, February-March issue, pp. 38–41.
Lacan, J. (1953). The function and field of speech and language in psychoanalysis. In: *Écrits* Bruce Fink (Trans.). New York: W. W. Norton, 2006.
Lacan, J. (1963). Kant with Sade. In: *Écrits*. Bruce Fink (Trans.). New York: W. W. Norton, 2006.
Lacan, J. (2006). *Écrits* Bruce Fink (Trans.). New York: W. W. Norton.
Lacan, J. (2013). *The Triumph of Religion preceded by Discourse to Catholics*. Bruce Fink (Trans.). Malden, MA: Polity Press.
Laing, R. D. (1960). *The Divided Self*. London: Tavistock Publishers.
Lake, R. C. (2010). The validity of schizophrenia versus bipolar disorder. *Psychiatric Annals, 40 (1)*: 77–87.
Lammers, A. C. (1994). *In God's Shadow: The Collaboration of Victor White and C. G. Jung*. Mahwah, MJ: The Paulist Press.
Leddy, M. J., De Roo, R., & Roche, D. (1992). *In the Eye of the Catholic Storm: The Church Since Vatican II*. Creal, M. (Ed.). Toronto: Harper Collins.
Libman, I. (2010). Personal communication with the author.

Maidenbaum, A. & Martin, S., (Eds.). (1991). *Lingering Shadows: Jungians, Freudians and Anti-Semitism*. London: Shambala.
Marcel, G. (1976). *Being and Having—An Existentialist Diary*. Gloucester, MA: Peter Smith.
Maritain, J. (1957). Freudianism and Psycoanalysis: A Thomist View, in Freud and the 20th Century, Nelson. B, (Ed.). New York: Unwin Hyman, pp. 226–54.
Marrus, M. (2006). The Missing: The Holocaust, the Church and Jewish orphans. *Commonweal. January 13th*, pp. 11–16.
Marrus, M. & Paxton, R. (1983). *Vichy France and the Jews*. New York: Schocken Books, 1981.
Masson, L. (1984). *The Assault on Truth: Freud's Suppression of the Seduction Theory*. New York: Harper Collins.
McFarland, R. (2007). Elective affinities: Exile and religious conversion in Alfred Doblin's *Schicksalreise* (Destiny's Journey), Karl Jakob Hirsch's *Heimkehr zu Gott* (Return to God), and Karl Stern's *The Pillar of Fire*". *Christianity and Literature*, 57 (1).
McGilchrist, I. (2009). *The Master and His Emissary: The Divided Brain and the Making of the Western World*. New Haven: Yale University Press.
McLellan, H. (1945). *Two Solitudes*. Toronto: MacMillan, 1961.
Merleau-Ponty, M. (1964). *The Primacy of Perception*. W. Cobb (Trans.). Evanston: Northwestern University Press.
Merton, T. (1948). *The Seven Storey Mountain*. New York: Harcourt Brace.
Michener, N. (1955). *Maritain on the Nature of Man in a Christian Democracy*. Hull, Canada: Editions "L'éclair".
Miller, D. & Halpern, D. (2013) (in press). The new science of cognitive sex differences. *Trends in Cognitive Science*, XX: 1–9.
Mowrer, Deane (1968). Interview with Karl Stern, July 6th, Tivoli Farm: NY (unpublished). *The Dorothy Day–Catholic Worker Collection*, Series W-9, Box 2, Milwaukee: Marquette University.
Nadeau, J. F. (2011). *The Canadian Führer*. Chodros, B., Hamovitch, E., & Joanis, S. (Trans.). Toronto: James Lorimer.
Neuhaus, D. (1988). Jewish conversion to the Catholic Church. *Pastoral Psychology*, 37 (1): 38–52.
Nietzsche, F. (1956). *The Birth of Tragedy and the Genealogy of Morals*. F. Golfing (Trans.). New York: Doubleday.
Noll, R. (1994). *The Jung Cult: Origins of a Charismatic Movement*. Princeton, NJ: Princeton University Press.
O'Hare, P. (1997). *The Enduring Covenant: The Education of Christians and the End of Anti-Semitism*. Valley Forge: Trinity Press International.

Olfman, S. (Ed.) (2007). *Bipolar Children: cutting edge controversy, insight and research*. Praeger Press.

Olfman, S. & Robbins. B. (Eds.) (2012). *Drugging our Children: How Profiteers and Pushing Antipsychotics on Our Youngest, and What we Can do to Stop it*. Denver, CO: Praeger Press.

Parker, I. (2011). *Lacanian Psychoanalysis: Revolutions in Subjectivity*. London: Routledge.

Parkin, A. (1987). *A History of Psychoanalysis in Canada*. Toronto: Toronto Psychoanalytic Society.

Parsons, W. (2013). *Freud and Augustine in Dialogue: Psychoanalysis, Mysticism and the Culture of Modern Spirituality*. Charlottesville: University of Virginia Press.

Pfister, O. (1928). The Illusion of a Future. In: Freud, S. (1927c). *The Future of An Illusion*. Commentary and introduction by Todd Dufresne (Ed.). Gregory Richter (Trans.). Guelph, Ontario: Broadview.

Post, R. (2010). Overlaps between schizophrenia and bipolar disorder. *Psychiatric Annals, 40 (2)*: 106–114.

Pound, M. (2007). *Theology, Psychoanalysis and Trauma*. London: SCM.

Roudinesco, E. (1999). *Jacques Lacan & Co., A History of Psychoanalysis in France, 1925–1985*, Chicago: University of Chicago Press.

Roudinesco, E. (2014). *Lacan: In Spite of Everything*. London: Verso.

Rudolph, K. (2004). Review of *Feminist Interpretations of Descartes*. Susan Bordo (Ed.). *Hypatia, 19 (2)*: 190–194.

Ruether, R. (1997). *Faith and Fratricide: The Theological Roots of Anti-Semitism*. Eugene, OR: WIPF & Stock Publishers.

Schaeder, G. (1973). *The Hebrew humanism of Martin Buber*. Detroit: Wayne State University Press.

Scheler, M. (1973). The Idols of Self Knowledge. *Selected Philosophical Essays*. Evanston, IL: Northwestern University Press.

Scheler, M. (2000). *Ressentiment*. Milwaukee: Marquette University Press.

Schore, A. (2003). *Affect Regulation & The Repair of the Self*. New York: W. W. Norton.

Schwartzwald, R. (1990). The "Civic Presence" of Father Marie-Alain Coutourier, O.P., in Québec. *Québec Studies, 10 (spring/summer issue)*, pp. 133–152.

Schwartzwald, R. (2004). Father Marie-Alain Coutourier, O.P., and the Refutation of Anti-Semitism in Vichy France. In: Ehrlich, L., Bolozky, S., Rothstein. R., Schwartz, M., Berkovitz, J., Young, J. (Eds.). *Textures and Meaning: Thirty Years of Judaic Studies at the University of Massachusetts, Amherst*. Published electronically by the Department of Judaic and Near Eastern Studies, University of Massachusetts, Amherst.

Schwartzwald, R. (2009). Les relations interculturelles en 1937 à travers la presse juive montréalaise d'expression anglaise. In: Lamonde, Y, & Saint-Jacques, D. 1937: *Un tournant culturel*. Québec: Les Presses de l'Université Laval.

Serlin, I. & Criswell, E. (2000). Women and Humanistic Psychology. In: *Handbook of Humanistic Psychology*, K. Schneider (Ed.). London: Sage.

Shaw, J. (1951). Meet the Karl Sterns. *The Catholic World*, pp. 424–430.

Shorter, E. (1997). *A Short History of Psychiatry*. New York: John Wiley & Sons.

Simon, S. (1999). A. M. Klein et Karl Stern: Le scandale de la conversion. *Etudes Francaises, 37 (3)*: 53–67.

Simon, S. (2002). Crossing town: Montreal in translation. *Profession*, pp. 15–24.

Slochower, H. (1966). Manicheanism and the Denigration of Women. Review of K. Stern, *The Flight From Woman*. *American Imago, 23 (2)*: 184–186.

Solomon, A. (2001). *The Noonday Demon: An Atlas of Depression*. New York: Simon and Schuster.

Stahnisch, F. (2010). German-Speaking émigré-neuroscientists in North America after 1933: Critical reflections on emigration-induced scientific change. In: Christian Fleck (Ed.). "Forced Migration of␣Scholars and Scientists in the 20th Century". A special issue of *Oesterreichische Zeitschrift fuer Geschichtswissenschaften* .Vienna. vol. 21, pp. 36–68.

Stein, E. (1933). *Life in a Jewish Family: 1891–1916*. Josephine Koeppel (Trans.). Washington DC: ICS Books, 1986.

Stern, K. (1945–1975). Letters to Dorothy Day. Series D-1, Box 21, Folder 4 of the Dorothy Day-Catholic Worker Collection, Department of Special Collections and University Archives, Raynor Memorial Libraries, Marquette University.

Stern, K. (1948a). Psychiatry and Its Assumptions. *The Commonweal*, vol. XLIX, 2, pp. 3–33.

Stern, K. (1948b). Religion & Psychiatry. *The Commonweal*, October 22nd, 1948, pp. 1–5.

Stern, K. (1951). *The Pillar of Fire*. New York: Harcourt, Brace and Co.

Stern, K. (1954). *The Third Revolution*. New York: Harcourt, Brace & Co.

Stern, K. (1956a). Dying and yet we live. Part 1. *The Catholic Worker, September issue*, p. 3 (text of an address delivered to the Edith Stein Guild on August 11th, 1956, in NYC).

Stern, K. (1956b). Dying and yet we live. Part 2. *The Catholic Worker*, October issue, p. 3 (text of an address delivered to the Edith Stein Guild on August 11th, 1956, in NYC).

Stern, K. (1959a). Group Psychology in the Atomic Era in Light of Christian Philosophy. In: *World Crisis and the Catholic: Studies Published on the*

Occasion of the Second World Congress for the Lay Apostolate, Rome. New York: Sheed and Ward.

Stern, K. (1959b). The use of dream interpretation in short-term psychotherapy. Delivered to the Annual Convention Canadian Psychiatric Association, St Mary's Hospital, Ottawa, June 5th.

Stern, K. (1960). *Through Dooms of Love*. New York: Farrar, Straus & Cudahy.

Stern, K. (1961). Death within life. Paper/panel honoring Gabriel Marcel, sponsored by The American Association of Existential Psychology and Psychiatry, November 12th, UN Plaza @ 46th Street (other panelists: Marcel, Adrian von Kaam, Tillich, Leslie Farber).

Stern, K. (1965a). *The Flight From Woman*. New York: Farrar, Straus & Giroux.

Stern, K. (1965b). Canadian House of Commons, February 26th. Standing Committee on External Affairs. Chairman: John R. Matheson, Esq. Minutes of proceedings and evidence, No. 37. Respecting: The subject-matter of Bill C-21, An act respecting genocide and Bill C-43, An act to amend the post office act (hate literature). Witness: Dr. Karl Stern, Psychiatrist in Chief. St Mary's Hospital, pp. 1773–1788 (Roger Duhamel, FRSC, Queen's Printer and Controller of Stationary, Ottawa).

Stern, K. (1966a). The Problem of Guilt. *Proceedings of The First Annual Loyola University Summer Institute in Pastoral Psychology, Loyola University: Los Angeles*. Reprinted in Stern, K. (1975). *Love and Success*. New York: Farrar Straus and Giroux.

Stern, K. (1966b). Psychoanalysis and philosophy. Workshop on: Teaching of Philosophy After Vatican II, June 17th, Catholic University of America, Washington, DC. Reprinted in Stern, K. (1975). *Love and Success*. New York: Farrar Straus and Giroux.

Stern, K. (1967). Neurosis and Personal Growth. *Institute of Man Symposium*, November 18th. Reprinted in Stern, K. (1975). *Love and Success*. New York: Farrar Straus and Giroux.

Stern, K. (1968). Interview with Deane Mowrer, July 6th, Tivoli Farm: NY (unpublished). *The Dorothy Day–Catholic Worker Collection*, Series W-9, Box 2, Milwaukee: Marquette University.

Stern, K. (1970). Thoughts on the Resurrection. *The Catholic Worker, February issue*, pp. 2–6.

Stern, K. (1975). *Love and Success*. New York: Farrar, Straus & Giroux.

Stern, K. (undated). Brief memorandum on the psychological problems associated with the priesthood and religious life. Unpublished paper, Karl Stern Archive.

Swales, P. (1989). Freud, Fliess and parricide: The role of Fliess in Freud's conception of paranoia. In: L. Spurling (Ed.). *Sigmund Freud: Critical Assessments, Volume 1*. London: Routledge.

Syrkin, M. (1951). From Jerusalem to Rome: *The Pillar of Fire* by Karl Stern, *The Nation, July 7th*, pp. 16–17.

Szasz, T. (1961). *The Myth of Mental Illness: The Foundations of Personal Conduct*. New York: Harper and Row.

Taylor, C. (1999). A Catholic Modernity? In: Heft (1999). Oxford: Oxford University Press.

Thavis, J. (2008). Pope reformulates Tridentine rite's prayer for Jews. *Catholic News Service, February 11th*.

Thavis, J. (2014). *The Vatican Diaries: A behind-the-scenes look at the power, personalities and politics at the heart of the Catholic Church*. New York: Penguin Books.

Thornton, E. (1983). *Freud and Cocaine: The Freudian Fallacy*. London: Blond & Briggs.

TIME (1956). Psychiatry and Faith, an interview with Karl Stern. August 1st.

Valenstein, E. (1986). *Great and Desperate Cures*. New York: Basic Books.

Vennari, J. (2013). Judaism and the Church: Before and after Vatican II. Available at: www.Sspx.org/en/news-events/news/Judaism-church-after-vatican II—1342.

Vogelin, E. (1999). *Hitler and the Germans*. Columbia: University of Missouri Press.

Warnes, H. (2009). Letter to the author.

Wistrich, R. (2010). *A Lethal Obsession: Anti-Semitism from Antiquity to the Global Jihad*. New York: Random House.

Yerushalmi, Y. (1991). *Freud's Moses: Judaism Terminable and Interminable*. New Haven: Yale University Press.

Zolli, E. (1954). *Before the Dawn*. San Francisco: Ignatius Press, 2008.

INDEX

Abella, I. 61
adolescent identity crisis 11, 188, 201
Advent sermon 44, 182, 195
Affect Regulation and the Repair of the Self 173
Albany Medical School 69
aliyah 42
Allan Memorial Institute of Psychiatry 70, 79, 95–96, 116
American Association of Existential Psychology and Psychiatry 121
American Imago 137
American Psychiatric Association 69
Angell, M. 159
Anglo-Saxon science 51
Anglo-Saxon theologians 101, 103
Answer to Job, An 103
anthroposophy 64, 71, 150
anti-Semitism 19, 36, 62, 64–65
   "knock on" effects 106

anti-Soviet propaganda 123
Arab–Jewish reconciliation 43
Ash, Scholem 91
Awad, G. 159

baptism 64–69
Bar Mitzvah 11–12, 14, 20
Barbusse, H. 10, 54
Baum, G. 127, 211, 214, 218
Belenky, M. 160
Bello, A. A. 197
Berdyaev, N. 123
Berlin Alexanderplatz 145
Beyond the Pleasure Principle 225
Bible, The 133
bima 11
bios 41
Blair, F. C. 62
Bloy, Léon 63
Bolshevik Revolution 18, 36
Borch-Jacobson, M. 159

248 INDEX

Bordo, S. 135, 175
Breggin, P. 33
Brigham Young University 208
Brown, William xv
Buber, Martin 11, 41–47, 91, 154
Burger, Franz 19, 39
Burghölzli Clinic in Zürich 69
Burston, D. xv, 11, 16, 39, 96, 159, 162, 165, 171, 188, 193, 196, 210, 215, 227
Burstyn, V. 175
Busch, Adolph 25

Cameron, Donald Ewan 69, 95–96, 116, 138
Canadian Chamber of Commerce 144
Canadian Jewry 152
Canadian Psychoanalytic Society 69–70
Canal Street synagogue 68, 90–91
Capitalism 36, 55, 84–85, 121, 123–124, 230
Carroll, J. 132, 202
Cartesian anxiety 135 see also Descartes, René
Catholic
   culture 114
   documents 186
   intellectual tradition 219
   intelligentsia 99
   psychoanalyst 163
   religious imagination 213
Catholicism 42, 52, 100, 127, 144, 151 see also Christianity
   conversion to 73, 83
   Jewish converts to 68
   mainstream 75–76
   Stern's emphasis on 88
Catholic Worker, The 66, 77, 92–94, 112, 124, 132, 146, 148, 150

CBC (Canadian Broadcasting Corporation) 128, 143
Christianity 41, 187
   Advent sermon 44, 182, 195
   and Freud 85–101
   conversion 181–182
   spiritual kinship with Judaism 45
   spirituality 225
   vs. Judaism 52–53
Christopher Award 81–85, 93
Civilization and Its Discontents 177
Cleghorn, R. 69–70, 95–96
Clinchy, B. M. 160
Cocks, C. 39
Collins, A. 96
Commonweal, The 74
Communism 82, 84–85, 121, 123–124
complicated man, A. 150–152
Concordia University 144, 202
Connelly, J. 143, 202
contra-sexual *analage* 133
Cooke, Evelyn 54
cosmic dilution 10
cosmological coherence 164
cosmology 62, 164
Coughlin, C. E. 72, 98
counter-cathexis 169
Couturier, M. -A. 63–64, 67, 94
Craddock, N. 159
creative illness 188
Crewes, F. 159
Crisis of the European Sciences and Transcendental Phenomenology, The 165
Criswell, E. 176
Crossan, J. D. 185
Crow, T. 159
crypto-Catholic movement 233
Cuban missile crisis 124–125

Davidman, H. J. 88
Davies, R. 26

Day, Dorothy 64–73, 76–78, 82–83, 91, 108–110, 112–113, 115, 118, 124, 138, 143–144, 150–151, 193, 200, 217–218, 230
De Beauvoir, S. 133–134, 152
defensive war 124
Delisle, E. 61, 63
Denova, R. 215
Der Jude 43
Descartes, René 126, 135–136, 176, 218 *see also* Cartesian
Desgroseilliers, R. 115, 159
Die Welt 43
Diefenbaker, John 62
Dionne, E. J. 195
Discourse to Catholics 224
Discovery of the Unconscious, The 39
Divided Self and The Myth of Mental Illness, The 118
Divinity of Christ 151
Dix, Otto 64
"*Dominus Iesus*" 214
Du Plessix Gray, F. 134
Dudek, L. 136
Duhamel, Roger 64
Dunlap, A. 222, 230
Duquesne University 121, 153

Earle, W. J. 230
École des Beaux-Arts 63
Edelman, G. 89–91
ego ideal 190
ego-strength 188, 191
Ellenberger, H. 39–40, 188
Elon, A. 50, 163
embryology of love 223
epiphany 182
Erikson, Erik xv, 11, 146, 187–189
esthetic aloofness 25
European Jewry 43

Fackenheim, Emile 211
family ordeal, the 138–142
Farmatorium 108–110, 153
Faulhaber, Cardinal 44
Feminist Interpretations of Descartes 135
feminist movement 132–137
Fisher, J. T. 66, 78, 83–84, 157
Fitzgerald, J. 157
Flamm, Frau 43–45
Flechsig, Paul 37
Flight from Woman 64, 73, 119, 126, 132–133, 135–137, 151, 171, 176, 183, 145, 223, 229
Flight to Objectivity: Essays on Cartesianism and Culture, The 135
forced sterilization 31–34
Foschi, R. 60
France, Vichy *see* Vichy regime
Frankel, Eugen 41, 44
Frankfurt Neurological Institute 23
Freud, Biologist of the Mind 158
Freud, S. 23, 34, 37–38, 55, 73–79, 85–101, 133, 146
  contention 163
  enlightenment positivism 164
  revenge 161
  theory of anti-Semitism 162–163
From Union Square to Rome 77, 82–83
Fromm, E. 149
Future of An Illusion, The 86, 133, 163

Gay, Peter xiv
Gemelli, Agostino 60
General Psychopathology 165
Georg, Stefan 37
German Enlightenment 17, 42
German General Medical Society for Psychotherapy 39
German Gnostic group 65

250 INDEX

German Institute for Psychiatric Research 31, 36, 75, 162
Germania 162
ghetto identity 106
Giannone, A. 60
Gilbert, M. 56–57
Gill, Eric 26
Gilligan, C. 160
Gilman, S. 163
Ginsberg, Asher 43
Giroux, Robert 81
Giuliani, A. 60
Goethean humanism 64
Goldberger, N. R. 160
Goldblatt, D. 23
Goldbloom, R. 23
Goldstein, Kurt 23, 34, 46
Göring, Hermann 39, 56
Göring, Matthias 39
Gradl, Herr 5
graven images 203
Greene, Graham 79, 86, 141
Groulx, A. L. -A. 63–64
Group Psychology and the Analysis of the Ego 112, 171
Gruenbaum, A. 159
Grynzspan, Herschel 55–57
Guttman, H. 138
gynophobia 175

Habonim 42, 71
Hackett, C. D. 227
hallowed presence 188
Halpern, D. 175, 222
halutzim 43, 209
haskalah 50
Haase, Ernst 24
Healy, D. xxi
Hebrew Catholics xx, 181
Hebrew-Christian religion 102
Hegel, Georg Wilhelm Friedrich 25, 42, 84, 186

Heller, B. 207
Hendry, Charles 128
Herschel, Abraham Joshua 211
Hertzberg, A. 187
Herzl, Theodor 43
Hesse, Hermann 34
Hewitt, M. 187
Hine, Daryl 110–111, 117, 152–158
hinge of history, the 186
Hiroshima 69–73
History of Psychoanalysis in Canada 159
Hitler and the Germans 195
Hitler, Adolf 18–19, 25, 30, 33, 35–36, 39, 52, 55, 61, 98 112, 120, 162, 193, 196, 202, 216
Hogenson, G. 148
homosexuality 111
    latent 150, 170
Hôpital de Nôtre Dame 58
Huber, Kati 26–27, 52
Huch, Ricarda 203–204
Husserl, E. 165–166, 197
Hyland, Herbert 58
hyper-masculine mentality 136, 160, 175

I and Thou 43
idealized object 194
identity crisis 11, 187–188, 201
In and Out: A Confessional Poem 110
Institute Pédagogiques, Montreal 67
International General Medical Society 39
International Psychoanalytical Association (IPA) 115, 152, 222, 225, 228–230, 233
interpersonal family communication 174
invisible Church 98, 191, 194–195
Isaac, Jules 211, 231

Jaspers, Karl 21, 24, 126, 165–169
Jewish bankers 72
Jewish community xx, 1, 5, 18, 45, 61, 68, 92, 106–107, 114, 126–127, 182, 190, 195–196, 198, 202–203, 215, 231
Jewish Enlightenment 50
Jewish Youth Movement 18
Jewry 17, 43–44, 91, 152, 209
John Birch Society 128
Jones, Ernest xiv–xv
Judaeo-Christian tradition 162, 198
Judaism 41–47
   and Catholicism 226–230
   Rabbinic 43
   Reform 42
   spiritual kinship with Christianity 45
   vs. Christianity 52–53
Jung, Carl Gustav xiv, 19, 38–41, 70, 73, 101–104, 133, 146, 148, 218
Jung Cult, The 40
Jung Judischer Wanderbund 13
just war 124

Kane, Paula 85–86
Kaplan, M. 57
Keller, James 81
Kennedy, John F. 124–125
   assassination 125
Kertzer, D. 57, 61, 72
kibbutzim 16, 43, 65–66, 209–210
King, McKenzie 62
Kirsch, T. 39, 159
Klages, Ludwig 8, 17, 19–20, 39–43, 55
Klein, A. M. 197, 202–203, 207
knowledge by connaturality 166–167
knowledge by disassembly 167
Koestler, A. 124, 183
Kohen, Frau 8, 14, 41, 68, 90, 189

Kotsko, A. 230
Kraepelin, Emil 31–32, 37–38, 138, 158–159
Kraepelinian psychiatry 69, 74, 97, 121, 159
Kramer, P. 159
Kristallnacht 55

L'Avennire d'Italia 60
L'Eau Vive 93–94
L'Osserartore Romano 215
Lacan, Jacques xv, 221–230, 233–234
Lacan: In Spite of Everything 222
Laing, Ronald D. xv, 118
Lake, R. C. 159
Lammers, A. C. 103
Landauer, Gustav 11
Laudenheimer, Rudolph 36–41, 46, 70
Laval University 144
Law for the Reestablishment of a Professional Civil Service 34
Lawrence, D. H. 41
Le Devoir 208
Le Feu 10, 54
leitmotifs 54
Lemieux, M. J. 99
Letter to An Apostate 207
Lewis, C. S. 82, 88
Lewy, Guenther 195
libidinal (counter-) cathexis 169
libidinal energy 168–169, 196
libido theory 132, 178
Libman, I. 106
Liebknecht, Karl 11
limbic systems 174
Living Corpse, The 34
Loeb, James 31
Love and Success 131, 145, 204
Luce, C. B. 73–74, 86, 93, 96
Luce, Henry 99

Lumen Gentium 214
Luxemburg, Rosa 11

Mager, Leo 35
Magic Flute 10
Magic Mountain, The 29–30
"Manicheanism and the denigration of woman" 137
Mann, Thomas 25, 29–30, 55
Marcel, G. 43
Maritain, J. 55, 61, 63, 67, 77, 82
Marrus, M. 61
Martin, Paul 128
Marx, Karl 42, 82, 84, 170–171
Marxism 11, 30, 36, 73, 83, 85, 123–124, 149, 181, 209
Massey, Vincent 62
Masson, L. 158
Master and His Emissary, The 176
masters of suspicion 171
Mathewson, John 128
Maurin, Peter 66, 78
Maurras, Charles 63
McCarthy, Joseph 98
McFarland, R. 209–210
McGilchrist, I. 175–178
McGill University 69–73
McLellan, H. 82, 158
Mein Kampf 52
Mendelsohnn, Felix 25
Mendelsohnn, Moses 43, 50
Menninger Clinic, Topeka 69
Merleau-Ponty, M. 166, 172, 175–176
Merton, T. xix, 81, 86, 91, 99
metaphysical sense 177, 191
metaphysics of the sexes 133, 176
Meyer, Adolf 69
Michener, N. 55
midrashim 46
Miller, D. 175, 222
minor hemisphere 174
Missa Solemnis 10

Mizrahi 44, 191, 210
Moabiter Krankenhaus (Moabit Hospital) 23–24
Montreal Gazette 128
Montreal General Hospital 115–116
Montreal Neurological Institute 58
Montreal Psychoanalytic Club 70
Montreal Star 136
Montreal's ethnic divides 60–61
   and anti-Semitism 62
Montreal's Fine Arts Museum 64
Montreal's Institute Pédagogiques 67
Montreal's Jewish community xx, 60, 68–69, 106, 126, 203
Montreal University 105
moral values 131–132
Moses and Monotheism 161, 163, 165, 227
Mounier, Emmanuel 43
Mowrer, Deane 150–151
Mussolini, Benito 63, 72

Nadeau, J. F. 63
National Socialism 24, 35, 84 *see also* Nazi
"natural conversation" 174
Nazi(s)
   and anti-Semitism 162, 196, 198, 203
   and Catholicism 44
   and Jung 39
   and *Kristallnacht* 55
   and Liselotte 51–53
   and psychiatry 31–32, 36
   and Zionism 42, 57
   anti- 41
   fleeing the 61, 113
   opposition to 34
   thugs 11
   triumph 34–36
   war-criminal 216
Nazism 74

INDEX   253

neo-Kraepelinian movement 159
Neuburger, Gottfried 90–91
Neugierde 123
Neuhaus, D. 82, 181, 197–198
New York Times Review of Books, The 119, 134
Niebuhr, Reinhold 82
Nietzsche, Friedrich 39, 52, 149, 162, 166, 170–171
Noll, R. 40
None is Too Many: Canada and the Jews of Europe 1933–1948 61
Nostra Aetate 186, 214, 231, 233

O'Hare, P. 185, 222, 228
Olfman, S. 159
On Hope 54
Oplaski, Adam 32
oral-passive orientation 224
orthodox Jewry 209
Osservatore Romano 71
Oussmanoff, Raissa 63
Oxford Etymological Dictionary 182

Pacelli, C. E. 72
Parker, I. 222, 228–230
Parkin, A. 159
Parsons, W. 192
participation mystique 172
Passion of the Christ, The 215
Paxton, R. 61
Penfield, Wilder 58, 69
Pétain, Philippe 63–64
Petliura, Symon 18
Pfister, O. 86–87, 100–101, 164
Philippe, Father Thomas 94
Pieper, Joseph 54–55, 95
Pillar of Fire, The xix–xx, 17, 23, 42, 53, 62, 64, 66–68, 75, 78, 81–83, 88–89, 92–93, 97, 99, 128, 137, 142, 145, 149, 153, 158, 162, 189–194, 199, 202–203, 205, 207–208, 210, 223, 229
Pillar of Salt, The 111, 153
Pillar of Smoke, The 142
Plato's *Symposium* 133
Plaut, Felix 31, 35
Pope Pius XI 60
Pope Pius XII 60
Post, R. 159
Post Office Act 128
Pound, M. 230
Prados, Miguel 69–70, 77, 96
"problem of guilt, The" 131
psychiatry 31–34
  "belligerent" materialism in 79
  classical 37
  Kraepelinian 69, 74, 97, 121, 159
  "philosophical superstructure" of 74
  psychodynamic 39
  Stern's doubts on 73–79
psychoanalysis, evolution of 166
psychoanalysis, terminology 168
psychoanalytic method 169
psychoanalytic theory of gender 132
psychodynamic psychiatry xv, xxi, 39, 121, 159

Québec nationalists 60–65, 77, 106, 115, 130, 202
Quiet Revolution 130, 132, 152, 223

Rabbinic Judaism 43
Race mixing 53
"R.C. Circuit" The 129
racism 31–34
Ratzinger, Cardinal 85
Red Nucleus 51
Reform Jews 42
"repetition compulsion" 121
Ressentiment 165
restless wanderers 195–196

"Return to Kraepelin!" 158
Review of Existential Psychology and Psychiatry, The 122
Robbins. B. 159
Rockefeller Foundation 31
Rockwell, George Lincoln 128–129
Rolland, R. 17, 19
Roman Catholic Church 100, 198
Roman Congregation for the Doctrine of the Faith 213
Roosevelt, Franklin D. 72
Roudinesco, E. 222, 226
Ruach Elohim 185
Rudolph, K. 135–136
Ruether, R. 206
Russ, Kaspar 5, 10, 68

Saul, King 38, 185
scathing dismissal, A. 152–158
Schaeder, G. 43
Scheler, M. 34
Schmid, Wilhelm 93
Schore, A. 174, 176
Schulz, Bruno 34, 39
Schwartzwald, Robert 61, 63–64
scientism xx–xxi, 74, 97, 131, 170–171
Scott, Clifford 69
Second Scroll, The 202–203
Second Sex, The 133–134
Second Vatican Council (Vatican II) 127
secular Jews 189
selective serotonin reuptake inhibitors (SSRIs) 159
Serlin, I. 176
Seven Story Mountain, The 81
sexual desire 132
Shavit, Shimon 92
Shaw, G. B. 17, 19
Shaw, J. 26, 92
Shorter, E. 31
Simon, S. 197, 202

Simons, Hugo 64
Slochower, H. 137
Solomon, A. 155
Soviet Communism 24, 124
Spanish Civil War 60
Spielmeyer, Walther 31, 46
Stahnisch, F. 23, 32, 35, 58, 95, 105
Stalin, Joseph 98
Stein, E. 82, 190, 197
Steiner, Rudolph 64–65
Sterba, Edith 69
sterilization, forced 31–34
Stern, Karl x, xv, 5, 8, 10–11, 13–14, 17–24, 26, 28–29, 32, 36–38, 41, 45, 47, 49–51, 53–54, 57, 59–62, 65–68, 71, 74–78, 84–87, 93, 98, 103, 113, 119, 122–123, 128–129, 131–133, 135–136, 138, 141, 146–147, 149, 162–164, 166–167, 169–171, 173, 175, 177, 179, 191–192, 195, 200, 203–206, 208–209, 223–224, 228
  adolescence 13–21
  and colleagues in London 52
  arrived in Montreal (June 1939) 59–64
  as medical student 22
  as pre-schooler 6
  as school boy 9
  at piano 58
  baptism 64–69
  Bar Mitzvah 11–12
  caught up with Liselotte 52
  challenge 161
  Christopher Award to 81–85
  circa 1935 40
  circa 1955 100
  doubts and misgivings about experience in Ebenburg 8
  experiment with prayer 16
  family 1–4

first analysis 36–41
fourth child died 70
from Judaism to Jesus 41–47
grandfather of 3–4
in London 49–53
in medical school 21–30
infancy and childhood of 1–13
inspiration from Franz Burger 19
intellectual activity 146
left Allan Memorial Institute
matricentric theory of human development 136
memories of kindergarten 5–7
move to Primrose Hill 53–59
one year old 2
personal loyalties 124
psychiatric profession 73–79
returned to Frankfurt as lecture assistant 28
Uncle Julius 10, 14–16, 58
vacations on Lake Mephremagog 76
went to school in Munich 8–11
with childhood friend 7
with colleagues in lab 29
Stern, Liselotte *see* von Baeyer, Liselotte
Swales, P. 159
Szasz, T. 118
Szold, Kfar 42, 65

Tablet, The 120
Tao TeChing 133
Tarule, J. M. 160
Thavis, J. 215, 232
Third Revolution, The 73, 95–102, 112, 154, 164, 168, 192, 223
Third Revolution: A Study of Psychiatry and Religion, The 96
This Hour Seven Days 128
Thornton, E. 158

Through Dooms of Love 74, 116, 118, 120, 122, 145
Tillich, Paul 43
Tolstoy, Leo 34
traitor complex 65, 67, 72, 90, 193, 200
Triumph of Religion, The 222
Troper, H. 61
Two Solitudes 82

UNESCO xx, 112
Université Québec a Montréal 211
Upanishads, The 133

Valenstein, E. 32
Valkyrie 13
Vennari, J. 245
Verdun Protestant Hospital 58
Vichy regime, France 61, 63–64, 213, 230
visible Church 67, 71, 73, 84, 98, 113, 194
Vogelin, E. 195
Volhard, Franz 23, 28–30, 39
vom Rath, Ernst 55
von Baeyer, Erich 24–25, 51
von Baeyer, Liselotte 26–27, 49–53, 55, 57, 59, 63–64, 67, 70, 76, 92, 107–112, 114–117, 139–142, 144, 146, 148, 153–154, 156–157, 190
von Weizsacker, Viktor 29
Voyer, Victorin 68, 79

Walsh, Noel 79, 96
Wandervogel movement 17, 192
Warnes, H. 146
Western capitalism 36
Western materialism 123
Wistrich, R. 57
Witakower, Eric 69
World Psychiatric Organization 69

Yishuv 16
Young Jewish Wanderers 13

zachor 185
Zilboorg, Gregory 89
Zionism 16–17, 41–47
    growing reservations about 46
    Karl's rejection of 43

Zionist 42–46
    milieu 43
    youth group 42
Zohar, The 133
Zolli, E. 82, 197